Indian America

Indian America

A TRAVELER'S COMPANION

EAGLE/WALKING TURTLE

John Muir Publications

Santa Fe, New Mexico

John Muir Publications, P.O. Box 613, Santa Fe, NM 87504

First edition. Second printing

Library of Congress Cataloging-in-Publication Data

Eagle Walking Turtle.
    Indian America, a traveler's companion / Eagle/Walking Turtle. — 1st ed.
      p. cm.
    Bibliography: p.
    Includes index.
    ISBN 0-945465-29-7
    1. Indians of North America. 2. United States—Description and travel—
1981— —Guide-books. I. Title.
E77.E117   1989
917.304'928—dc20   89-42940
                                                       CIP

Editor: Sheila Berg
Designer: Joanna Hill
Typeface: Baskerville
Typesetter: G&S Typesetters, Inc.
Printer: McNaughton & Gunn, Inc.

Distributed to the book trade by:
W. W. Norton & Company, Inc.
New York, New York

Cover painting, "Spirit Bull," Eagle/Walking Turtle

This book is dedicated to the Native People of Turtle Island.

May they last, and last, and last . . .

And may there always be more of the spirit of the people over the land.

Contents

Preface

Indian America is your guide to the world of the native people of America. Because many tribes may not be located on major highways, it is suggested that you consult a road atlas in addition to the information provided here.

It is important to realize that some tribes have a very small population and do not practice ceremonies; some do not welcome visitors. For this reason, you may find limited information for some tribes within these pages. But it is also important to know that most tribes welcome the public and cordially invite you to attend powwows and ceremonies and visit their reservations.

The brief histories accompanying the listings will most often end at the turn of the century. This is when Native Americans experienced dislocation from their lands and the intrusion of white culture and, for all intents and purposes, ceased the practice of their own cultures free of non-Indian influence.

Welcome to Indian country. Enjoy your journey.

Acknowledgments

A lot of people have had a lot of patience to withstand the torment that I placed on them to conduct this project and the goal I have to document Indian America in the 1980s. Some of those people are my mother, Leola; my wife, Woman Above; my son, Blue Bird; and my grandson, Yellow Horse. My good friend and spiritual relative Dan Chisholm passed on to the other side just before publication of *Indian America*. I have lived life better because of his wisdom.

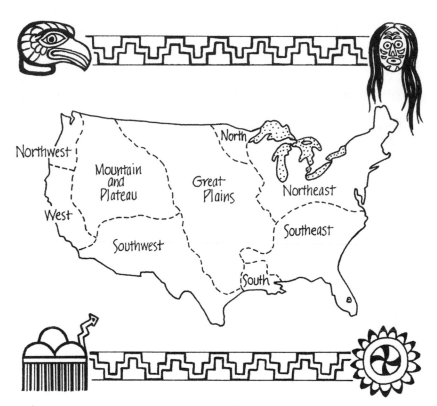

Native American Cultural Areas

Introduction

When the first Europeans arrived here on Turtle Island (our name for the North American continent), they found our ancestors. They were a docile, peaceful people, living in harmony with their environment and respecting the whole of all living things. They were (and are) a spiritual people. As more people arrived from Europe, our people were displaced from their lands and forced to move westward in search of new places to live and hunt or farm to support their families. Then, later, government policies moved whole tribes to the West to make room for the arriving immigrants from the old world.

In this journey through Indian America you will find that Native Americans may live in less than perfect living conditions. You may see that we have not always been able to make the changes necessary to move from one culture to another. You may be reminded of the atrocities committed against us by racial prejudice, greed, and government policies. You may even be appalled by what you see. But do not forget that the heart of the people lives on in the spirit of the past before our culture was torn apart by the changes brought by the industrial revolution—when buffalo herds were wide as day and the Earth stayed young. And when you attend a sacred ceremony, or even a powwow, your own past will swell up within your own heart and remind you of your own heritage when your ancestors lived in tribes and were close to the Earth.

Indian America is divided into nine regions. These differentiate between tribes that lived in different ways. The Great Plains people are hunters who had previously been farmers from the eastern United States. The Mountain and Plateau people live in the high elevations of the West. The Northeastern and Northern people live in the cold areas where the lakes and trees cover the land. The Northwest people live where the land meets the big water of the Pacific. The Western people are those who live in the coastal deserts and inlands between the big water and the mountains. The

Southwestern people are those who live in mud houses in the pueblos and those who roam the inland deserts between the mountains. The Southeastern and Southern people live in the wet and swampy places beyond our plains.

We will explore how Native Americans live today. Often, it will be up to you to discover how a tribe is living now by visiting their community or reservation or nation. Tribes will not always be willing to share their life-styles with outsiders, but all celebrations or powwows listed within these pages are open to the public and you are cordially invited. This journey through Indian America is important to you as a guide for finding Native American arts, ceremonies, powwows, and other aspects of our culture that are found in our communities today.

And we will touch on spirit and philosophy and the Beauty Path. The Beauty Path is the journey our spirit takes on its way through the whole of all living things for the time of eternity, before we came to live on our Earth Mother and after we leave Her to go live with our Sky Father again. There goes the Beauty Path, the path to sacred places like Black Mesa, Devils Tower, Bear Butte, Harney Peak, the four sacred mountains of the Navajo, and the prayer mountains and sacred lakes of the Pueblo people. The Beauty Path is the direction we are always facing.

You do not need to be afraid to be here in Indian Country. The people are kind and good and generous. Be extremely respectful at our ceremonies. Wear clothing that reflects that respect, and maintain a quiet and courteous attitude, and follow the manners of the Indian people who are there. You will learn that the Beauty Path and the sacred places you may be seeking are right beneath your feet. Look up to pray with the Creator and look down to pray with your Earth Mother. All places are sacred and the Beauty Path is always ahead. Our church is not just on Sunday. It is all the time and everywhere, not just in a building but in the mountains, in the hills, in the woods and streams, and in the plains and valleys. The black road of life is hard and, probably, the red road of spirit is harder. Walking in balance between the two is hardest of all. But it is good. It is very, very good.

When you arrive here with us in Indian Country you will find people with dark complexions, black eyes, and dark to black hair. Our housing is built with the help of HUD, and now it is often out of style with modern America. Some are Easter egg houses in pink, turquoise, and blue, stucco houses to imitate adobe in the South-west, and urban development solar-heated styles similar to the one you may live in. Even shacks and log houses and beer cans and puppies and wrecked cars in the yard. That dome-shaped structure behind the house is a sweat lodge. And you will still see tipis, which are probably for Peyote meetings of the Native American Church. But what you find will depend on what part of our country you are in. Reservations can vary greatly in America. Watch for bumper stickers on our cars: America is Indian Country; Custer Wore Arrow Shirts; Have Tipi, Need Squaw; If You Ain't Indian You Ain't; and more. Indian humor is dry, but you know what you are laughing at.

Our people face the same obstacles in life that all people do. We want happiness and success and a good life. Despair is evident here with us too. We have alcoholics, drug addicts, school dropouts, and unemployment. We also have hardworking people; family people making it in the world. You may find some prejudice here against non-Indians. It may be generations before it passes away, but the sacred circles of man still intertwine and we all know it. We will form into one great hoop. Change is a natural part of evolution.

And there already is a great hoop. It is so big that everything is within it, because it is the hoop of all living things in the universe, and all that live in it are our relatives. If you stand on a high hill, like the one at Pojoaque Pueblo that faces west toward the Jemez Mountains, and you look from North to South, you can see its shape and know that it is true. The great hoop of all living things has four quarters, and each is sacred, for each has mysterious pow-ers of its own, and it is by those powers that we all live. Also, each quarter has its own sacred colors and sacred objects, and these stand for its power.

> Look first towards that place where the sun goes down and its color is blue gray like the thunder clouds, and it has the power to make life and to destroy life. The bow stands for the lightning that destroys for food, and the wooden cup stands for the rain that makes life.
>
> Next is the place where the great white giant lives, and its color is white like the snows. It has the power of healing, for thence come the cleansing winds of the winter. The white wing feathers of the goose stand for that wind of cleansing and a sacred white herb stands for the healing.

Next is the place whence comes the light, where all the days of men are born; and its color is red like the sunrise. It has the powers of wisdom and powers of peace. The morning star stands for wisdom, for it brings the light that we may see and understand; and the pipe is for the peace that understanding gives.

Next is the place of the summer, and the color of it is yellow like the sun. Thence comes the power to grow and flourish. The sacred staff of six branches is for the power to grow, and the little hoop is for the life of the people who flourish as one.

Then at the place whence comes the power to grow, a road begins, the good red road of spirit that all men should know; and it runs straight across the hoop of the world to the place whence comes the power of cleansing and healing, to the place of white hairs and the cold and the cleansing of old age.

And then there is a second road, the hard black road of difficulties that all men must travel. It begins at the place whence comes the days of men, and it runs straight across the hoop of this world to the place where the sun goes down and all the days of men have gone and all their days shall go; far beyond is the other world, the world of spirit.

It is a hard road to travel, a road of trouble and need. But where this black road of difficulties crosses the good red road of spirit at the center of the hoop of the world, that place is very holy, and there springs the Tree of Life. For those who look upon the Tree, it shall fill with leaves and bloom and singing birds; and it shall shield them as a sheo [prairie hen] shields her chickens.

So, with these words, Blue Spotted Horse expressed where the safety and everlasting life of our spirit lies beneath the Tree of Life.

Look now for the center. The place of our beginning is there. Is it in the mountains near Abiquiu, New Mexico? A great flattop mountain is there. Some say it is the place of original Creation. It is the home of the Deer People, the original inhabitants of this continent. So, some of us came by the Bering Strait. Some of us went the other way, too. Some of us were already here. Ask the elders of the people; they know. The center of the spiraling circle of the Beauty Path begins in your own heart. And it grows and spins outward, counterclockwise in the way of all spirit things, as your spirit matures and expands and gains momentum until it springs open like a coiled spring. So, the center is found at all sacred places and all sacred places are everywhere and always in your own heart. It is good. It is very, very good.

A society can be measured by how well its most fortunate members have treated the least fortunate. Native American people, as a whole, have been extremely compassionate to those less fortunate than themselves. Praise to the Creator, through ceremony, is translated into our concern for the welfare of all life and to the alleviation of suffering for all living things. Beatitude of the spirit for all living things in the beauty of creation will be ours through ceremony and praise of the Creator.

We are all native peoples living on our Mother Earth. We have been displaced and moved and our lives have changed and are changing. But, we are of one spirit; we all share in the goodness of sharing one life-force. And we are now in the process of a beautiful transformation of returning to live closer to the beauty of creation again. Our spirit is emerging to a new awareness that will protect our existence and the environment of our Mother Earth.

But hold fast! There is more . . .

THE GREAT PLAINS

MONTANA:
Blackfeet /
Flathead /
Chippewa Cree /
Gros-Ventre /
Assiniboine / Sioux /
Crow / N. Cheyenne

WYOMING:
Northern Arapahoe / Shoshone
KANSAS: Iowa / Kickapoo / Potawatomi /
Sac and Fox

OKLAHOMA: Absentee - Shawnee /
Apache / Otoe- Missouria / Caddo /
Pawnee / Cheyenne-Arapahoe /
Potawatomi / Ponca / Comanche /
Delaware / Iowa / Kaw / Sac and Fox /
Kickapoo / Kiowa / Tonkawa /
Wichita / Cherokee / Chickasaw /
Choctaw / Creek / Eastern Shawnee /
Miami / Modoc / Osage / Ottawa /
Peoria / Quapaw / Seminole / Seneca-Cayuga /
Wyandotte

NORTH DAKOTA: Turtle Mountain
Chippewa / Devils Lake Sioux /
Arikara - Hidatsa - Mandan /
Standing Rock Sioux

SOUTH DAKOTA:
Cheyenne River
Sioux / Crow Creek
Sioux / Santee Sioux /
Brule Sioux / Oglala
Sioux / Rosebud
Sioux / Sisseton-
Wahpeton
Sioux / Yankton
Sioux

IOWA: Mesquakie

NEBRASKA: Santee
Sioux / Winnebago /
Omaha

MISSOURI:
Eastern Shawnee

The Great Plains of North America stretch from the Mississippi River in the east to the Rocky Mountains in the west and from Texas in the south to the Canadian Provinces in the north. It is an area of about a million square miles and the terrain consists of bluffs and crags, of flat-topped mesas several hundred feet high, of richly wooded valleys and glistening streams. It contains rugged terrain in terraces, cliffs, and chasms with colors ranging from spectacular to the very drab; but mostly the Great Plains are grasslands.

This is the land of our people. Nomadic in nature, they followed the migrations of the buffalo and wandered the plains with spiritual respect for their environment and for all living things. The land was unbroken before the Europeans brought the plow; the grasses were as high as a horse's flanks and the buffalo herds stretched as wide as day; and the earth stayed young. When the winds of winter blew from the north down our plains, our people stayed in river bottoms in the trees out of the hard winds and close to water. In the summers of growth and warmth from the south, when the winds blew up clouds full of rains and the sun brought life, our people hunted the buffalo and followed the happiness of freedom, always in respect for life and thankful for the blessings from Grandfather, the Creator.

There was time then. Time to develop one of the greatest cultures ever to exist on our Mother Earth. Our people developed into a culture rich in beautiful art forms. Spiritually moving ceremonies in praise for our Grandfather the Creator, definite ways of living, rich in their grasp of human values and morality—the people of the plains were exceptional indeed.

The buffalo gave the people time. Food and everything needed for life, including shelter, came from the buffalo. The meat was used for food. The hide provided clothing and covers for tipis and bedding. The bones were used for cooking utensils and weapons. Sinew was formed into thread for sewing, and even the fat of the animal was used for light. When the buffalo was plentiful and easy to hunt, the people had time to do beautiful artwork with quills and willow and buckskins. And dances and songs and chants developed for social entertainment and spiritual appreciation of the creation of all living things.

Medicines for the body and spirit evolved with time also. Sage, cedar, and sweetgrass were used in the sacred ceremonies of our people. The Creator provided the knowledge of how to use these sacred medicines through the Medicine People found in every tribe.

The people cared for each other, and the old were cared for in the home. Young people were praised for their caring and for their aid to the elders of the tribe. The elders taught the young the ways passed down to them from their elders in years gone by; the circle was never broken. The sacred hoop of the people was whole and round. And it was good. It was very, very good.

The men formed societies for the protection and well-being of the whole of all the people. The women formed societies dedicated to caring and embracing the welfare of all the people. And they bore the babies and raised the children. And it was good. It was very, very good.

The heartbeat of our Mother Earth was heard and felt with the drum, and the flute from Father Sky played the prayers of the people. It is true that life could still be difficult and often was, but it was difficult in an honorable and clean way. The people never forgot to maintain their respect for the whole of all living things; they never forgot to play the drum to keep the heartbeat of Mother Earth alive; they never forgot to pray the flute to romance the heartbeat of all living things.

With the coming of the intruders to the plains the circle was broken. The buffalo was exterminated by a society of people who were not in tune with the goodness of all living things. Without the buffalo, the culture of our people broke apart and suffered permanent wounds that will never heal without leaving scars.

The tribes in these pages are descendants of our people, and you can find among them remnants of this great culture. You can still hear the drum play out the heartbeat of our Mother Earth in ceremony and powwow across the plains. And you will hear the flute pray in the homes and in the open spaces of the wind. The Medicine People use sage, cedar, and sweetgrass, and the sweet smell carries the healing forward from the past into the future in the Sweat Lodge, Offerings Lodge, Native American Church, and sacred dances of our people across the land.

Join with them to honor their ancestors and to honor our Creator, our Mother Earth, our Moon, our Sun, and the whole of all living things in the whole of all Creation. You will find that it is good. It is very, very good.

Aho . . .

They made us many promises, more than I can remember, but they never kept but one; they promised to take our land, and they took it.

—Unidentified Old
Teton Sioux

The Great Spirit raised both the white man and the Indian. I think he raised the Indian first. He raised me in this land it belongs to me. The white man was raised over the great waters, and his land is over there. Since they crossed the sea, I have given them room. There are now white people all about me. I have but a small spot of land left. The Great Spirit told me to keep it.

—Mahpiua Luta
(Red Cloud) of the
Oglala Sioux

This war did not spring up here in our land; this war was brought upon us by the children of the Great Father who came to take our land from us without price, and who, in our land, do a great many evil things. The Great Father and his children are to blame for this trouble. . . . It has been our wish to live here in our country peaceably, and do such things as may be for the welfare and good of our people, but the Great Father has filled it with soldiers who think only of our death.

—Sinte-Faleshka
(Spotted Tail) of the
Brule Sioux

If a man loses anything and goes back and looks carefully for it he will find it, and that is what the Indians are doing now when they ask you to give them the things that were promised them in the past; and I do not consider that they should be treated like beasts, and that is the reason I have grown up with the feelings I have.

—Tatanka Yotanka
(Sitting Bull), Sioux

There was not hope on earth, and God seemed to have forgotten us. Some said they saw the Son of God; others did not see Him. If He had come, He would do some great things as He had done before. We doubted it because we had seen neither Him nor His works.

The people did not know; they did not care. They snatched at the hope. They screamed like crazy men to Him for mercy. They caught at the promise they heard He had made.

The white men were frightened and called for soldiers. We had begged for life, and the white men thought we wanted theirs. We heard that soldiers were coming. We did not fear. We hoped that we could tell them our troubles and get help. A white man said the soldiers meant to kill us. We did not believe it . . .

—Red Cloud, Sioux,
after Wounded Knee

. . . today, by reason for the immense augmentation of the American population, and the extension of their settlements throughout the entire West, covering both slopes of the Rocky Mountains, the Indian races are more seriously threatened with a speedy extermination than ever before in the history of the country.

—Donehogawa (Ely Parker),
the first Indian Commissioner
of Indian Affairs

No white person or persons shall be permitted to settle upon or occupy any portion of the territory, or without the consent of the Indians to pass through the same.

—Treaty of 1868

One does not sell the earth upon which the people walk.

—Tashunka Witko
(Crazy Horse), Sioux

If we make peace, you will not hold it.
—Gall, Hunkpapa
Sioux

We, too, have children, and we wish to bring them up well.
—Red Cloud,
Oglala Sioux

My heart is very strong.
—Satanta, Kiowa

May the white man and the Indian speak truth to each other today.
—Blackfoot, Crow

The whites think we don't know about the mines, but we do.
—Blackfoot, Crow

This country south of the Arkansas is our country.
—Kicking Bird, Kiowa

Osages have talked like blackbirds in spring; nothing has come from their hearts.
—Governor Joe, Osage

The Tonkawa killed him—it make my heart hot.
—Quanah Parker,
Comanche

I want my people follow after white way.
—Quanah Parker,
Comanche

Some white people do that, too.
—Quanah Parker,
Comanche

We want the privilege of crossing the Arkansas to kill buffalo.
—Black Kettle,
Cheyenne

It is our great desire and wish to make a good, permanent peace.
                                          —Little Raven,
                                              Arapahoe

I am the man that makes it rain.
                                          —Lone Wolf, Kiowa

You sent for us; we came here.
                                          —Tall Bull, Cheyenne

Do not ask us to give up the buffalo for sheep.
                                          —Ten Bears,
                                              Comanche

Teach us the road to travel, and we will not depart from it forever.
                                          —Satank, Kiowa

I love the land and the buffalo and will not part with it.
                                          —Satanta, Kiowa

We preferred our own way of living.
                                          —Crazy Horse, Sioux

I see that my friends before me are men of age and dignity.
                                          —Spotted Tail, Sioux

I feel that my country has gotten a bad name.
                                          —Sitting Bull, Sioux

You are living in a new path.
                                          —Sitting Bull, Sioux

I bring you word from your fathers the ghosts.
                                          —Kicking Bear, Sioux

We love the Great Spirit . . .
                                          —Petalesharo, Pawnee

By peace our condition has been improved in the pursuit of civilized life.

—John Ross, Cherokee

They have not got forked tongues.

—Washakie, Shoshone

The only good Indian is a dead Indian.

—General Sheridan

Sac and Fox Tribal Council
Route 2, Box 56C
Tama, IA 52339
(515) 484-4678

Mesquakie, "foxes" (Muskwakiwuk, red earth people)

Location: To find Tama, look in your atlas between Marshalltown and Cedar Rapids on U.S. Highway 30.

Public Ceremony or Powwow Dates: During the second weekend in August, beginning on Thursday and running through Sunday, you will find the Mesquakie celebration powwow.

Art Forms: Arts and crafts are offered for sale during the powwow. The Mesquakie are known for their intricate beadwork, which features Eastern Woodlands floral designs.

Visitor Information: The village that is built for the powwow is likely to show wigwams and Plains-style tipis.

The Mesquakie are an Algonquian tribe whose home at the latter part of the seventeenth century was along the Fox River, Wisconsin. They joined with the Sauk for protection from other warring tribes early in the eighteenth century.

KANSAS

Iowa of Kansas Executive Committee
Route 1, Box 58A
White Cloud, KS 66094
(913) 595-3258

Iowa (Sleepy Ones)

Visitor Information: The Iowa live today in two locations, here and on a reservation in Oklahoma.

Traditional and linguistic evidence proves that the Iowa sprang from the Winnebago, who appear to have been the mother stock of some other of the southwestern Siouan tribes; but the closest affinity of the Iowa is with the Oto and Missouri, the difference in language being merely one of dialect. Iowa chiefs in 1883 said that their people and the Oto, Missouri, Omaha, and Ponca "once formed part of the Winnebago Nation."

Kickapoo of Kansas Tribal Council
Route 1, Box 157A
Horton, KS 66349
(913) 486-2131

Kiwigapawa (he stands about)

Location: The reservation is seven miles west of Horton.

Public Ceremony or Powwow Dates: The Kickapoo hold an annual powwow about the third weekend in July from Friday through Sunday at their powwow grounds. You will see traditional dancing as well as powwow dancing. The traditional Kickapoo Green Corn Dance is also done.

Art Forms: Arts and crafts are sold at the powwow. You will find leatherwork, beadwork, wood carvings, and jewelry. Local Kickapoo artists as well as artists from other tribes in the area are there. For buying at other times, check with the senior citizens center in the housing area for information about individuals who live nearby.

Visitor Information: The community has a bingo enterprise for visitors who like to play games of chance.

Joe Vetter, Iowa Indian, December 18, 1903
Photo by Thomas W. Smillie; Courtesy Museum of New Mexico, Neg. No. 87000

This tribe belongs to the central Algonquian language group. They share a close ethnic and linguistic connection with the Sauk and Foxes. They are more closely related to the Miami, Shawnee, Menominee and the Peoria than to the Chippewa, Potawatomi, and Ottawa. All of these tribes were living near the portage between the Fox and Wisconsin rivers from 1667 to 1670. Alloa, Columbia County, Wisconsin, is the probable locality, about 12 miles south of the mixed village of the Mascouten, Miami, and Wea.

Prairie Band Potawatomi Tribal Council
Route 2, Box 50A
Mayetta, KS 66509
(913) 966-2255

Potawatomi (Potawatamink or Potawaganink, people of the fire)

Location: This band of the Potawatomi is located west of Mayetta. Look for the bingo signs along Highway 75 at Mayetta.

Public Ceremony or Powwow Dates: The tribe holds their annual pow-wow during the summer. Call for dates and times.

Art Forms: Call the tribal office for details on art and craft work available from tribal members.

Visitor Information: The tribe has a herd of buffalo that stays behind the tribal complex. I am always in awe of the beauty and size of these great animals. Be sure to look at the old photographs on the walls of the hall at the tribal office.

In 1616, written record places the Potawatomi on the west shores of Lake Huron. The Potawatomi, Chippewa, and Ottawa were originally one people. In 1908 there were 1,769 Potawatomi in Oklahoma; 676 of the Prairie Band in Kansas; and 78 in the Calhoun County, Michigan, Band.

Sac and Fox of Missouri Tribal Council
P.O. Box 38
Reserve, KS 66434
(913) 742-7471

Sauk (Osa Kiwug, people of the yellow earth)
Foxes (Muskwakiwuk, red earth people)

Location: The tribal offices and store are located in Reserve. Follow the signs from Highway 73.

Visitor Information: The tribe operates a small arts and crafts shop next to the tribal office building.

The Sauk are an Algonquian tribe whose home at the early part of the seventeenth century was on the eastern peninsula of Michigan. In 1909, the total Sauk and Fox population was 975. All were on reservations in Iowa, Oklahoma, and Kansas.

The Foxes are also an Algonquian tribe. Their home at the latter part of the seventeenth century was along Fox River, Wisconsin. They joined with the Sauk for protection from other warring tribes early in the eighteenth century.

MISSOURI

Eastern Shawnee Business Committee
P.O. Box 350
Seneca, MO 64865
(417) 776-2435

Shawnee (Shawun, south)

Visitor Information: This tribe usually participates in events around Miami, Oklahoma. Read more about them under the Miami tribe of Oklahoma.

This tribe is formerly of South Carolina, Tennessee, Pennsylvania, and Ohio. Linguistically, the Shawnee belong to the group of central Algonquian dialects, very closely related to Sauk and Fox. As embodied in the Walum Olum, the traditional history of the Delawares, they, the Shawnee, and the Nanticoke were originally one people.

Keo-kuk, Jr. (Watchful Fox), Head Chief of the Fox, 1868
Photo by A. Zeno Shindler; Courtesy Museum of New Mexico, Neg. No. 56181

MONTANA

Blackfeet Tribal Business Council
P.O. Box 850
Browning, Montana 59417
(406) 338-7276

Siksika (Blackfoot People)
Pikuni

Location: The town of Browning is the hub of the Blackfeet reservation, where you will find the Blackfeet Tribal Business Council, the Bureau of Indian Affairs, the Blackfeet Public Health Service hospital, the Manpower office, the Blackfeet Native American Programs office, the Blackfeet Housing Authority, the Browning public schools, and the Blackfeet Community College.

Public Ceremony or Powwow Dates: The North American Indian Days celebration is held in Browning the second week in July. It is an intriguing way to see authentic Indian tradition. Tipis are pitched on the powwow grounds for four days of Indian dancing, games, sports events, and socializing. The celebration is located at the Blackfeet Tribal Fairgrounds, adjacent to the Museum of the Plains Indian. Comprising one of the largest gatherings of U.S. and Canadian tribes, the celebration is an unforgettable experience. Once you hear and feel the mystery of the drum, the traditional and fancy dancing, the many proud native people, you will begin to understand their endurance in times of hardship which enabled them to keep at least some of their lands.

Art Forms: You will find traditional forms among these Plains Indians, which include quill work, beadwork, leather work, feather work, and moccasins. Call the tribal office for more information.

Visitor Information: The Blackfeet Indian Reservation, one of the outstanding recreation areas in North America, is on 1.5 million acres of panoramic beauty. The location is ideal for vacationers since it is next to Glacier National Park and within easy driving distance of Yellowstone National Park. The eight major lakes and 175 miles of rivers and streams offer prime fishing. The reservation offers a summer and winter playground of hiking, camping, fishing, hunting, boating, picnicking, swimming, horseback riding,

Manny Shot, Blackfoot
Photo by H. Pollard; Courtesy Museum of New Mexico, Neg. No. 111167

rodeos, water skiing, snow skiing, and snowmobiling. A nine-hole golf course is located in East Glacier. The Blackfeet were among the most powerful Indian tribes of the Northwest Plains. At one time, their territory extended west of the Rocky Mountains from the North Saskatchewan River to the headwaters of the Missouri River (now called Yellowstone National Park).

The Blackfeet Indian Reservation is located in the mountains of northern Montana. On the north, it borders the Canadian province of Alberta and to the south includes Glacier County. The western boundary is at the base of the magnificent Rocky Mountains, which make up Glacier National Park. The majority of the land consists of high rolling plains, historically the hunting grounds for the Blackfeet people. Elevation varies from 3,400 feet to the east to over 9,000 feet at Chief Mountain to the west.

Browning has been the headquarters for the Blackfeet Indian Reservation since 1895. The town was named after the Indian Affairs Commissioner of that time, Daniel Browning. You will find motels, cafes, gift shops, and automobile services. Relax, enjoy, and let a part of history come alive in nature's wilderness on the Blackfeet Reservation.

The modern Blackfeet Nation descended from three of the most powerful Indian tribes in the northwestern plains: the Northern Piegans (Pikuni), the Blackfeet (Sisaka) or Southern Piegans, and the Blood (Kainai) Indians. All speak a common language. The Bloods ranged primarily in Canada, while the Northern Piegans inhabited the high plains along the eastern slopes of the Rockies on both sides of the United States-Canada border. The Blackfeet dwelled almost exclusively in Montana, a territory also occupied by the Gros Ventre and Assiniboine, a distant relative of the Dakota or Sioux Indians. Observers on the early frontier spoke erroneously of these two latter tribes as members of the Blackfeet. However, these two tribes, along with the Shoshoni to the south, were inveterate enemies of the Blackfeet. When the early missionaries and treaty-makers first attempted to contact these tribes, they were often caught in tribal wars being fought between the Blackfeet and their enemies.

The non-Indian population, which had migrated from the European countries in their quest for freedom, began their westward move from the eastern part of the United States in search of furs, land, and riches. The 1700s saw the entrance of the fur trade in

Blackfeet Territory, with the buffalo robe becoming an important item of trade. The westward expansion of the white society demanded more land for settlers, fur companies, railroads, and the businesses and military establishments necessary for protection of the railroads and settlers. Thus, the Blackfeet people's land was needed and the Treaty-Making Era began.

In exchange for land, the U.S. government ratified treaties with the Blackfeet people promising peace, protection, agricultural goods, services, education, money, and inviolate land—promises that usually were not kept.

At the end of the Treaty-Making Period (1871), the United States had other methods of securing more land. Through presidential orders and congressional acts, the Blackfeet land base dwindled to its current size. From an original territory that extended from the Yellowstone River to the Saskatchewan River in Canada and from the Continental Divide to the confluence of the Missouri and Yellowstone rivers, the Blackfeet's land was reduced to a small 1.5-million-acre tract of land in northwestern Montana.

In the early times, the buffalo contributed a great deal to the Blackfeet's existence: meat for the staple diet, hides for the lodges and clothing, robes for the lodges, and bones for some of the tools. The Blackfeet at that time required very little else to maintain their way of life.

Although the Blackfeet had only a minor interest in trapping, they were skillful hunters. Therefore, as the fur trade entered the Blackfeet Territory in the mid-1700s, the buffalo became a vital part of the trade. In 1874, the northwestern buffalo herd was estimated at four million; by 1879, five years later, there were only a few buffalo left on the plains; by 1883–84, the buffalo were virtually exterminated. Some had been killed to feed the railroad crews, but most had been massacred for their hides. Their naked carcasses spotted the prairies where they rotted and became fair game for bone pickers.

With their natural economy gone, the Blackfeet became dependent on the government for food and supplies. The government was ill prepared for such a crisis. Winter rations were greatly underestimated by Agent John Young. His ignorance of the government caused a catastrophe during the winter of 1883–84 as the annuities for the Indians did not arrive. Some 600 Piegans starved or froze to death that winter. Bones and bodies were scattered about until public health officers hauled them away for burial on a small ridge to the east. This burial grounds became known as "Ghost Ridge."

The arrival of missionaries among the Blackfeet is another part of the history of the tribe. They came to the tribes in the early 1800s to bring Christianity and education. In 1859, the first mission school was opened for the Blackfeet Indians near Choteau, Montana, which was reservation land at that time. Three log cabins were erected and called the St. Peters Mission. In 1883, a small one-room mission school was opened at Robare. The Catholics, or "Black Robes," were the first religious group to have an impact on the Blackfeet, although other religious groups were present.

The government and public schools began providing educational services in the late 1800s and early 1900s. Willow Creek School was established by the government in 1892. In 1904, the Cut Bank boarding school was opened for 125 students. The first government day school opened at Heart Butte, Old Agency, and Starr School in 1915. The first public school opened at Four Persons Agency in Choteau in 1872 and closed in 1876 because of poor attendance. Altyn opened a school for white children only in 1898 in the Babb valley. The first public school in Browning opened in 1905 with an enrollment of 20 students. Government boarding schools off the reservation, such as Carlisle Indian School, were the primary source of education for many years with many of the Indian children taken from their homes forcibly to attend these schools.

A particularly interesting event in the history of the reservation took place in 1903–04. A fence was built around the entire reservation with exits only at Whiskey Gap on the Canadian line, Robare on Birch Creek, and Cut Bank. Whether or not an Indian was allowed to leave the reservation was the decision of the "agent" or superintendent of the Bureau of Indian Affairs. It was also necessary for whites to obtain a pass to enter. Regular line riders patrolled the fences to ensure they remained intact and that those within stayed in and those without stayed out. According to records, the real reason for the fence was to ensure that the Indian cattle did not mingle with those of the whites; but, whatever the reasons, the fence was gone by 1909.

Discovery of oil in the Swift Current Valley between Babb and Many Glacier made history. Three wells were drilled. At Boulder Creek, oil was found. Although none of these wells proved to have commercial value, they did lead to later exploration and oil industry expansion on the reservation. The next major event that affected the Blackfeet was the Allotment Act of 1907. All of the 2,450 Blackfeet people on the tribal rolls were allotted land (320 acres). Some acreage was reserved for the town site of Browning and Babb with all remaining lands sold under the Homestead Act.

The Great Northern Railroad's promotional campaign brought more people to this area to seek their fortune. This, in turn, led to the need for more organized communities. The "Old West" with its lawless, untamed frontiers was gone. The farmer migrated west, bringing an end to the open range. Towns with local governments, churches, and law and order were established. It was during this time that the right to patent land was granted to Indians by the U.S. government. Those who obtained trust patents could now trade their land to another Indian or sell it to anyone if he had obtained a fee patent. In 1919, the government realized that the acreage allotted to the Indians was not enough to sustain them, so an additional 80 acres was given to each Indian. Many of the new allotments were in choice locations, and as a result, some Indians had patents forced on them so they would have to sell their land. In any case, most of them did not understand what the patent process was, and they sold their property for unbelievably low prices. It wasn't unusual for a man to trade his acreage for one horse. Also, many Indian people lost their lands to local merchants for grocery and supply bills.

In February 1919, Glacier County was established. On December 1, 1919, Browning became incorporated; the battle for the county seat between Browning and Cut Bank was on. Browning had the advantage of being near the center of the county and was the site of the Blackfeet Agency. A vote was held, and a few Blackfeet who had their land patents at the time cast their vote for Browning, even though the majority of Indians could not vote. If they could have, Browning would almost certainly be the county seat for Glacier County. (Indians were not granted full status as citizens with the right to vote until 1924, although they did fight in World War I for the United States prior to 1924.)

The Indian Reorganization Act (IRA) passed by Congress in 1934 allowed for tribes to organize a tribal government and made provisions for education (Johnson O'Malley funds) and a credit program, among others. With the reestablishment of tribal powers in 1935, the Blackfeet formed the Blackfeet Tribal Business Council with a constitution outlining the powers and authority. Since 1934, the Blackfeet have made slow but steady progress toward becoming the proud and industrious people they were prior to the arrival of the white man approximately 200 years before. In the fifty years since the IRA, the Blackfeet tribe has made progress in all areas—economic development, education, social services, increasing the tribal land base, population, improved health standards, physical systems, housing, and management skills. The population has increased from a low of 2,000 members in 1920 (a result of a smallpox epidemic along with the massacre of many Blackfeet women and children) to 13,200 enrolled tribal members as of January 1988 (an increase of approximately 630% in 68 years).

Other congressional acts were enacted which resulted from various studies such as the Merriam Report and the Kennedy Subcommittee on Indian Education, which pointed out the needs of Indian people. These included the Civil Rights Act of 1968, the Indian Self-Determination Act and Education Assistance Act of 1975, the Elementary and Secondary Education Act, and others that led to increased self-government and decision making by tribes. These acts provided for expanded opportunities for improved education, improved housing, improved social services, health care, economic development activities, and other services that tribes took advantage of.

Although the quality of life and the standard of living for the Blackfeet people have improved dramatically in the last fifty years, a great deal remains to be done. A tribal plan identifies the needs and priorities for continued progress for the Blackfeet Reservation and tribe.

Chippewa Cree Business Committee
Box 137
Box Elder, MT 59521
(406) 395-4282

Chippewa (Ojibway, "to roast till puckered up," referring to the puckered seam on their moccasins)
Cree (contraction from Kristinaux, French form of Kenistenoag, given as one of their own names)

Location: The reservation is located 15 miles south of U.S. Highway 2 on State Highway 234 near Havre.

Cree Woman with Fur Robe, 1926
Photo by Edward S. Curtis; Courtesy Museum of New Mexico, Neg. No. 122943

Public Ceremony or Powwow Dates: Rocky Boy Indian Days is usually the first weekend in August. Call the tribal office for dates and times.

Art Forms: Call the tribal office for the names of individuals who do traditional forms of arts and crafts.

Visitor Information: The tribe sells permits for fishing and camping. Tipis can be rented for camping, and there are trailer hookups. The Bear Paw Ski Bowl offers good skiing during the winter.

In 1776, before smallpox had greatly reduced them, the population of the Cree proper was estimated at about 15,000. In 1908, it was between 2,500 and 3,000.

Confederated Salish and Kootenai Tribal Council
Box 278
Pablo, MT 59855
(406) 675-2700

Salish (Okinagan: salst, "people")
Kuronaqa (one of their names for themselves)

Location: Look in your atlas in northwest Montana for the Flathead Indian Reservation.

Public Ceremony or Powwow Dates: Be sure to head for Arlee, Montana, for the Fourth of July powwow.

Art Forms: Look for arts and crafts for sale at the powwow.

Visitor Information: At the powwow, the people celebrate with a rodeo, carnival, rock music, traditional Indian music, and hand games. Tipis are set up on the grounds. This is fun!

The Salish are a large and powerful division of the Salishan family, to which they gave their name, inhabiting much of western Montana and centering around Flathead Lake and Valley. A more popular designation for this tribe is Flatheads, given to them by the surrounding people, not because they artifically deformed their heads but because, in contrast to most tribes farther west, they left them in their natural condition, flat on top.

The Salish lived primarily by hunting. With the related Pend d'Oreille and Kootenai, they ceded to the United States their lands in Montana and Idaho, by the treaty of Hell Gate, Montana,

Unidentified woman, Flathead (Salish)
Photo by Edward S. Curtis; Courtesy Museum of New Mexico, Neg. No. 103019

July 16, 1855. They also joined in the peace treaty signed at the mouth of Judith River, Montana, October 17, 1855. Lewis and Clark estimated their population in 1806 to be 600. Their probable number in 1853 was 325, a diminution said to be due to wars with the Siksika (Blackfeet). The number of Flatheads under the Flathead Agency in Montana (1909) was 598.

The Kootenai are a distinct linguistic stock who inhabit parts of southeast British Columbia and northern Montana and Idaho, from the lakes near the source of Columbia River to Pend d'Oreille Lake. Their legends and traditions indicate that they were driven westward by the Siksika, their hereditary enemies. The two tribes now live on amicable terms, and some intermarriage has taken place. Before the buffalo disappeared from the plains from over-hunting and destruction by the whites, they often had joint hunting expeditions. In 1890, the number of Kootenai in Idaho and Montana was 400 to 500; in 1905, the Flathead Agency, Montana, reported 554.

Crow Tribal Council
P.O. Box 159
Crow Agency, MT 59022
(406) 638-2601

Crows (translated from French *gens des corbeaux,* of their own name, Absaroke, crow, sparrowhawk, or bird people)

Location: Crow Agency is located on Interstate Highway 90 south of Hardin, Montana.

Public Ceremony or Powwow Dates: The Crow Fair is generally held in August. This is one of the biggest powwows in the lower 48 states and is considered one of the best. The Crow love tipis and the area will be filled with them. Call the tribal office for dates and times.

Art Forms: The Crow are known for their fabulous beadwork, usually in floral designs. Look for the beautiful beaded horse gear during the parade for the Crow Fair. The visitors center at the Custer Battlefield also has arts and crafts.

Visitor Information: There is traditional dancing, powwow dancing, Indian food, arts and crafts sales, and more during the fair. The Crow flatten their roach headdresses and are distinctive during the dancing.

Perits-har-sts and wife, Crow Indians, Washington, D.C., 1873
Photo by Ulke; Courtesy Museum of New Mexico, Neg. No. 58639

Custer Battlefield National Monument is located 2 miles southeast of Crow Agency on Interstate Highway 90, exit 510.

The Crow are a Siouan tribe forming part of the Hidatsa tribe. According to tradition, their separation from the Hidatsa was probably about 1776. One story has it that this separation was the result of a factional dispute between two chiefs who were desperate men with a nearly equal number of followers. They were then residing on the Missouri River. One of the two bands, which afterward became the Crows, withdrew and migrated to the vicinity of the Rocky Mountains, where they continued to roam until forced onto the reservation. Since their separation from the Hidatsa, their history has been similar to that of most tribes of the plains, their chief enemies being the Siksika and the Dakota. At the time of Lewis and Clark (1804), they dwelled chiefly on the Bighorn River; in 1817, they were located on the Yellowstone and the east side of the Rocky Mountains; in 1834, they lived on the south branch of the Yellowstone.

The tipis of the Crows were exactly like those of the Sioux, set up without any regular order. On the poles, instead of scalps, there were small pieces of colored cloth, chiefly red, which floated like streamers in the wind. According to one observer, the camp swarmed with wolflike dogs. The Crows were a wandering tribe of hunters, only occasionally planting a few small patches of tobacco. They lived at that time in some 400 tipis and are said to have possessed between 9,000 and 10,000 horses. In stature and dress, they were similar to the Hidatsa and were proud of their long hair. The women have been described as skillful in various kinds of work and their shirts and dresses of bighorn leather, as well as their buffalo robes, embroidered and ornamented with dyed porcupine quills, as particularly handsome. The men were skilled in making weapons, especially their large bows, covered with horn of the elk or bighorn and often with rattlesnake skin. The Crows are skillful horsemen and could throw themselves from side to side during battle. Their dead were usually placed on scaffolds elevated on poles in the prairie. The population was estimated by Lewis and Clark (1804) at 350 lodges and 3,500 individuals; in 1829 and 1834, at 4,500; in 1843, there were 400 tipis. Their number in 1890 was 2,287; in 1904, 1,826. The Crows have been officially classified as Mountain Crows and River Crows, the former so-called because

*Curley, Crow Indian scout for Gen. G. Custer at Battle of Little Big Horn in 1876
Photo by Finn; Courtesy Museum of New Mexico, Neg. No. 2511*

of their custom of hunting and roaming near the mountains away from the Missouri River, the latter, because they left the mountain region about 1859 and occupied the country along the river. There were no ethnic, linguistic, or other differences between them.

Fort Belknap Community Council
P.O. Box 249
Harlem, MT 59526
(406) 353-2205

Gros Ventre (Big Bellies)
Assiniboine-Sioux (u sin, "stone"; u pwawa, "he cooks by roasting"; one who cooks with a stone)

Location: This reservation is located in north central Montana straight north of Billings.

Public Ceremony or Powwow Dates: Call the tribal office for dates and times.

Some writers have confused the Gros Ventre with the Hidatsa. They are very distinct tribes and are not related to each other. The name was given to them by the French and later by others to (1) the Atsina, or Hitunena, a detached band of the Arapahoe, and (2) the Hidatsa, or Minitari. In the Lewis and Clark narrative of 1806 the former are distinguished as Minitarees of Fort de Prairie and the latter as Minitarees of the Missouri, although there is no justification for applying the name Minitari to the Atsina. The two tribes have also been distinguished as Gros Ventre of the Missouri (Hidatsa) and Gros Ventre of the Prairie (Atsina). The name as applied to the Atsina originates from the Indian sign by which they are designated in the sign language—a sweeping pass with both hands in front of the abdomen, intended to convey the idea of "hungry." A clue to its application to the Hidatsa is that the Hidatsa formerly tattooed parallel stripes across the chest and were thus sometimes distinguished in picture writings. The gesture sign to indicate this style of tattooing would be sufficiently similar to that used to designate the Atsina to lead the careless observer to interpret both as "Gros Ventre." The ordinary sign now used by the southern Plains tribes to indicate the Hidatsa is interpreted to mean "spreading tipis," or "row of lodges."

Tipi, Gros Ventre
Photo by V. C. Traphagen; Courtesy Museum of New Mexico, Neg. No. 77735

Chief Red Whip, Gros Ventre, 1913
Photo by Joseph A. Dixon; Courtesy Museum of New Mexico, Neg. No. 68011

The Assiniboine are a large Siouan tribe, originally constituting a part of the Yanktonai. The Jesuits encountered them about 1640 in the vicinity of Lake Alimibeg, between Lake Superior and Hudson Bay. In 1829, the estimated Assiniboine population was 8,000; and before the smallpox epidemic of 1836, during which 4,000 of them perished, 10,000. In 1836, the number was 6,000. The U.S. Indian report of 1843 placed the number at 7,000. In 1890, they numbered 3,008; in 1904, 2,600.

Fort Peck Executive Board
P.O. Box 1027
Poplar, MT 59255
(406) 768-5311

usini u pwawa (cook with stones)

The Assiniboine are a large Siouan tribe, originally constituting a part of the Yanktonai. Their separation apparently preceded the appearance of the whites about 1640. In 1658, they were in the vicinity of Lake Alimibeg, between Lake Superior and Hudson Bay. Estimates of their population range from 8,000 in 1829 down to 2,600 in 1904. Smallpox brought by encroaching whites killed most of the members of the tribe.

Northern Cheyenne Tribal Council
Lame Deer, MT 59043
(406) 477-6248

Sha-Hi'yena, Shai-ena (from Sioux)

Shai-ela (from Teton)

Cheyenne

Location: This reservation is in south central Montana bordering the Wyoming state line.

Public Ceremony or Powwow Dates: The Northern Cheyenne hold a powwow, usually in July. They often hold stick-games and other interesting events.

Art Forms: The Northern Cheyenne do traditional forms of artwork. Individual artisans can be contacted through the tribal office.

Visitor Information: The Northern Cheyenne Tribal Museum, Lame Deer, presents the history and culture of the Cheyenne Indian people.

The Cheyenne are of the greater Algonquian family. They call themselves Dzi tsi stas, apparently nearly equivalent to "people alike," that is, "Our People"; with a slight change of accent, it might also mean "gashed ones," from ehistai, "he is gashed," or possibly "tall people."

The popular name has no connection with the French *chien*, "dog," as has sometimes been erroneously supposed. In the sign language they are indicated by a gesture that has often been interpreted to mean "cut arms" or "cut fingers," being made by drawing the right index finger several times rapidly across the left but which appears really to indicate "striped arrows," by which name they are known to the Hidatsa, Shoshone, Comanche, Caddo, and probably other tribes, in allusion to their old-time preference for turkey feathers for winging arrows.

The earliest authenticated habitat of the Cheyenne, before the year 1700, seems to have been that part of Minnesota bounded roughly by the Mississippi, Minnesota, and upper Red rivers. The Sioux, living at that time closer to the Mississippi, to the east and southeast came in contact with the French as early as 1667, but the Cheyenne are first mentioned in 1680, under the name of Chaa, when a party of that tribe, described as living on the head of the great river, the Mississippi, visited La Salle's Fort on the Illinois River to invite the French to come to their country, which they represented as abounding in beaver and other fur animals. The veteran Sioux missionary, Williamson, says that according to concurrent and reliable Sioux tradition, the Cheyenne occupied the upper Mississippi region prior to the Sioux and were found by them already established on the Minnesota. At a later period, they moved over to the Cheyenne branch of Red River, North Dakota, which thus acquired its name, being known to the Sioux as "the place where the Cheyenne plant," showing that the latter were still an agricultural people. This westward movement was due to pressure from the Sioux, who were themselves retiring before the Chippewa, then already in possession of guns from the east.

Driven out by the Sioux, the Cheyenne moved west toward the Missouri River, where their further progress was opposed by the

Honii-Watoma (Wolf Robe), Cheyenne, 1909
Photo by DeLancey Gill; Courtesy Museum of New Mexico, Neg. No. 86994

Sutaio, a people speaking a closely related dialect, who had preceded them to the west and were then apparently living between the river and the Black Hills. After a period of hostility, the two tribes made an alliance, some time after which the Cheyenne crossed the Missouri below the entrance of the Cannonball River and later took refuge in the Black Hills around the heads of the Cheyenne River of South Dakota. Lewis and Clark found them there in 1804, since which time their movement was constantly west and south until they were confined to reservations. Up to the time of Lewis and Clark, they carried on desultory war with the Mandan and Hidatsa, who probably helped to drive them from the Missouri River. They seem, however, to have kept on good terms with the Arikara.

According to their own story, the Cheyenne, while living in Minnesota and on the Missouri River, occupied fixed villages, practiced agriculture, and made pottery but lost these arts on being driven out into the plains to become roving buffalo hunters. On the Missouri, and perhaps also farther east, they occupied earth-covered log houses. Some Cheyenne had cultivated fields on the Little Missouri River as late as 1850. This was probably a recent settlement, as they are not mentioned in that locality by Lewis and Clark. At least one man among them still understood the art of making beads and figurines from pounded glass, as formerly practiced by the Mandan. In a sacred tradition recited only by the priestly keeper, they still tell how they "lost the corn" after leaving the eastern country. One of the starting points in this tradition is a great fall, apparently St. Anthony's Falls on the Mississippi, and a stream known as the "River of Turtles," which may be the Turtle River tributary of Red River, or possibly the St. Croix, entering the Mississippi below the mouth of the Minnesota and anciently known by a similar name.

Although the alliance between the Sutaio and the Cheyenne dates from the crossing of the Missouri River by the latter, the actual incorporation of the Sutaio into the Cheyenne camp circle probably occurred within the last two hundred years, as the two tribes were regarded as distinct by Lewis and Clark. The Cheyenne say also that they obtained the Sun Dance and the buffalo head medicine from the Sutaio but claim the Medicine Arrow Ceremony as their own from the beginning. Up to 1835, and probably until reduced by the cholera epidemic of 1849, the Sutaio retained their distinctive dialect, dress, and ceremonies and camped apart from the Cheyenne. In 1851, they were still to some extent a distinct people but exist now only as one of the component divisions of the Southern Cheyenne tribe. Under the name Staitan, they are mentioned by Lewis and Clark in 1804 as a small and savage tribe roving west of the Black Hills. There is some doubt as to when or where the Cheyenne first met the Arapahoe, with whom they have long been confederated; neither do they appear to have any clear idea as to the date of the alliance between the two tribes, which has continued. Their connection with the Arapahoe is a simple alliance, without assimilation, while the Sutaio have been incorporated bodily.

Their modern history may be said to begin with the expedition of Lewis and Clark in 1804. Constantly pressed farther into the plains by the hostile Sioux, they established themselves next on the upper branches of the Platte, driving the Kiowa, in turn, farther to the south. They made their first treaty with the government in 1825 at the mouth of the Teton River, on the Missouri, at the present site of Pierre, South Dakota. In consequence of the building of Bent's Fort on the upper Arkansas in Colorado in 1832, a large part of the tribe decided to move down and make permanent headquarters on the Arkansas, while the rest continued to rove about the headwaters of the North Platte and Yellowstone rivers. This separation was made permanent by the treaty of Fort Laramie in 1851, the two sections being now known respectively as Southern and Northern Cheyenne. The distinction is purely geographic, although it has served to hasten the destruction of their former compact tribal organization.

The Southern Cheyenne are known in the tribe as Sowonia, "Southerners," while the Northern Cheyenne are commonly designated as O Mi Sis eaters, from the division most numerously represented among them. Their advent to the Arkansas brought them into constant collision with the Kiowa, who, with the Comanche, claimed the territory to the south. The old men of both tribes told of numerous encounters during the next few years, chief among these being a battle on an upper branch of Red River in 1837, in which the Kiowa massacred an entire party of 48 Cheyenne warriors of the Bowstring society, and a battle in summer 1838, in which the Cheyenne and Arapahoe attacked the Kiowa and Comanche on Wolf Creek, northwest Oklahoma, with considerable

Sun Dance Pledgers, Cheyenne, 1911
Photo by Edward S. Curtis; Courtesy Museum of New Mexico, Neg. No. 65118

loss on both sides. About 1840, the Cheyenne made peace with the Kiowa in the south, having already made peace with the Sioux in the north. Since this time all these tribes, together with the Arapahoe, Kiowa, Kiowa Apache, and Comanche, usually acted as allies in the wars with other tribes and with whites. For a long time the Cheyenne were friends with the western Sioux, after whom they patterned many details of their dress and ceremony. They seem not to have suffered greatly from the smallpox epidemic of 1837–39, having been warned in time to escape to the mountains. But in common with other prairie tribes, they suffered terribly from cholera in 1849, several of their bands being nearly exterminated. They lost about 200 lodges, estimated at 2,000 souls, or about two-thirds of their whole number before the epidemic.

Their peace with the Kiowa enabled them to extend their incursions farther to the south, and in 1853, they made their first raid into Mexico but with disastrous results, losing all but three men in a fight with Mexican lancers. From 1860 to 1878, they were prominent in border warfare, acting with the Sioux in the north and with the Kiowa and Comanche in the south. And they probably lost more in conflict with the whites than any other tribe of the plains, in proportion to their number. In 1864, the southern band suffered a severe blow in the notorious Chivington massacre in Colorado and again in 1868 at the hands of Custer in the battle of the Washita. They took a leading part in the general outbreak of the southern tribes in 1874–75. The Northern Cheyenne joined with the Sioux in the Sitting Bull War in 1876 and were active participants in the victory over Custer. Later in the year they received such a severe blow from General Mackenzie that they were forced to surrender. In the winter of 1878–79, a band of Northern Cheyenne under Dull Knife, Wild Hog, and Little Wolf, who had been brought down as prisoners to Fort Reno to be colonized with the southern portion of the tribe in what is now Oklahoma, made a desperate attempt at escape. Of an estimated 89 men and 146 women and children who broke away on the night of September 9, about 75, including Dull Knife and most of the warriors, were killed in the pursuit that continued to the Dakota border, in the course of which about 50 whites lost their lives. Thirty-two of the Cheyenne slain were killed in a second break for liberty from Fort Robinson, Nebraska, where the captured people had been confined. Little Wolf, with about 60 followers, got through in safety to the north. At a later period, the Northern Cheyenne were assigned to the present reservation in Montana. The Southern Cheyenne were assigned to a reservation in west Oklahoma by treaty of 1867 but refused to remain there until after the surrender of 1875, when a number of the most prominent warriors were deported to Florida for a term of three years. In 1901–02, the lands of the Southern Cheyenne were allotted in severalty and the Indian people were offered American citizenship. Those in the north seemed to hold their own in population, while those of the south steadily decreased. In 1904, the Southern Cheyenne numbered 1,903; and the Northern Cheyenne, 1,409.

Although originally an agricultural people of the timber country, the Cheyenne for generations were a typical prairie tribe, living in skin tipis, following the buffalo over great areas, traveling and fighting on horseback. They commonly buried their dead in trees or on scaffolds but occasionally in caves or in the ground. Polygamy was permitted, as was usual among the prairie tribes. Under their old system, before the division of the tribe, they had a council of 44 elective chiefs, four of whom constituted a higher body, with power to elect one of their own number as head chief of the tribe. In all councils that concerned the relations of the Cheyenne with other tribes, one member of the council was appointed to argue as the proxy or "devil's advocate" for the alien people. This council of 44 is still symbolized by a bundle of 44 invitation sticks, kept with the sacred medicine arrows and formerly sent around when occasion arose to convene the assembly.

This set of four medicine arrows, each of a different color, constitutes the tribal palladium that they claim to have had from the beginning of the world and is exposed with appropriate rites once a year if previously "pledged" and on those rare occasions when a Cheyenne has been killed by one of his own tribe, the purpose of the ceremony being to wipe away from the murderer the stain of a brother's blood. The rite did not die with the final separation of the two sections of the tribe in 1851. The bundle is still religiously preserved by the Southern Cheyenne. Besides the public ceremony there is also a rite spoken of as "fixing" the arrows, held at shorter intervals, which concerns the arrow priests alone. The public ceremony is always attended by delegates from the Northern Cheyenne. No woman, white man, or even mixed blood of the tribe has ever been allowed to come near the sacred arrows.

Their great tribal ceremony for generations has been the Sun Dance (Offerings Lodge), which they themselves say came to them from the Sutaio, after emerging from the timber region into the open plains. So far as known, this ceremony belongs exclusively to the tribes of the plains or to those in close contact with them. The Buffalo Head Ceremony, which was formerly connected with the Sun Dance but has been obsolete for many years, also came from the Sutaio. The modern Ghost Dance Spirituality was enthusiastically taken up by the tribe at its first appearance, about 1890, and the Peyote Ceremony is now popular with the younger men. They also had until the early 1900s a Fire Dance, something like that credited to the Navajo, in which the initiated performers danced over a fire of blazing coals until they extinguished it with their bare feet. In priestly dignity the keepers of the Medicine Arrow (Cheyenne) and Sun Dance (Sutaio) ceremonies stood first and equal.

At the Sun Dance, and on other occasions where the whole tribe was assembled, they formed their camp circle in eleven sections, occupied by as many recognized tribal divisions. As one of these was really an incorporated tribe, and several others have originated by segregation within the memory of old men still living in 1905, the ancient number did not exceed seven. While it is quite probable that the Cheyenne may have had the clan system in ancient times while still a sedentary people, it is almost as certain that it disappeared so long ago as to be no longer even a memory.

The Northern Cheyenne were known as the most aggressive of all warrior tribes until they were defeated, with the loss of the chief, Tall Bull, by General Carr's forces in 1869.

NEBRASKA

Omaha Tribal Council
P.O. Box 368
Macy, NE 68039
(402) 837-5391

Omaha (Dhegiha)

Location: The Omaha Reservation is located in northeast Nebraska bordering the Winnebago Reservation.

The Omaha are one of the five tribes of the so-called Dhegiha group of the Siouan family, the other four being the Kansa, Quapaw, Osage, and Ponca. Earliest contact with the Europeans places them on the Ohio and Wabash rivers.

Santee Sioux Tribal Council
Route 2
Niobrara, NE 68760
(402) 857-3302

Sioux (Isanyati)

Location: The reservation is located in northeastern Nebraska straight west of Sioux City, Iowa.

The Santee Sioux are an eastern division of the Dakota. The Mdewakanton and Wahpekute, sometimes also the Sisseton and Wahpeton, comprise part of this division.

Winnebago Tribal Council
Winnebago, NE 68071
(402) 878-2272

Winnebago (Winipig)

Location: The reservation is located in northeast Nebraska on the Missouri River.

Public Ceremony or Powwow Dates: The annual powwow is usually held in late July, but you must call the tribal office for exact dates and times.

The Winnebago were in Wisconsin on Green Bay when the Frenchman Nicolet encountered them. They are culturally similar to the Iowa, Oto, and Missouri.

NORTH DAKOTA

Devils Lake Sioux Tribal Council
Sioux Community Center
Fort Totten, ND 58335
(701) 766-4221

Sioux

Location: The Fort Totten Reservation is located in northeast central North Dakota close to Devils Lake on Federal Highway 2.

In 1908, the tribes placed on this reservation were the Assiniboine, Cuthead (Pabaksa), Santee, Sisseton, Yankton, and Wahpeton Sioux.

Standing Rock Sioux Tribal Council
Fort Yates, ND 58538
(701) 854-7231

Sioux

Location: This reservation is located in south central North Dakota and north central South Dakota. Look straight south of Bismarck, North Dakota, on your map.

Public Ceremony or Powwow Dates: Call the tribal office for dates and times of their powwow at Little Eagle, South Dakota. It is usually held in July.

In 1908, the tribes placed on this reservation were the Blackfeet (Sihasapa), Hunkpapa, and Lower and Upper Yanktonai Sioux.

Three Affiliated Tribes
Fort Berthold Tribal Business Council
P.O. Box 220
New Town, ND 587634
(701) 627-4781

Arikara, Hidatsa, and Mandan

Location: The Three Affiliated Tribes occupy west central North Dakota within six counties: McLean, McKenzie, Mountrail, Dunn,

Bear's Teeth, Arikara, 1908
Photo by Edward S. Curtis; Courtesy Museum of New Mexico, Neg. No. 103168

Mercer, and Ward. Look on your map of North Dakota, northwest of Bismarck and southeast of Williston on the Missouri River.

Public Ceremony or Powwow Dates: The powwows held on the Fort Berthold Reservation are colorful annual events and visitors are welcome. There is no admission charge for the powwows, and many concession stands are available. The organizers do not allow any alcohol or drugs on the grounds during the events. Law enforcement personnel will strictly enforce these regulations.

The Arikara Celebration is held annually at White Shield, North Dakota, the second weekend of July. The Mandaree Celebration is held annually at Mandaree, North Dakota, the third weekend of July. The Little Shell Celebration is held at New Town, North Dakota, the second weekend of August, and the Twin Buttes Celebration is held at Twin Buttes, North Dakota, the third weekend of August.

Art Forms: You will find beadwork and star quilts handmade by local artisans. Call the tribe at the main office phone number for more information.

Visitor Information: The nearby cities of New Town and Parshall, North Dakota, have all services needed by the traveler. The Three Affiliated Tribes Museum is located in New Town.

The Fort Berthold Reservation is the home of the Mandan, Hidatsa, and Arikara tribes, who joined together as the Three Affiliated Tribes under the Indian Reorganization Act of June 18, 1934, with a Federal Corporation Charter ratified April 23, 1937, with a subsequent amendment November 27, 1961. They operate under a constitution and by-laws approved June 28, 1936, with subsequent amendments.

All three tribes lived in permanent earth-lodge villages for many centuries before the coming of the white man. Despite a basic similarity of economic and social life, these village peoples differed markedly in language and customs. The Mandan and Hidatsa speak a Siouan dialect, while the Arikara are members of the Caddoan linguistic group, being related closest to the Pawnee.

When first visited by traders and explorers in the middle eighteenth century, the Mandan Hidatsa lived very near their present location. The Hidatsa had three earth-lodge villages at the mouth of the Knife River, north of the present town of Stanton, North

Dakota, and the Mandan had a half dozen or more villages near the mouth of the Heart River at Mandan, North Dakota. The Arikara were located in central South Dakota with some of their villages ranging as high as the Grand River area.

The village people seem to have been moving slowly upstream in a long-term migration that began well back in prehistoric times. In the latter third of the eighteenth century, this migration was sharply accelerated because of the ravages resulting from the smallpox epidemic. This influenced the Mandan to a greater degree than the other tribes, so that at the beginning of the nineteenth century they had moved to a location a few miles south of the Hidatsa. The Hidatsa controlled the hunting to the north, and the Arikara controlled the hunting to the south.

The Mandan and Hidatsa were the "farmers, merchants, and bankers" of the northern plains. Evidence has been found which indicates that these people were dealing with the native peoples of the deep Southwest. The Arikara, however, insisted on acting as brokers between the agricultural Hidatsa and Mandan in their bartering with the Mexican and deep Southwest people in trading for corn during the recurrent droughts that often plagued the Southwest.

The year 1837 marks the last of the violent smallpox epidemics that hit the general area. This epidemic resulted in the decimation of the Mandan tribe to a point where it could no longer exist as an independent unit. The Hidatsa were also hard hit. But inasmuch as members of this tribe were out on the prairies for their annual summer buffalo hunts, the Hidatsa were affected to a lesser degree by the ravages of smallpox.

The Arikara, who had been increasingly harassed by the Sioux coming in on them from both south and east, chose this time to abandon their villages. When the Arikara found the Mandan's villages empty, they moved into the hastily abandoned houses. In the meantime, the Mandan and Hidatsa, over a period of years, continued to move slowly upstream where they finally constructed a new village in a beautiful bend on the Missouri River. This location was the famous "Like a Fishhook Village."

Recorded history relating to the Fort Berthold Reservation area dates back to the 1790s when early explorers traversed the area and slightly later when the Lewis and Clark Expedition traveled on their Missouri River voyage through the Louisiana Territory. However, definitive history of the reservation begins with the Treaty of Fort Laramie of 1851, which defined the boundary of the Gros Ventre (a misnomer for the Hidatsa), Mandan, and Arikara Indian nations, now called the Three Affiliated Tribes. The Fort Laramie Treaty established a vast area of land vaguely described as the entire right bank of the Missouri River from the mouth of the Yellowstone River and from the mouth of the Powder River to the headwaters of the Heart River. This territory, which included parts of Montana, Wyoming, North Dakota, and South Dakota, was named Fort Berthold in honor of an American Fur Company founder, Bartholomay Berthold.

Between 1851, when the Fort Laramie Treaty was signed, and 1891, a succession of executive orders and congressional acts changed the size of the reservation from a maximum of roughly 13,500,000 acres to a gross area (including white-owned land) of approximately 930,000 acres. During 1954, the reservation lost an additional 152,300 acres of land to the U.S. Army Corps of Engineers for the filling of the Garrison Reservoir (Lake Sakakawea). The waters of Lake Sakakawea inundated most of the well built up bottom and access roads and divided the reservation into five isolated segments that are not contiguous one with the other. The flooding of the bottom lands destroyed the long-established Indian population centers, with the Tribal Agency itself being moved to the city of New Town. Since 1954, several small communities have sprung up, the principal ones being White Shield, Mandaree, and Twin Buttes.

The immense loss of natural resources occasioned by the flooding of Lake Sakakawea was cause for only a part of the adjustments that have had to be made by the Indian people. No attempt was made to reestablish duplicates of the small Indian villages that existed; thus Indian families were forced to relocate on isolated holdings scattered throughout the reservation. Consequently, social and clan lines were crossed and recrossed with former neighbors becoming widely separated. This extreme stress on the Indian people has been partly responsible for movement off the reservation.

Turtle Mountain Tribal Council
Belcourt, ND 58316
(701) 477-6451

Ojibwa (Chippewa)

Location: The reservation is located in north central North Dakota just south of Manitoba, Canada.

The range of the Chippewa was along both shores of Lake Huron and Lake Superior extending across Minnesota to Turtle Mountains, North Dakota. This band is the Pembina.

OKLAHOMA AREA INDIAN EVENTS

The tourist is advised to check with the Oklahoma City Native American Indian Center for latest listings and dates of each event: (405) 232-2512, 2830 South Robinson, Oklahoma City, OK 73103.

January
New Year's Powwow
Oklahoma City, OK

April
Trade Fair and Powwow
Shawnee, OK

May
Delaware Powwow
Copan, OK

Pawnee Indian Veterans Memorial Day Dance
Pawnee, OK

Kiowa Blackleggings Society Armed Forces Day Observance
Anadarko, OK

June
Osage Tribal Ceremonial Dances
Greyhorse, OK

Osage Tribal Ceremonial Dances
Pawhuska, OK

Hub City Inter-Tribal Powwow
Clinton, OK

El Reno Inter-Tribal Exposition
El Reno, OK

Cheyenne-Arapaho Indian Powwow
Clinton, OK

Greyhorse Indian Exposition/Powwow
Fairfax, OK

Potawatomie Inter-Tribal Powwow
Shawnee, OK

Absentee Shawnee Little River Powwow
Little Axe, OK

Sequoyah Inter-Tribal Powwow
Elk City, OK

July
Kiowa Tia-Piah Society of Carnegie
Carnegie, OK

Kiowa Tia-Piah Society of Oklahoma
Lawton, OK

Oklahoma City Indian Hills Powwow
Oklahoma City, OK

Ardmore Indian Association Powwow
Ardmore, OK

Kiowa-Apache Blackfeet Society Ceremonials
Ft. Cobb, OK

Sac & Fox Powwow
Jim Thorpe Memorial
Stroud, OK

Otoe-Missouri Powwow
Highway 177
Red Rock, OK

Kiowa Gourd Clan Ceremonies
Carnegie, OK

Quapaw Powwow
Quapaw, OK

Kiowa Oh-Ho-Mah Powwow
west of Anadarko, OK

Annual Tulsa Powwow
Tulsa, OK

Arapaho Tribal Powwow
Canton, OK

Feather and Buckskin Society Powwow
South of Guthrie, OK

Sac and Fox Veterans Club Powwow
Shawnee, OK

Indian Hills Powwow
Oklahoma City, OK

August
Ottawa Powwow
Quapaw, OK

Wichita Tribal Powwow
north of Lawton, OK

Redbone Blackfeet Society Powwow
near Ft. Cobb, OK

Star Hawk Society Powwow
Colony, OK

American Indian Exposition
Anadarko, OK

Annual Choctaw Festival
Talihina, OK

Ponca Indian Fair and Powwow
Ponca City, OK

Cheyenne-Arapaho Exposition
Canton, OK

Kihekah Steh Club Annual Powwow
Skiatook, OK

Ed Mack's Veteran's Powwow
Shawnee, OK

September
Cheyenne-Arapaho Powwow
Canton, OK

Osage Indian Day Celebration
Tribal Dances
Hominy, OK

Indian Powwow
Eufaula, OK

Ottawa Powwow
Quapaw, OK

Oklahoma City Powwow Club hosts a Powwow the last Friday of each month, September through May.

October
Five Civilized Tribes Art Show
Five Civilized Tribes Museum
Muskogee, OK

Pawnee Bill Oklahoma Indian Art Show
Pawnee, OK

American Indian Student Association Powwow
University of Oklahoma
Norman, OK

November
Kiowa Tia-Piah Society Veterans Day Powwow
Carnegie, OK

Indian Veterans Celebration
Pawhuska, OK

Pawnee Indian Veterans Day Dance
Pawnee, OK

December
Pawnee Indian Veterans Christmas Day Dance
Pawnee, OK

OKLAHOMA

Absentee-Shawnee Executive Committee
P.O. Box 1747
Shawnee, OK 74801
(405) 275-4030

Shawnee (Shawun, "south")

Visitor Information: All three branches of the Shawnee Tribe are located in Oklahoma today. Shawnee stomp dance leaders and shell shakers dance traditional forms during stomp dance competitions at powwows. Look for them at the Quapaw powwow.

This tribe is formerly of South Carolina, Tennessee, Pennsylvania, and Ohio. Linguistically, the Shawnee belong to the group of Central Algonquian dialects and are very closely related to Sauk and Fox. The tradition of the Delawares, as embodied in the Walum Olum, makes them, the Shawnee, and the Nanticoke originally one people.

The Apache Tribe
Route 2, Box 121
Apache, OK 73006
(405) 588-2298

Apache (probably from Apachu, "enemy," the Zuni name for the Navajo, who were designated "Apaches de Nabaju" by the early Spaniards in New Mexico)

Visitor Information: After the Apache wars with the blue coats in the Southwest were over in 1886, Chiricahua Apache Chief Geronimo was imprisoned at Fort Sill north of Lawton, Oklahoma. The guardhouse and cell where Geronimo and his warriors were imprisoned is still here. Many of Geronimo's people still live in the area today.

Nai-chi-ti (Nachez) and wife, Chiricahua Apache, ca. 1882
Photo by Ben Wittick; Courtesy School of American Research Collections in the
Museum of New Mexico, Neg. No. 15903

Apache Business Committee
P.O. Box 1220
Anadarko, OK 73005
(405) 247-9493

Apache (probably from apachu, "enemy," the Zuni name for Navajo)

Visitor Information: This Indian community has several tribes living in it or nearby. They are the Apache, Arapahoe, Caddo, Cheyenne, Comanche, Delaware, Kiowa-Apache, Kiowa, and Wichita. There are also other tribes represented by marriage, employment, and choice. Please see the Oklahoma events calendar at the beginning of the Oklahoma section for more details on celebrations and powwows.

The Apache call themselves N de, Dine, Tinde, or Inde, "People."

Caddo Tribal Council
P.O. Box 487
Binger, OK 73009
(405) 656-2344

Caddo (Hasinai)

Visitor Information: The Caddo people live out their traditions in song, music, and dance. Labor Day is their biggest single celebration with three days of dancing, but the whole season of June through September is busy with dances. Call the tribal office for dates and times and arrangements.

According to tribal traditions, the lower Red River of Louisiana was the early home of the Caddo, from which they spread to the north, west, and south.

Tennyson Berry (Sekûñtekûñ or War Bonnet), Kiowa-Apache, 1913
Photo by DeLancey Gill; Courtesy Museum of New Mexico, Neg. No. 59438

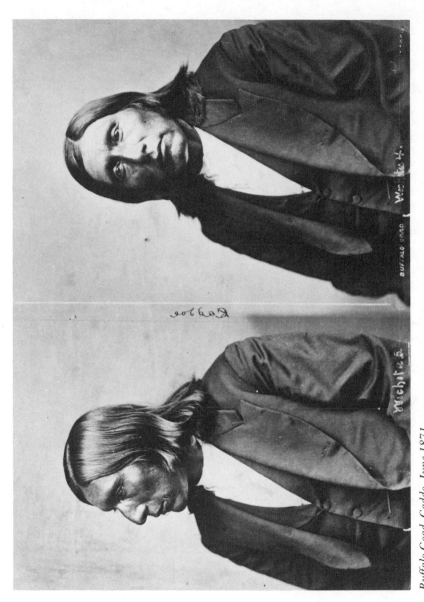

Buffalo Good, Caddo, June 1871
Photo by Jeremiah Gurney and Son; Courtesy Museum of New Mexico, Neg. No. 4853

Cherokee Nation of Oklahoma
P.O. Box 948
Tahlequah, OK 74465
(918) 456-0671

United Keetoowah Cherokee Council
2450 South Muskogee Avenue
Tahlequah, OK 74464
(918) 456-5491

The tribal name is a corruption of Tsalagi or Tsaragi, the name by which they commonly called themselves, and which may be derived from the Choctaw *chiluk ki*, "cave people," in allusion to the numerous caves in their mountain country. They sometimes also call themselves Ani-Yun-wiya, "real people," or Ani-Kitu hwagi, "people of Kituhwa," one of their most important ancient settlements. Their northern kinsmen, the Iroquois, called them Oyata ge ronon, "inhabitants of the cave country," and the Delawares and connected tribes called them Kittuwa, from the same settlement already noted.

Location: The Cherokee Heritage Center, Tsa-la-gi, is three miles south of Tahlequah on Highway 62, then one mile east. Tsa-la-gi Lodge is one mile more down Highway 62, four miles south of Tahlequah.

Public Ceremony or Powwow Dates: The Cherokee National Holiday is celebrated in early September. The Fall Festival is usually held in Jay, Oklahoma, around October. The Red Bird Smith ceremonial grounds near Vian, Oklahoma, host stomp dances each August 17 honoring Red Bird Smith. Call the tribal office for dates, times, and arrangements to attend ceremonials.

Art Forms: Traditional arts and crafts are sold at the Heritage Center.

The Cherokee seem to be identical with the Rickohockans, who invaded central Virginia in 1658, and with the ancient Talligewi, of Delaware tradition. It is said the Cherokee were driven southward from the upper Ohio River region by the combined forces of the Iroquois and Delawares.

Traditional, linguistic, and archaeological evidence shows that the Cherokee originated in the north, but they were found in possession of the south Allegheny region when first encountered by DeSoto in 1540. Their relations with the Carolina colonies began 150 years later. In 1736, the Jesuit Priber started the first mission among them and attempted to organize their government on a "civilized" basis. In 1759, under the leadership of Oconostota, they began war with the English of Carolina. In the Revolution, they aided the Americans and continued the struggle almost continuously until 1794. During this period, parties of the Cherokee pushed down the Tennessee River and formed new settlements at Chickamauga and other points around the Tennessee-Alabama line. Shortly after 1800, missionary and educational work was established among them, and in 1820, they adopted a regular form of government modeled on that of the Iroquois Confederacy. In the meantime, large numbers of the more conservative Cherokee, wearied by the encroachments of the whites, had crossed the Mississippi and made new homes in the wilderness in what is now Arkansas. A year or two later Sequoya, a celebrated Cherokee chief, invented the alphabet.

At the height of their prosperity, gold was discovered near the present Dahlonega, Georgia, within the limits of the Cherokee Nation, and at once powerful agitation was begun for the removal of the Indians. After years of hopeless struggle under the leadership of their great chief, John Ross, they were compelled to submit to the inevitable, and by the treaty of New Echota, December 29, 1835, the Cherokee sold their entire remaining territory and agreed to move beyond the Mississippi to a country there to be set apart for them—the Cherokee Nation in Indian Territory. Their removal, known as the Trail of Tears, was accomplished in the winter of 1838–39. It caused terrible hardship and the loss of nearly one-fourth of their number: the unwilling Indians were driven out by military force and made the long journey on foot. On reaching their destination, they reorganized their national government, established their capital at Tahlequah, and admitted to equal privileges the earlier emigrants, known as "old settlers."

A part of the Arkansas Cherokee had previously gone down into Texas, where they had obtained a grant of land in the east part of the state from the Mexican government. The later Texan revolutionists refused to recognize their rights, and in spite of the efforts of General Sam Houston, who defended the Indian claim, a conflict broke out, resulting in 1839 in the killing of the Cherokee chief, Bowl, with a large number of his men, by the Texan troops and the expulsion of the Cherokee from Texas.

When the main body of the tribe was removed to the West, several hundred fugitives escaped to the mountains, where they lived as refugees, until 1842, when through the efforts of William H. Thomas, an influential trader, they received permission to remain on lands set apart for their use in west North Carolina. They constitute the present eastern band of Cherokee, residing chiefly on the Qualla Reservation in Swain and Jackson counties, with several outlying settlements. (See **North Carolina**, Cherokee, for more details on this tribe today.)

The Cherokee in the Cherokee Nation were for years divided into two hostile factions, those who had favored and those who had opposed the treaty of removal. Hardly had these differences been settled when the War Between the States was declared. Being slaveowners and surrounded by southern influences, a large part of each of the Five Civilized Tribes of the territory (Cherokee, Chickasaw, Choctaw, Creek, Seminole) enlisted in the service of the Confederacy, while others adhered to the National Government. The territory of the Cherokee was overrun by both armies in turn. By the close of the war, they were devastated. By treaty in 1866, they were readmitted to the protection of the United States but obliged to liberate their Negro slaves and admit them to equal citizenship. In 1867 and 1870, the Delawares and Shawnee, respectively, numbering together about 1,750, were admitted from Kansas and incorporated with the Nation. In 1889, the Cherokee Commission was created for the purpose of abolishing the tribal governments and opening the territories to white settlement, with the result that after 15 years of negotiation, an agreement was made by which the government of the Cherokee Nation came to a final end on March 3, 1906. The Indian lands were divided, and the Cherokee Indians, native and adopted, became citizens of the United States without a reservation.

The Cherokee have seven clans: Wolf, Deer, Bird, Paint, Ani Saha ni, Ani Ga tagewi, Ani Gi la hi. In ancient times, there were fourteen. The wolf clan is the largest.

Cheyenne-Arapaho Business Committee
P.O. Box 38
Concho, OK 73022
(405) 262-0345

Cheyenne (Shai-ela)
Arapaho (Inunaina)

Location: The Southern Cheyenne and Southern Arapaho share their tribal office in Concho, Oklahoma.

Public Ceremony or Powwow Dates: The Southern Arapaho usually have a powwow over Labor Day weekend. The Southern Cheyenne participate in the American Indian Exposition each year at Anadarko. Call the tribal office for dates and times. The Southern Arapaho attend the Sun Dance (Offerings Lodge) with the Northern Arapahoe in Wyoming each year. The Southern Cheyenne hold a Sun Dance (Offerings Lodge) in Oklahoma each year.

Art Forms: Please call the tribal office to find local artisans who do traditional beadwork and other Plains-style artwork.

Visitor Information: Please read more about the Arapahoe and Cheyenne under Wyoming and Montana in the Great Plains section. These are big tribes and very typical of Plains Indians.

Chickasaw Nation of Oklahoma
P.O. Box 1548
Ada, OK 74820
(404) 436-2603

Chickasaw

Location: The tribal headquarters is at Arlington and Mississippi streets in Ada.

Public Ceremony or Powwow Dates: Chickasaw Nation Annual Day is held the first Saturday in October five miles north of Ada at Byng School. The princess of the Chickasaw Nation is selected, there is gospel and country music, lunch is served, and the governor gives his annual address.

Visitor Information: The Chickasaw Nation is a very progressive community. Included among their enterprises are woodwork items ranging from cabinets to chests. A trading post is planned, and a proposal has been presented for a tribal museum.

The Chickasaw are a Muskhogean tribe, closely related to the Choctaw in language and customs, although the two tribes were mutually hostile. The earliest written history places the Chickasaw in northern Mississippi. In the eighteenth century, they were located in Pontotoc and Union counties, where the headwaters of the Tombigbee meet those of the Yazoo River and its affluent, the Tallahatchie. The DeSoto narratives place them in this area in 1540 under the name Chicaza.

They were on the Trail of Tears in the 1830s.

Choctaw Nation of Oklahoma
P.O. Drawer 1210
16th and Locust Streets
Durant, OK 74701
(405) 924-8280

Choctaw (possibly a corruption of the Spanish *Chato*, "flat," or "flattened," alluding to the custom of these people to flatten the head)

Location: The location of the tribal headquarters is 16th and Locust streets in Durant. The museum is on the third floor.

Public Ceremony and Powwow Dates: The Choctaw Nation of Oklahoma Labor Day Festivities are held in Tuskahoma. From Friday through Monday, games, the princess contest, and traditional dancing are held. The stickball game is particularly interesting to watch and has its roots in the traditional game played for centuries. Talihina, Oklahoma, has a parade on Saturday which features the Choctaw Nation.

Art Forms: The museum in the old Choctaw Council House in Tuskahoma has a gift shop. Traditional Choctaw diamond pattern women's dresses and men's shirts are for sale.

Visitor Information: The Choctaw tribe is of the Muskhogean group, formerly occupying middle and southern Mississippi, their territory extending for some distance east of the Tombigbee River, probably as far as Dallas County, Georgia. They were also on the Trail of Tears when removed to Indian Territory from Mississippi in 1832. (Read more under **Mississippi,** Choctaw.)

Citizen Band of Potawatomi Indians of Oklahoma
Route 5, Box 151
Shawnee, OK 74801
(405) 275-3121

Location: The tribal complex is located on the south side of Shawnee at 1901 Gordon Cooper Drive.

Public Ceremony and Powwow Dates: The annual powwow is always held the last weekend in June. The public is welcome.

Art Forms: Members of this tribe do beautiful paintings, using both traditional subject matter and progressive styles, and ribbon work and beadwork.

Visitor Information: Tribal enterprises include the Potawatomi Tribal Store where visitors spend more than $1 million annually in cigarette and gas sales; the trading post operated within the tribal museum which handles artwork, jewelry, souvenirs, and craft supplies; the bingo hall, which seats 500 people and takes in $10,000 to $20,000 in monthly tribal income; the Fire Lake Golf Course in the area, with a full line pro shop and snack bar; and the swap meet, a weekend flea market held on tribal powwow grounds.

The Citizen Band Potawatomi Tribe has $5-1/2 million invested—approximately $3 million in grants and $2 million in enterprises and interest income. The tribe maintains jurisdiction over approximately 264 acres held in trust and has the ability to purchase and place land in trust anywhere within its old reservation boundaries, an area totaling more than 30 square miles.

Originally an Algonquin-speaking woodland tribe from the Great Lakes region, the Potawatomi are part of the Three Fires Confederacy with the Chippewa and Ottawa Nations and were removed from the north in 1838, first to Iowa and then Kansas. They accepted U.S. citizenship in 1861 and purchased allotments in Indian Territory. They are one of the five bands in the Potawatomi Nation.

The tribe has over 11,000 members who are governed by a constitutional form of government with referendum representation. Five elected business committee members are authorized constitutionally to act on behalf of the tribe on all matters except claims and treaties.

Comanche Tribal Business Committee
P.O. Box 908
Lawton, OK 73502
(405) 247-3444

Comanche

Location: The tribal office is located in Lawton, Oklahoma.

Public Ceremony and Powwow Dates: The annual powwow is held in Sultan Park, Walters, Oklahoma, during July. This is a celebration of homecoming powwow that remembers the time that Comanche warriors returned to the home camp. There are Black Crow Society dances and other traditional Comanche dances as well as powwow dancing.

In April, the Comanche dance the Little Pony Society dances at Apache Park, Apache, Oklahoma. Medicine men's dances are also done during this celebration. Call the tribal office for dates and times at the above number.

Visitor Information: The people of the tribe live in the vicinity of Lawton, Cache, and Apache, Oklahoma.

The Comanche are one of the southern tribes of the Shoshonean stock, and the only one of that group living entirely on the plains. Their language and traditions show that they are a comparatively recent offshoot from the Shoshone of Wyoming, both tribes speaking practically the same dialect. Traditionally, the two tribes lived adjacent to each other in southern Wyoming. Since that time, the Shoshone were beaten back into the mountains by the Sioux and other prairie tribes, while the Comanche were driven steadily southward by the same pressure. In this southerly migration, the Penateka, a division of the Comanche, seem to have preceded the rest of the tribe. The Kiowa say that when they themselves moved southward from the Black Hills region, the Arkansas was the north boundary of the Comanche.

In 1719, the Comanche are mentioned under their Siouan name of Padouca as living in what now is western Kansas. It must be remembered that from 500 to 800 miles was an ordinary range for a prairie tribe and that the Comanche were equally at home on the Platte and in the Bolson de Mapimi of Chihuahua. As late as 1805,

Mum-shu-kawa, Comanche, 1914
Photo by DeLancey Gill; Courtesy Museum of New Mexico, Neg. No. 86998

the North Platte was still known as Padouca Fork. At that time they roamed over the country around the source of the Arkansas, Red, Trinity, and Brazos rivers in Colorado, Kansas, Oklahoma, and Texas. For nearly two centuries they were at war with the Spaniards of Mexico and extended their raids far down into Durango. They were friendly to the Americans generally but became bitter enemies of the Texans, by whom they were dispossessed of their best hunting grounds, and carried on a relentless war against them for nearly forty years. They have been close confederates of the Kiowa since about 1795. In 1835, they made their first treaty with the U.S. government and by the treaty of Medicine Lodge in 1867 agreed to go to their assigned reservation between the Washita and Red rivers, in southwest Oklahoma; but it was not until after the last uprising of the southern prairie tribes in 1874–75 that they and their allies, the Kiowa and Apache, finally settled on it. They were probably never a large tribe, although supposed to be populous on account of their wide range. They were terribly wasted by war and disease. They numbered 1,400 in 1904 and were attached to the Kiowa Agency, Oklahoma.

The Comanche were nomadic buffalo hunters, constantly on the move, cultivating little from the ground, and living in skin tipis. They were long noted as the finest horsemen of the plains and bore a reputation for dash and courage. They have a high sense of honor and hold themselves superior to the other tribes with which they are associated. Their language was the trade language of the region and more or less understood by all the neighboring tribes.

The clan system seems to be unknown among the Comanche. They have, or still remember, twelve recognized divisions or bands and may have had others in former times. Of these all but five are practically extinct, and the Kwahari and Penateka are the most important.

Creek Nation of Oklahoma
P.O. Box 580
Okmulgee, OK 74447
(918) 756-8700

Creek Nation of Oklahoma
Alabama-Quassarte Tribal Town
P.O. Box 404
Eufaula, OK 74432
(918) 689-3398

Kialegee Tribal Town
928 Alex Noon Drive
Wetumka, OK 74883

Thlopthlocco Tribal Town
8433 East 64th Place
Tulsa, OK 74133
(918) 582-9201

Creek (from the English because of the many creeks in their homeland)

Location: The Creek Nation Tribal Capitol Complex is located on Highway 75 at Loop 56 north of Okmulgee, Oklahoma.

Public Ceremony or Powwow Dates: The Creek ceremonies are held all summer from May until September. Stomp dances are held on weekends. Dancing will often begin between 10:00 p.m. and 1:00 a.m. and then continue until dawn. Then, after some weeks of doing stomp dances, the Green Corn Ceremonial is performed according to lunar phases. Call the tribal office for dates and times.

Art Forms: The gift shop in the Creek Council House Museum at 112 West Sixth in the Town Square of Okmulgee, has arts and crafts for sale. The telephone number is (918) 756-2324.

Visitor Information: The Creek Indian Nation is a very progressive tribe. The Creek Council House design of the past century inspired the design of the auditorium. The Creek Nation is organized into about nineteen towns. Many Creek people spend their weekends camping at the town's ceremonial grounds while the stomp dances are in progress. The ceremonial grounds of each town are arranged in a rectangle with brush arbors around the edge where people sit. At the center of the ground is the sacred fire, which the stomp dancing revolves around. During Green Corn time, there is fasting, drinking of the sacred drink, and ritual scratching—all for purification and health.

To make sure visitors are welcome during the stomp dances and Green Corn Ceremonial, call the tribal office for arrangements.

The Creeks are a confederacy forming the largest division of the Muskhogean family. They received their name from the English on account of the numerous streams in their country. During early historic times the Creeks occupied the greater portion of Alabama and Georgia, residing chiefly on the Coosa and Tallapoosa rivers, the two largest tributaries of the Alabama River, and on the Flint and Chattahoochee rivers. They claimed the territory on the east from the Savannah to St. Johns River and all the islands, thence to Apalache Bay, and from this line northward to the mountains. The south portion of this territory was held by dispossession of the earlier Florida tribes. At an early date, they sold to Great Britain their territory between the Savannah and Ogeechee rivers, all the coast to St. Johns River, and all the islands up to Tidewater, reserving for themselves St. Catherine, Sapelo, and Ossabaw islands, and from Pipemakers Bluff to Savannah. Thus occupying a leading position among the Muskhogean tribes, the Creeks were sufficiently numerous and powerful to resist attacks from the northern tribes, such as the Catawba, Iroquois, Shawnee, and Cherokee, after they had united in a confederacy.

For more than a century before their removal to the West between 1836 and 1840, the people of the Creek Confederacy occupied some 50 towns, in which six distinct languages were spoken: Muscogee, Hitchiti, Koasati, Yuchi, Natchez, and Shawnee. About half the confederacy spoke the Muscogee language, which thus constituted the ruling language and gave name to the confederacy. The meaning of the word is unknown. Although an attempt has been made to connect it with the Algonquian *maskeg*, "swamp," a southern origin is probable. The people speaking the related Hitchiti and Koasati were contemptuously designated as "Stincards" by the dominant Muscogee. While the Seminole were still a small group confined to the extreme north of Florida, they were frequently spoken of as Lower Creeks. To the Cherokee, the Up-

per Creeks were known as Ani-Kusa, from their ancient town of
Kusa, or Coosa, while the Lower Creeks were called Ani-Kawita,
from their principal town, Kawita, or Coweta. The earlier Seminole
emigrants were chiefly from the Lower Creek towns.

The history of the Creeks begins with the appearance of De-
Soto's army in their country in 1540. Tristan de Luna came in contact with part of the group in 1559, but the only important fact that
can be drawn from the record is the deplorable condition the people were in as a result of the Spanish invasion. The Creeks came
prominently into history as allies of the English in the Apalachee
wars of 1703–1708, and from that period continue almost uniformly as treaty allies of the South Carolina and Georgia colonies,
while hostile to the Spaniards of Florida. The only serious revolt of
the Creeks against the Americans took place in 1813–14; this was
the well-known Creek War in which General Jackson took a prominent part. This ended in the complete defeat of the Indians and
the submission of Weatherford, their leader, followed by the cession of the greater part of their lands to the United States. The
extended and bloody contest in Florida, which lasted from 1835 to
1843 and is known as the Seminole War, secured permanent peace
with the southern tribes. The removal of the larger part of the
Creek and Seminole people and their black slaves to the lands assigned them in Indian Territory took place between 1836 and 1840
and is today known as the Trail of Tears due to the deaths of so
many on the way.

The Creek were proud, haughty, and arrogant, brave and val-
iant in war. They were devoted to decoration and ornament and
very fond of music. Ball play was their most important game. Marriage outside the clan was the rule; descent was in the female line.
In government it was a general rule that where one or more clans
occupied a town, they constituted a tribe under an elected chief, or
miko, who was advised by the council of the town in all important
matters, while the council appointed the "great warrior," or tusten-
uggi-hlako. They usually buried their dead in a square pit under
the bed where the deceased had slept. Certain towns were conse-
crated to peace ceremonies and were known as "white towns,"
while others set apart for war ceremonials were designated as "red
towns." They had several orders of chiefly rank. Their great spiritual ceremony was the annual puskita, of which the lighting of the
new fire and the drinking of the black drink were important
accompaniments.

The early statistics of Creek population are based on mere estimates. It is not known what numerical relation the mixed bloods hold to the full bloods and their former black slaves, or the number of their towns (having a square for festivities) and villages (having no square). In the last quarter of the eighteenth century, the Creek population may have been about 20,000, occupying from 40 to 60 towns. Estimates made after their removal to Indian Territory place the population between 15,000 and 20,000. In 1904, the "Creeks by blood" living in the Creek Nation numbered 9,905, while Creek freedmen numbered 5,473. The number of acres in their reservation in 1885 was 3,215,395, only a portion of which was tillable, and 90,000 were actually cultivated.

In 1904 the Creek Nation in Indian Territory was divided into 49 townships, three of which were inhabited solely by blacks. The capital was, and is, Okmulgee. Their legislature consisted of a House of Kings (corresponding to the Senate) and a House of Warriors (similar to the U.S. House of Representatives), with a head chief as executive. Several volumes of their laws have been published.

Delaware Executive Committee
P.O. Box 825
Anadarko, OK 73005
(405) 247-2448

Lenape
Leni-lenape (real men or genuine men)

Location: The tribal office of the western Oklahoma Delaware is in Anadarko. Another group of Delaware live near Copan, Oklahoma.

Public Ceremony or Powwow Dates: The Copan community holds its powwow in late May or early June. The Anadarko community of Delaware participates in celebrations in the Anadarko, Oklahoma, area. Call the tribal office above for more information.

The original homeland of the Delaware includes New York City and much of New Jersey, Delaware, and Pennsylvania. Some of the people still live in this area, but most members of the tribe are living in Ontario, Oklahoma, and Wisconsin today.

The Delaware are a confederacy, formerly the most important of the Algonquian stock, occupying the entire basin of the Delaware River in eastern Pennsylvania and southeastern New York,

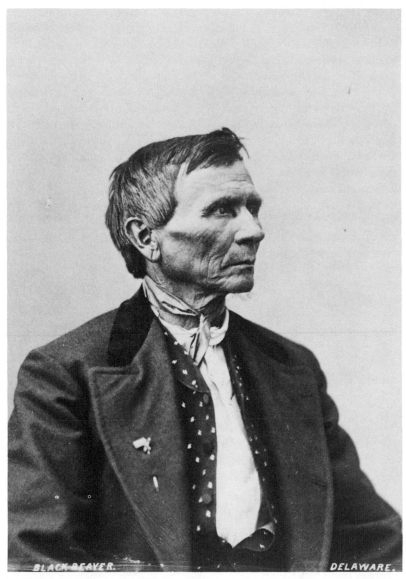

Black Beaver, Delaware, 1872
Photo by Alexander Gardner; Courtesy Museum of New Mexico, Neg. No. 87531

together with most of New Jersey and Delaware. The English knew them as Delawares, from the name of their principal river; the French called them Loups, "wolves," a term probably applied originally to the Mahican on the Hudson River and afterward extended to the Munsee division and to the whole group.

To the more remote Algonquian tribes, the Delaware, together with all their related tribes along the coast far up into New England, were known as Wapanachki, "easterners," or "eastern land people," a term that appears also as a specific tribal designation in the form of Abnaki. By virtue of admitted priority of political rank and of occupying the central home territory, from which most of the related tribes had diverged, they were accorded by all the Algonquian tribes the respectful title of "Grandfather," a recognition also accorded by the Huron as a courtesy. The Nanticoke, Conoy, Shawnee, and Mahican claimed close connection with the Delaware and preserved the tradition of a common origin.

The Lenape, or Delaware proper, were composed of three principal tribes: Munsee, Unami, and Unalachtigo. Some of the New Jersey bands may have constituted a fourth. Each of these had its own territory and dialect, with more or less separate identity. The Munsee, in fact, were frequently considered an independent people.

Iowa of Oklahoma Business Committee
Iowa Veterans Hall
P.O. Box 190
Perkins, OK 74059
(405) 547-2403

Iowa (Sleepy Ones)

Visitor Information: The Iowa today live in two locations, here and on a reservation in northeast Kansas near the Sac and Fox.

Traditional and linguistic evidence proves that the Iowa sprang from the Winnebago, who appear to have been the mother stock of some other of the southwestern Siouan tribes. But the closest affinity of the Iowa is with the Oto and Missouri, the difference in language being merely one of dialect. Iowa chiefs in 1883 said that their people and the Oto, Missouri, Omaha, and Ponca "once formed part of the Winnebago Nation."

Kaw Business Committee
Drawer 50
Kaw City, OK 74641
(405) 269-2552

Kansa

This is a southwestern Siouan tribe. Their linguistic relations are closest with the Osage and are close with the Quapaw.

Kickapoo of Oklahoma Business Committee
P.O. Box 58
McLoud, OK 74851
(405) 964-2075

Kiwigapawa ("he stands about")

This tribe belongs to the central Algonquian language group. They share a close ethnic and linguistic connection with the Sauk and Foxes. They are more closely related to the Miami, Shawnee, Menominee, and the Peoria than to the Chippewa, Potawatomi, and Ottawa. All of these tribes were living near the portage between the Fox and Wisconsin rivers from 1667 to 1670. Alloa, Columbia County, Wisconsin, is the probable locality, about 12 miles south of the mixed village of the Mascouten, Miami, and Wea.

Kiowa Business Committee
P.O. Box 369
Carnegie, OK 73015
(405) 654-2300

Kiowa (Ga-i-gwu, or Ka-i-gwu, "principal people")

Location: The tribal complex is located in Carnegie, 1/4 mile west of the four-way stop (Highways 9 and 58) on Highway 9.

Public Ceremony or Powwow Dates: In the fall, there is a powwow to raise funds for the museum. Traditional Kiowa dances as well as powwow dancing are featured. Over the Fourth of July weekend, the museum has an arts and crafts show with Kiowa Gourd Society dances.

Art Forms: The Kiowa are artistic people, and among their tribal rolls are listed some of the most famous painters who do traditional and contemporary Indian art.

Kishkinniequote (Jim Deer), Kickapoo, 1907
Photo by DeLancey Gill; Courtesy Museum of New Mexico, Neg. No. 59443

Apiatou, Kiowa
Courtesy Museum of New Mexico, Neg. No. 46986

Visitor Information: Don't miss the museum and the mural work depicting Kiowa history.

A history of the Kiowa people will show that they at one time resided in the area around the upper Yellowstone and Missouri, but they were more widely known to have lived near the upper Arkansas and Canadian rivers in Colorado and Oklahoma and to have constituted a distinct linguistic form. They are noticed in Spanish records as early as 1732. Their oldest tradition, which agrees with the concurrent testimony of the Shoshone and Arapahoe, locates them about the junction of Jefferson, Madison, and Gallatin forks, at the extreme head of the Missouri River, in the neighborhood of the present Virginia City, Montana. They afterward moved down from the mountains and formed an alliance with the Crows, with whom they continued on friendly terms. From here they drifted southward along the base of the mountains, driven by the Cheyenne and Arapahoe, with whom they finally made peace about 1840. After that, they commonly acted in concert with the latter tribes.

The Sioux claim to have driven them out of the Black Hills, and in 1805, they were reported by Lewis and Clark as living on the North Platte. According to the Kiowa account, when they first reached the Arkansas River, they found their passage opposed by the Comanches, who claimed all the country to the south. A war followed, but peace was finally concluded when the Kiowa crossed over to the south side of the Arkansas and formed a confederation with the Comanche. In connection with the Comanche, they carried on a constant war on the frontier settlements of Mexico and Texas, extending their incursions as far south as Durango. Among all the prairie tribes they were noted as the most predatory and warlike.

The Kiowa made their first treaty with the U.S. government in 1837 and were put on their present reservation jointly with the Comanche and Kiowa Apache in 1868. Their last uprising was in 1874–75 in concert with the Comanche, Kiowa-Apache, and Cheyenne. While probably never very numerous, they were greatly reduced by war and disease. Their last terrible blow came in spring 1892, when measles and fever destroyed more than 300 of the three confederated tribes.

The Kiowa do not have a clan system, and there is no restriction on intermarriage. The Kiowa Apache, associated with them, form a component part of the Kiowa camp circle.

Although brave and warlike, the Kiowa are considered gentle and considerate. In person, they are dark and well built, forming a contrast to the more slender and brighter complexioned prairie tribes farther north. Their language is very nasal and throaty sounding. In the early 1900s their chief was Lone Wolf, but his title was disputed by Apiatan. Their reservation was between the Washita and Red rivers in southwest Oklahoma. In 1901, their lands were allotted and opened to settlement. The population was 1,165 in 1905.

Miami Business Committee
P.O. Box 636
Miami, OK 74355
(918) 540-2890

Miami (Omaumeg, "people on the peninsula")

Public Ceremony or Powwow Dates: The Oklahoma Indian Heritage Days Celebration is usually held in late May and the exact date can be obtained by calling the tribal offices. The Quapaw powwow and the Ottawa powwow, held in July and late summer, respectively, can be great fun. Call the tribal office for dates and times.

Art Forms: The senior citizens of this tribe are restoring their traditional art forms.

Visitor Information: The Miami today live in Oklahoma and Indiana. They can be found at the Quapaw powwow and are cosponsors of the Heritage Days Celebration. Both are held in Miami, Oklahoma.

Intertribal offices and a gift shop are located here just behind the Welcome Center off westbound Highway I-44. Exit at Miami on Steve Owens Boulevard and take the access road on the 1400 block parallel to the freeway. The telephone number is (918) 542-4486.

The Inter-Tribal Council is made up of representatives of the Eastern Shawnee, Seneca-Cayuga (Iroquois), Peoria (Illinois), Ottawa, Miami, Wyandot, Quapaw, and Modoc tribes (originally from northern California and southern Oregon).

The earliest written information is from Gabriel Druillettes in 1658. He called the Miami the Oumamik and said they were living at St. Michel at or about the mouth of Green Bay, Wisconsin.

Modoc Tribe of Oklahoma
P.O. Box 939
Miami, OK 7435
(918) 542-1190

Modoc (Moatokni, "southerners")

Visitor Information: The Modoc Tribe was originally in northern California and southern Oregon. The famous Modoc War waged by Chief Captain Jack in 1873 against the settlers was not unique as it was in response to attacks on the Indian people by the settlers. In the late 1950s, the reservation was terminated in the west. Today, Modoc people still live at Sprague River, Oregon, and near Miami, Oklahoma, where many were taken after the Modoc War.

Read more about them under the Miami tribe of Oklahoma.

This is a Lutuamian tribe, forming the southern division of that people in southwest Oregon. The Modoc language is practically the same as Klamath, the dialect differences being extremely slight. The Modoc lived on Little Klamath Lake, Modoc Lake, Tule Lake, Lost River Valley, and Clear Lake and extended at times as far east as Goose Lake.

Osage Tribal Council
Tribal Administration Building
Pawhuska, OK 74056
(918) 287-4622

Osage (corruption of Wazhazhe, their own name, by French traders)

Location: The museum is on Grandview Avenue in Pawhuska.

Public Ceremony or Powwow Dates: In June, the Osage have ceremonial dances in Homin, Oklahoma, and Tribal Ceremonial Dances in Pawhuska. The Kiehkah Steh Club powwow in Skiatook is in August. Call the tribal office for dates and times.

Art Forms: Arts and crafts can be found at the museum. Finger woven sashes are one of the many art forms to be found there.

> The beings which ultimately became men originated in the lowest of the four upper worlds which Osage Spirituality postulates and ascended to the highest where they obtained souls. Then they descended until they came to a red oak tree on which the lowest world

Sho-she, Osage
Photo by DeLancey Gill; Courtesy Museum of New Mexico, Neg. No. 87005

rests and by its branches reached our earth. They were divided into two sections, the Tsishu, or peace people, who kept to the left, living on roots, etc. . . . and the Wazhazhe (true Osage), or war people, who kept to the right and killed animals for their food. Later these two divisions exchanged commodities, and after some time the Tshihu people came into possession of four kinds of corn and four kinds of pumpkins, which fell from the left hind legs of as many different buffaloes. Still later the tribe came upon a very warlike people called Hangka-utadhantse, who lived on animals, and after a time the Tsishu people succeeded in making peace with them, when they were taken into the nation on the war side. Originally there were seven Tsishu gentes, seven Wazhazhe gentes, and seven Hangka gentes, but in order to maintain an equilibrium between the war and peace sides after adopting the Hangka, the number of their gentes was reduced to five and the number of Wazhazhe gentes to two.

(taken from Osage tribal literature)

The first written historical record of the Osage locates them on the Osage River. This was about 1673. They are a southern Siouan tribe of the western division. They are classed with the Omaha, Ponca, Kansa, and Quapaw, with whom they originally constituted a single body living along the lower course of the Ohio River.

The tribe has three bands: the Pahatsi, or Great Osage; Utsehta, or Little Osage; and Santsukhdhi, or Arkansas Band.

Otoe-Missouria Tribal Council
P.O. Box 68
Red Rock, OK 74058
(405) 723-4434

Oto (from Wat ota, "lechers")
Missouri ("great muddy," referring to the Missouri River)

Oto-Missouria

Location: The tribal office is in Red Rock.

Public Ceremony or Powwow Dates: Their annual powwow is usually in July in Red Rock. Call for exact dates and times.

The Oto are one of the three Siouan tribes forming the Chiwere group, the others being the Iowa and Missouri. The languages differ only slightly. The earliest written record places them above Green Bay, Wisconsin.

The Missouri are a tribe of the Chiwere group of the Siouan family. Their name for themselves is Niutachi. The most closely allied tribes are the Iowa and the Oto. According to tradition, after having parted from the Winnebago at Green Bay, the Iowa, Missouri, and Oto moved westward to the Iowa River, where the Iowa stopped.

Ottawa Business Committee
P.O. Box 110
Miami, OK 74355
(918) 540-1536

Ottawa (adawe, "to trade")

Visitor Information: The Ottawa live today in Canada and Oklahoma. Their powwow is usually in August near Miami, Oklahoma. For more information, read about them under the Miami tribe of Oklahoma.

On the French River near its mouth on the Georgian Bay, Champlain in 1615 met 300 men of a tribe that, he said, "we call les cheueux releuez." He said that their arms consisted only of the bow and arrow, a buckler of boiled leather, and the club; that they wore no breechclout and their bodies were much tattooed in many fashions and designs; and that their faces were painted in diverse colors, their noses pierced, and their ears bordered with trinkets.

Pawnee Business Council
P.O. Box 470
Pawnee, OK 74058
(918) 762-3624

Pawnee (pariki, "horn," the dressing of the scalp-lock, by which the hair was stiffened with fat and made to stand erect and curved like a horn)

Location: The location of the tribal office is east of town on the main street in Pawnee.

Public Ceremony or Powwow Dates: The Fourth of July weekend is the time to be in Pawnee, Oklahoma, for one of the best powwows in the world. Four days of dancing, hand games, and celebrating

White Horse, Pawnee, ca. 1868–69
Photo by William H. Jackson; Courtesy Museum of New Mexico, Neg. No. 31255

make your trip to Pawnee worthwhile no matter how far you traveled. The four bands of the Pawnee join together for this great powwow. They are the Chaui or Grand Pawnee, the Kitkehahki or Republican Pawnee, the Pitahaurat or Tapage Pawnee, and the Skidi or Wolf Pawnee.

Art Forms: The Pawnee do some fine arts and crafts, including Peyote stitch on fans, staffs, and rattles. My friend Anthony Davis shows some of the best I have ever seen.

Visitor Information: There is a traditional-style roundhouse located 1/2-mile beyond the tribal headquarters.

The Pawnee call themselves Chahiksichahiks, "Men of Men." In 1702, there were 2,000 families living in the central plains where west Nebraska and east Wyoming are today. Disease brought by settlers dwindled the tribe to 649 survivors in 1906.

Peoria Business Committee
P.O. Box 1527
Miami, OK 74355
(918) 540-2535

Peoria (Peouarea, "carrying a pack on his back")

Visitor Information: The Illinois tribe is known as the Peoria today and live in northeast Oklahoma. They participate in Indian Heritage Days and the stomp dances after powwows like the Quapaw powwow. Read about the Peoria under the Miami tribe of Oklahoma.

This is one of the principal tribes of the Illinois Confederacy. In 1688, they lived on a river west of the Mississippi above the mouth of the Wisconsin River, probably the upper Iowa River.

Ponca Business Committee
P.O. Box 2, White Eagle
Ponca City, OK 74601
(405) 762-8104

Ponca

Location: The tribal office is located in White Eagle.

Public Ceremony or Powwow Dates: The annual powwow is usually held in August, but check with the tribal office for dates and times.

Little Soldier, Ponca, 1914
Photo by DeLancey Gill; Courtesy Museum of New Mexico, Neg. No. 87008

Art Forms: Call the tribal office for individuals who do arts and crafts.

Visitor Information: The White Eagle Tribal Park is the location of the powwow grounds and the fairgrounds. The museum here has information on about 12 tribes, but the Ponca, Tonkawa, Kaw, Otoe, and Osage are the prominent ones shown.

The Ponca are one of the five tribes of the so-called Dhegiha group of the Siouan family, forming with the Omaha, Osage, and Kansa the upper Dhegiha or Omaha division. The Ponca and Omaha have the same language, differing only in some dialects. In 1906, the tribe totaled 833 members.

Quapaw Tribal Business Committee
P.O. Box 765
Quapaw, OK 74363
(918) 542-1853

Quapaw (Ugakhpa, "downstream people")

Public Ceremony or Powwow Dates: The Quapaw hold their powwow over the Fourth of July weekend at Quapaw, Oklahoma. This is a real Plains-style powwow with war dancers both straight and fancy. There are round dances, rabbit dances, Plains-style stomp dancing, and even the Oklahoma two-step. After the powwow, Eastern Woodlands and Southern style stomp dances go on all night. Read more about the Quapaw under the Miami tribe of Oklahoma.

This is a southwestern Siouan tribe forming one of the two divisions of the Dhegiha group. When the group separated, the Quapaw went down the Mississippi and the Omaha, Kansa, Ponca, and Osage went up the Missouri.

Sac and Fox Tribal Office
Route 2, Box 246
Stroud, OK 74079
(918) 968-3526

Location: Six miles south of Stroud, on State Highway 99, is. the location of the tribal complex.

Public Ceremony or Powwow Dates: Their world-famous outdoor powwow is held the second weekend in July. The annual all-Indian

Memorial Stampede Rodeo is held each summer, but you must call the tribe for exact dates and times.

Art Forms: The drum is sacred, the otter is a mythical animal, the sun and moon are considered special to the Sac and Fox. Naming and adopting ceremonies are still observed. The Swan or Crane Dance is unique to the Sac and Fox and, as described by the famed warrior Black Hawk, is still observed each year at the powwow. Eleven ancient Sac and Fox clans are still maintained: Fish, Peace, Fox, Warrior, Bear, Wolf, Thunder, Beaver, Potato, Eagle, and Deer. The Sac and Fox are known for their fine ribbonwork, usually done in floral designs to reflect their woodland heritage.

Visitor Information: The Sac and Fox people are proud to share their rich heritage and history with all visitors and encourage guests to stop and see the old and new sites and structures in their nation's capital. Most of the sites and buildings are open for public viewing, but some are strictly for ceremonial use by tribal members. Three historic sites, the brick vault once a part of the old agency office building, the water tower base that once served the Sac and Fox Mission School, and the old Sac and Fox Cemetery where many tribal chiefs are buried are all open to the public. Chief Keokuk's brick home, built in 1879 and located a few miles west of the capitol grounds, is privately owned and listed on the National Register of Historic Sites.

One of the Sac and Fox sites you may want to see while visiting the capitol grounds is the Sac and Fox Tribal Courthouse. Housed in the oldest building on the capitol grounds, it was once two council houses (c. 1930), brought together for a community building (c. 1960) and dedicated as a courthouse in 1986. Open during business hours, it houses several historic tribal photographs and a 1936 wall mural painted by a tribal member. Court is held here regularly. Also see the Sac and Fox Tribal Office, which has an art gallery. At the Bark House and swimming pool, food, drink, and Indian crafts can be purchased. The Sac and Fox National Public Library also contains the tribal archives and a display area. Other important buildings on the capitol grounds are the Black Hawk clinic, food warehouse, and community building. There is also an RV campground.

Black Hawk was their famous war chief who led the last great Indian attack against the United States. He wrote eloquently of his

Mishewauk, Sac and Fox
Photo by Keystone View Co.; Courtesy Museum of New Mexico, Neg. No. 90585

people in an autobiography published in 1872. Moses Keokuk was the government chief who led the Sac and Fox into Indian Territory. He was well educated and a great orator. William Jones was born in Stroud and educated at the Sac and Fox Mission School, Hampton Institute, Phillips Academy, and Harvard and Columbia universities. He was a brilliant ethnologist who wrote about his tribe until his untimely death while on an expedition in the Philippines.

Jim Thorpe was born at a Sac and Fox village south of the agency town and educated at the Sac and Fox Mission School and at Carlisle in Pennsylvania. He won the pentathlon and decathlon at the 1912 Olympics and later played professional football and baseball. He was named the world's greatest athlete in 1950.

The story of the Sac and Fox begins in the upper peninsula of the Great Lakes region of the United States. The Sac, or Sauk (from the French word Saukie), or people of the yellow earth, and the Fox, or people of the red earth, were two separate but neighboring tribes. For protection and survival they banded together in 1804. In 1869, Sac and Fox tribesmen came to Indian Territory and settled on 759,000 square miles of land they purchased in what became Lincoln, Payne, and Potawatomie counties. It was their final homeland after a succession of moves from Wisconsin through Illinois, Iowa, Missouri, and Kansas forced on them by the western migration of white settlers.

After the 500 tribesmen dispersed into several villages across the reservation, they built traditional bark houses for summer and cattail houses for winter. In 1885, they wrote and adopted a constitution and established a court system, a police department, a mission school, and a large farming operation. All of this government activity was centered at the Sac and Fox Agency, a historical point dating from the time of the Civil War and a landmark in Indian Territory. The agency site marked the crossing of many trails and was a halfway point on the famous Sac and Fox Trail between Pawnee and Shawnee. It was a stagecoach stop, a military post, and a meeting place for cowboys, Indian traders, hunters, homeseekers, gamblers, and outlaws long before the opening of Indian Territory to settlers. Many colorful descriptions of life at the Sac and Fox Agency abound in Oklahoma history. The agency was really a town with many substantial buildings that stood on streets running parallel to what is now the north-south highway through the capitol grounds.

The years between 1869 and 1910 saw the Sac and Fox Agency town flourish, and more than 25 businesses and dwellings are listed on the agent's inventories. A sawmill was the first structure built in 1869 and was followed by two frame houses, two large brick homes, two oak stockade buildings, a blacksmith shop, a bank, a doctor's office, a post office, a commissary, a cotton gin, a cobbler's shop, a smoke house, a church, a log calaboose (jail), a photography studio, a hotel, two general merchandise stores, a drugstore, and even a little weather station. A council house stood on the ceremonial grounds near the pond and was the site of feasts, powwows, councils, and ceremonials. There were also baseball fields and a horse-racing track. The Sac and Fox Mission School was begun by Quaker missionaries in 1870, on the eastern edge of the capitol grounds. Many Sac and Fox children were forced to attend and were punished for speaking their native Indian language. A handsome three-story brick classroom building was erected in 1873 at a cost of $8,500. Girls' and boys' dormitories, a laundry, a large dairy barn, horse stables, and a water tower and sewer system completed the campus. The water tower legs can still be seen on the site, but all of the buildings were torn down many years after the school closed in 1917. The Sac and Fox Agency and Mission School were moved to Shawnee in 1917 and 1919 and soon the old town was abandoned. The pews and bell of the Sac and Fox church were moved to the Only Way Church north of Stroud, the bank and cotton gin to Chandler, the post office closed, the agency office building moved to another location to become a cafe, and the other buildings demolished.

In 1960, two council houses from the north and south part of the reservation, each built in the 1930s, were brought together on the capitol grounds to serve as a community building, tribal offices, and a museum. This historic structure, containing a handpainted Indian mural done in 1936, is the oldest occupied building on the capitol grounds and began serving as the Sac and Fox Tribal Courthouse in 1986. The Sac and Fox Agency office building was the center of the agency town, and inside it was a sturdy brick vault (probably constructed of brick made in a kiln on the capitol grounds) where money, supplies, and documents were kept over the years. When the office was torn down in the 1950s, the vault was saved and still stands as a testament of the strength of the Sac and Fox Nation. Despite a forced move to Indian Territory, smallpox epidemics, Deep Fork flooding, poor farm soil, drought, often cruel treatment by the government, and the white settlers that arrived in the Sac and Fox land run on September 22, 1891, the Sac and Fox Nation has endured and continues to build a modern nation on the capitol grounds on the site of the landmark Sac and Fox Agency.

Seminole Nation of Oklahoma
P.O. Box 1495
Wewoka, OK 74884
(405) 257-6287

Sim a no le, or Isti simanole, "separatist," "runaway," from the Creek language

Location: The Seminole Nation Museum is one mile southeast of the junction of U.S. Highway 270 and State Road 56 in Wewoka.

Public Ceremony or Powwow Dates: Stomp dances are held regularly and some are open to visitors. In September, the tribe holds Seminole Nation Days in the town of Seminole. Call the tribe for dates, times, and arrangements to attend public ceremonies.

Art Forms: The museum has a good craft shop and art gallery that features traditional and contemporary Seminole work, including patchwork clothing and other arts and crafts from tribal artisans.

The Seminole are a Muskhogean tribe originally from Florida. Please see the Florida Seminole for more information.

Seneca-Cayuga Business Committee
P.O. Box 1283
Miami, OK 74355
(918) 542-6609

Seneca ("place of the stone")
Cayuga (Kweniogwen, "the place locusts were taken out")

Visitor Information: Now part of the Iroquois Confederacy, the Seneca and Cayuga are two of the Six Nations who joined together centuries ago in the East. They have managed to preserve their heritage and become progressive in today's world as well. This part of the Confederacy holds their Green Corn Ceremony in July or August in Miami, Oklahoma. Call the tribal office for dates, times, and etiquette required to attend. Also, read more about them under the Miami tribe of Oklahoma.

The Cayuga are from Cayuga Lake, New York. This council was composed of four clan phratries, which formed the pattern for the Five Nations of the Iroquois. This prominent tribe occupied western New York between Seneca Lake and the Geneva River and had their council fire at Tsonontowan, near Naples in Ontario County.

Susquehannock Nation
c/o The Seneca Cayuga
P.O. Box 1283
Miami, OK 74355
(918) 542-6609

The Susquehanna people are part of the Iroquois Nation. In 1608, they were located on the lower portion of the Susquehanna River and its affluents. Captain John Smith used Sasquesahannocks in his text and Sasquesahanough on his map.

Tonkawa Business Committee
P.O. Box 70
Tonkawa, OK 74653
(405) 628-2561

Titskanwatitch, or Tonkaweya, "they all stay together"

This prominent tribe is of the Tonkawan linguistic family, which during most of the eighteenth and nineteenth centuries lived in central Texas. In 1778, the tribe consisted of 300 warriors besides women, old men, and children. In 1908, there were only 48 survivors of the tribe as a result of both smallpox and the massacre of 137 men, women, and children by Delawares, Shawnee, and Caddo in 1862.

Wichita Executive Committee
P.O. Box 729
Anadarko, OK 73005
(405) 247-2425

Kitikitish (Kirikirish)

When Coronado encountered the Wichita in 1541, the Kitikitish were living in the area around the great bend of the Arkansas River and northeastward in central Kansas. In 1772, the tribe consisted of 3,500 members. Smallpox reduced that number to 310 in 1902.

Wyandotte Business Committee
P.O. Box 250
Wyandotte, OK 74370
(918) 678-2297

Wyandot

The Wyandot live in Oklahoma today and participate in Indian Heritage Days at Miami, Oklahoma. Read more about them under the Miami tribe of Oklahoma.

Yuchi Tribe of Oklahoma
c/o The Creek Nation
P.O. Box 580
Okmulgee, OK 74447
(918) 756-8700

Yuchi ("situated yonder," probably given by some member of the tribe in answer to the inquiry, "Who are you?")

This tribe is coextensive with the Uchean family. Investigations point to the conclusion that the Westo referred to by early Carolina explorers and settlers, and for whom the Savannah River was originally named, were the Yuchi.

SOUTH DAKOTA

Sioux

The Sioux are the most populous linguistic family north of Mexico, next to the Algonquian. The name is taken from a term applied to the largest and best-known tribal group or confederacy belonging to the family, the Sioux or Dakota, which is an abbreviation of Nadowessioux, a French corruption of Nadowe-is-iw, the name given them by the Chippewa (Ojibwa). It signifies "snake," "adder," and, by metaphor, "enemy."

Before contact with whites, the majority of Sioux lived in an area extending from the west bank of the Mississippi northward from the Arkansas nearly to the Rocky Mountains, except for certain sections held by the Pawnee, Arikara, Cheyenne, Arapahoe, Blackfeet, Comanche, and Kiowa. The Dakota proper also occupied territory on the east side of the river, from the mouth of the Wisconsin to Mille Lacs, and the Winnebago lived around Lake Winnebago and the head of Green Bay. Northward Sioux tribes extended some distance into Canada, in the direction of Lake Winnipeg. A second group of Sioux tribes, embracing the Catawba, Sara or Cheraw, Saponi, Tutelo, and several others, occupied the central part of North Carolina and South Carolina and the piedmont region of Virginia, while the Biloxi dwelled in Mississippi along the Gulf Coast, and the Ofo on the Yazoo River in Mississippi.

According to tradition, the Mandan and Hidatsa reached the upper Missouri from the northeast and, pushed by the Dakota, moved slowly upstream to their present location. Some time after the Hidatsa reached the Missouri, internal troubles broke out, and a part of that tribe, now called the Crows, separated and moved westward to the neighborhood of the Yellowstone River. The Dakota formerly inhabited the forest region of southern Minnesota and do not seem to have moved onto the plains until hard pressed by the Chippewa, who had been supplied with guns by the French. According to all the evidence available, traditional and otherwise, the so-called Chiwere tribes—Iowa, Oto, and Missouri—separated from the Winnebago or else moved westward to the Missouri from the same region. The five remaining tribes of this group—Omaha, Ponca, Osage, Kansa, and Quapaw—undoubtedly lived together as one tribe at some time and were probably located on the Mississippi. Those moving farther down became known as "Downstream People," Quapaw, while those who went up were the "Upstream People," Omaha. The Omaha moved northwest along the river and divided into the Osage, Kansa, Ponca, and Omaha proper. More remote migrations must have taken place, but the facts are not definitely known.

The eastern Sioux were encountered by Captain John Smith in 1608, but after that time, their numbers decreased rapidly through Iroquois attacks and European aggression. Finally, the remnants of the northern tribes of the eastern Sioux accompanied the Tuscarora northward to the Iroquois and were adopted by the Cayuga in 1753. On the destruction of their village by Sullivan in 1779, they separated. The southern tribes of this eastern Sioux group consolidated with the Catawba and steadily decreased in population. Some of the eastern Sioux tribes may have been reached by de Soto.

The first known meeting between any western Sioux and the whites was in 1541, when de Soto reached the Quapaw villages in eastern Arkansas. The earliest mention of the main northwestern group is probably that in the Jesuit Relation of 1640, where mention is made of the Winnebago, Dakota, and Assiniboine. As early as 1658, Jesuit missionaries had heard of the existence of thirty Dakota villages in the region north from the Potawatomi mission at St. Michael, around the head of Green Bay, Wisconsin. In 1680, Father Hennepin was taken prisoner by the same tribe.

In 1804–05, Lewis and Clark passed through the center of this region and encountered most of the Sioux tribes. After this, there were many expeditions into and through their country. Traders settled among them and were followed by permanent settlers, who pressed the Sioux into narrower and narrower areas until they were finally removed to Indian Territory or confined to reservations in the Dakotas, Nebraska, and Montana. Throughout this period, the Dakota proved themselves most consistently hostile to the intruders. In 1862, there was a bloody Santee uprising in Minnesota which resulted in the removal of all the eastern Dakota from that state, and in 1876, the outbreak among the western Dakota and the cutting off of Custer's command occurred. Later still, the Ghost Dance spread among the Sioux proper, culminating in the massacre of men, women, and children at Wounded Knee, South Dakota, on December 29, 1890, when their gathering for this event was misconstrued as a hostile action.

It is impossible to make general statements about the customs and habits of these people that will be true for the entire group. Nearly all of the eastern tribes and most of the southern tribes belonging to the western group raised corn, but the Dakota (except some of the eastern bands) and the Crows depended almost entirely on buffalo and other game animals, the buffalo entering very deeply into the economic and spiritual life of all the tribes of this section.

In the east, the habitations were bark and mat wigwams, but on the plains, earth lodges and skin tipis were used. Formerly, they had no domestic animals except dogs, which were used to transport tipis and all other family belongings, including children (the travois). The introduction of horses constituted a new epoch in the life of all Plains tribes, facilitating their migratory movements and the pursuit of the buffalo and doubtless contributing largely to the ultimate ability of the Sioux to conduct sophisticated warfare against the intruding whites.

Taking the reports of the U.S. and Canadian Indian offices as a basis and making a small allowance for bands or individuals not counted, the total number of Indian people of Sioux stock in 1908 was approximately 40,800.

Cheyenne River Sioux Tribal Council
P.O. Box 590
Eagle Butte, SD 57625
(605) 964-4155

Sioux

Location: The reservation is located in north central South Dakota on U.S. Highway 212.

Public Ceremony or Powwow Dates: The Cultural Center in Eagle Butte is your best source of information on powwows sponsored by the Cheyenne River Sioux Tribal Council and held sometime during the summer months. Labor Day weekend provides the opportunity to hold a powwow, rodeo, buffalo feast, and celebration. Call the tribal office for dates and times.

Art Forms: Sioux arts and crafts, including dance outfits and beadwork, can be purchased in the Cultural Center.

Visitor Information: The weekly bingo enterprise holds gaming each Friday. Call the Cultural Center for time and prizes to be awarded.

In 1908, the tribes on this reservation were the Blackfeet (Sihasapa), Miniconjou, Sans Arcs, and Two Kettle (Oohenonpa) Sioux.

Crow Creek Sioux Tribal Council
P.O. Box 658
Fort Thompson, SD 57339
(605) 245-2221

Sioux

Location: The reservation is located in central South Dakota north of Interstate Highway 90.

In 1908, the tribes on this reservation were the Lower Yanktonai, Lower Brule, Miniconjou, and Two Kettle (Oohenonpa) Sioux.

Flandreau Santee Sioux Executive Committee
Flandreau Field Office
Box 283
Flandreau, SD 57028

Sioux (Isanyati)

Location: Flandreau is in extreme eastern South Dakota east of Interstate Highway 29 on State Highway 34. Pipestone National Monument is just east of Flandreau in Minnesota.

Public Ceremony or Powwow Dates: The Santee Sioux have their annual powwow in July at Flandreau. Call for exact dates and times.

Visitor Information: This is the location of the Bureau of Indian Affairs school that so many Indian young people, especially those from the plains, have attended.

This tribe is a part of the Santee who separated from the Mdewakanton and Wahpekute of the Santee Agency, Nebraska, in 1870 and settled in 1876 at Flandreau.

Lower Brule Sioux Tribal Council
Lower Brule, SD 57548
(605) 867-5821

Sioux (SichangXu)

Location: The reservation is located in south central South Dakota north of Interstate 90 on State Highway 47.

Public Ceremony or Powwow Dates: The annual powwow is usually held in August. Call the tribal office for dates and times.

Visitor Information: The tribe has a herd of buffalo and elk that may be observed by arrangement with the tribal office. Hunting and fishing permits are also available from the tribe.

In 1908, the tribes on this reservation were the Lower Brule and Lower Yanktonai Sioux.

Oglala Sioux Tribal Council
Pine Ridge, SD 57770
(605) 867-5821

Sioux (to scatter one's own)

Location: The Pine Ridge Reservation is in southwest South Dakota southeast of Rapid City. A small part of the reservation is in northwestern Nebraska north of Rushville.

Public Ceremony or Powwow Dates: Powwows can take place at any time. May, June, and August are the most popular months, however. Call the tribal office for dates and times. The most famous Sun Dance (Offerings Lodge) in the world is in August.

Art Forms: The Sioux are known for fine beadwork and quillwork and all other traditional forms of Plains Indian art.

Visitor Information: My whole family danced at the Little Big Horn Centennial Powwow held at Manderson, South Dakota, in June 1979 to honor Crazy Horse. We were made welcome. There was a feast of buffalo stew, and the people enjoyed our company as we did theirs. . . . Aho. Black Elk (the cousin of Crazy Horse) made his home near here.

In 1908, the tribes on this reservation were the Brule, Oglala Sioux, and Northern Cheyenne.

Rosebud Sioux Tribal Council
Rosebud, SD 57570
(605) 747-2381

Sioux

Location: The Rosebud Reservation is in south central South Dakota bordering Nebraska.

Public Ceremony or Powwow Dates: Powwows usually begin in June and continue through August. The Spotted Tail Powwow is in August, when the Rosebud Tribal Fair is held. Rosebud Powwow Days is in August. Call the tribal office to get the exact dates and times.

In 1908, the tribes on this reservation were the Loafer (Waglukhe), Miniconjou, Oglala, Two Kettle (Oohenonpa), Upper Brule, and Wahzhazhe Sioux.

Not Afraid of Pawnee or Padani-Kokipi-Sni, Yankton Sioux
Photo by DeLancey Gill; Courtesy Museum of New Mexico, Neg. No. 87015

Sisseton-Wahpeton Sioux Tribal Council
Route 2, Agency Village
Sisseton, SD 57262
(605) 698-3911

Sioux (Lake Village)

Location: This agency is located in extreme northeast South Dakota.

Public Ceremony or Powwow Dates: The annual powwow is held in July. Call the agency for exact times and dates.

This is one of the original seven tribes of the Sioux.

Yankton Sioux Tribal Business and Claims Commission
P.O. Box 248
Marty, SD 57361
(605) 384-3641

Sioux (End Village)

Location: This office is located in southeastern South Dakota close to Yankton.

Public Ceremony or Powwow Dates: Call the tribal office for dates and times of the powwow held at Lake Andes near Fort Randall around the first of August.

This tribe is one of the primary seven divisions of the Dakota.

TEXAS

Alabama-Coushatta Tribe of Texas
Route 3, Box 640
Livingston, TX 77351
(409) 563-4391

Alabamu (alba ayamule, "I open or clear the thicket")

Location: To get to the tribal complex, take Highway 190 seventeen miles east from Livingston, Texas.

Public Ceremony or Powwow Dates: At the tribe's reconstructed Indian Village and Museum of Alabama and Coushatta Culture and History, you will find traditional and other kinds of Indian dances. The dances are usually on weekends. You may find the tribe doing the Green Corn Thanksgiving Dance and the girl's basket dance. Other dances done are the buffalo, round, snake, boys or men's hoop, and general friendship dances.

Art Forms: The Alabama-Coushatta do fine river cane baskets.

Visitor Information: The Inn of the Twelve Clans restaurant and the arts and crafts shop are the first places to visit. Then go to the Indian Chief Railroad, Indian Country and Big Thicket tours, the tribal council house, and the tribal dance square.

Guided tours of the Big Thicket Wilderness are offered by tribal members. You can canoe, camp, swim, and fish at tribal facilities. For campers, there is a grocery store, camper hookups, laundromat, and showers. Lake Tombigbee is located in the center of the camping area.

From mid-June through August, the tribe presents the outdoor drama, "Beyond the Sundown," the story of Indian history during the Texas fight for independence.

The Alabama gave the state their name but, along with the Coushatta, were driven west to Texas. Both tribes' original homeland was in Alabama, where they were members of the Creek Confederacy. Today, the Alabamu and Coushatta live mostly in Texas and Oklahoma, with a few Coushattas living near Kinder, Louisiana. Over 500 members of the tribe now live near Livingston, Texas, on the reservation. For further information, please see the Coushatta of Louisiana.

This is a Muskhogean tribe of the Creek Confederacy which formerly dwelled in southern Alabama. It is clear that the Alibamu and Koasati were closely related, as their languages are practically identical. When first contacted by the whites, the home of the tribe was on the Alabama River, a short distance below the junction of the Coosa and Tallapoosa rivers. Their early history is uncertain, but according to tradition, they had migrated from a westerly locality. They are mentioned in the Creek legends under the name Atilamas, as one of four tribes contending for the honor of being considered the most ancient and valorous. The chroniclers of DeSoto's expedition in 1541 locate the town of Alibamo a short distance northwest of the Chicasa, in northwest or central Mississippi. The history of the tribe recommences with the appearance of the French in Mobile Bay in 1701–02. The French soon became involved in war with the tribe, who, joining the Cherokee, Abihka, and Catawba in 1708, descended the Alabama River to attack Fort Louis and the Mobile Indians in that vicinity but retired after burning some villages. In 1713 the French established Ft. Toulouse in their country to hold them in check and to protect French traders. The site of the fort was occupied in 1812 by Ft. Jackson. After the cession in 1763 by France to Great Britain, the fort was abandoned, and at that time, a part of the tribe moved to the banks of the Mississippi and established a village 60 miles above New Orleans. This band numbered about 120, including 30 warriors. The tribe subsequently moved to west Louisiana. In 1890, some were still living in Calcasieu Parish, others lived in the Creek Nation in Indian Territory, and a party of about 200 lived in Polk County, Texas.

Little has been recorded concerning the character and customs of the Alibamu, but it is evident from their early history that they were warlike. According to one observer, "They did not conform to the customs of the Creeks, and the Creek law for the punishment of adultery was not known to them. They cultivated the soil to some extent and had some hogs, horses, and cattle. Though hospitable, it was their custom, when a white person visited them, as soon as he had eaten, what was left was thrown away and everything which had been used by the white person was washed."

WYOMING

Northern Arapahoe Business Council
P.O. Box 396
Ft. Washakie, WY 82514
(307) 332-6120, 332-5006, 856-3461

Arapahoe (Inunaina or Our People)
  (Tirapihu or Larapihu or Trader from the Pawnee)
  (Blue Sky Men or Cloud Men from the Sioux and Cheyenne)

Location: The Wind River Indian Reservation is located in central Wyoming. Communities include the following: Beaver Creek, St. Stephens, Lower Arapahoe, 17-Mile, Mill Creek, and Ethete.

Black Coal (Niâwâsis), Chief of Northern Arapahoe
Photo by John K. Hillers; Courtesy Museum of New Mexico, Neg. No. 37929

Public Ceremony or Powwow Dates: There are several powwows and a Sun Dance (Offerings Lodge) held each year. The Wyoming Indian High School Powwow and Yellow Calf Memorial Powwow are usually held in May at Ethete. The Community Powwow is held in June at Arapahoe. The Sun Dance and Ethete Celebration are held in July at Ethete. Arapahoe Language Camp is held at Heil's Corner in July. August is the month for the Northern Arapahoe powwow at Arapahoe. During Labor Day there is a powwow at Ethete, and the Christmas holidays provide a time for powwow celebrations through the New Year in both the Arapahoe and Ethete communities. Call the tribal office for dates and times.

The Sun Dance is open to the public, but extreme courtesy is required not only from the general public but from Indian people as well. Do not take any cameras, recording equipment, sketch pads, or food and drink close to the Offerings Lodge. Women who are on their moon are not allowed close to the Offerings Lodge. No shorts or halter tops or scanty clothing is to be worn close to the Offerings Lodge. When standing close to the lodge entrance, it is best to stand to the side and not in the center, to allow the dancers and others who are in the process of conducting the ceremony to pass in and out of the lodge. Maintain a courteous and quiet attitude.

Art Forms: There are arts and crafts available from several gift shops and galleries on the reservation. Call the Visitors Bureau, North American Indian Heritage Center, Box 275, St. Stephens, WY 82524, (307) 856-6688, for locations to purchase fine beadwork, feather work, quill work, and other types of Plains-style art. Northern Arapahoe art designs are expressed in geometric patterns.

Visitor Information: The Wind River Indian Reservation has in operation a great natural hot springs pool near Ft. Washakie, Wyoming, and the Arapahoe tribe operates the Ethete store and the Great Plains store in Arapahoe. Fishing permits are available at the tribal fish and game offices in Ft. Washakie.

The tribe also operates "Singing Horse Tours." These day-long excursions into Wyoming's Indian Country give visitors to the area the opportunity to experience the rich cultures and histories of the Arapahoe and Shoshone tribes of the Wind River Indian Reservation. On the tour, you will hear the commentary of tribal members on the history and culture of the two tribes. The itinerary includes the Riverton Museum in Riverton; the Mission Heritage Center, Nature Window Gallery, Rendezvous Gift Shop, and Indian Heritage Center Gallery in St. Stephens; the Pioneer Museum in Lander; Warm Valley Arts and Crafts, Mid-West Art Gallery, Sacajawea Site, Washakie Site, Robert's Mission, and Living History Indian Village in Ft. Washakie; and other historical places of interest in the area. For more information on the tours and the fine lecture series offered by the tribe, write or call the Visitors Bureau, North American Indian Heritage Center, Box 275, St. Stephens, WY 82524, (307) 856-6688.

According to the traditions of the Arapahoe, they were once a sedentary, agricultural people, living far to the northeast of their more recent habitat, apparently around the Red River Valley of northern Minnesota. From this point, they moved southwest across the Missouri, apparently about the same time that the Cheyenne moved out from Minnesota, although the date of the formation of the permanent alliance between the two tribes is uncertain. The Atsina, afterward associated with the Siksika, appear to have separated from the parent tribe and moved off toward the north after their emergence into the plains. The division into Northern and Southern Arapahoe is largely geographic, originating within the last century and made permanent by the placing of the two bands on different reservations. The Northern Arapahoe, in Wyoming, are considered the nucleus or mother tribe and retain the sacred tribal articles—a tubular pipe, one ear of corn, and a turtle figurine, all of stone.

Since they crossed the Missouri, the drift of the Arapahoe, as is true of the Cheyenne and Sioux, has been west and south. The Northern Arapahoe made lodges on the edge of the mountains near the head of the North Platte River, while the Southern Arapaho continued down toward the Arkansas. Around 1840, they made peace with the Sioux, Kiowa, and Comanche. They remained at war with the Shoshone, Ute, and Pawnee, however, until they were confined to reservations. They generally maintained a friendly attitude toward the whites. By the treaty of Medicine Lodge in 1867, the Southern Arapaho, together with the Southern Cheyenne, were placed on a reservation in Oklahoma, which was thrown open to white settlement in 1892. At the same time, Indians received allotments in severalty, with rights of American citizen-

Scabby Bull, Arapahoe, 1898
Photo by DeLancey Gill; Courtesy Museum of New Mexico, Neg. No. 86992

ship. The Northern Arapahoe leased their present reservation on Wind River in Wyoming in 1876, after having made peace with their hereditary enemies, the Shoshoni, who lived on the same reservation. The Atsina division, usually regarded as a distinct tribe, is associated with the Assiniboine on the Fort Belknap Reservation in Montana. They numbered, respectively, 889, 859, and 535 in 1904—a total of 2,283, compared to a total of 2,638 ten years earlier.

As a people, the Arapahoe are much given to ceremonial observances. The annual Sun Dance is the greatest tribal ceremony, and they were active propagators of the ghost-dance religion years ago. In arts and home life, they were a typical Plains tribe. They bury their dead in the ground, unlike the Cheyenne and Sioux, who deposit them on scaffolds or on the surface of the ground in boxes. They have a military organization common to most of the Plains tribes and have no trace of the clan system, although the former is actually very similar to the latter.

Among themselves, they recognize five main divisions, each speaking a different dialect and apparently representing as many originally distinct but related tribes: 1.) Nakasinena, Baachinena, or Northern Arapahoe. Nakasinena, Sagebrush Men, is the name used by themselves. Baachinena, Red Willow Men, is the name by which they were commonly known to the rest of the tribe. The Kiowa distinguished them as Tagyako, "Sagebrush People," a translation of their proper name. They are considered the mother tribe of the Arapahoe, being indicated in the sign language by the sign for "Mother People." 2.) Nawaunena, "Southern Men," or Southern Arapaho, called Nawathineha, "Southerners," by the Northern Arapaho. The Kiowa know them as Ahayadal, the name given to the wild plum. The sign for them is made by rubbing the index finger against the side of the nose. 3.) Aaninena, Hitunena, Atsina, or Gros Ventres of the Prairie. The first name, said to mean "White Clay People," is what they call themselves. Hitunena, or Hitunenina, "Begging Men," "Beggars," or more exactly "Spongers," is the name used for them by other Arapahoe. The same idea is intended to be conveyed by the tribal sign that has commonly been interpreted as "Big Bellies," whence the name Gros Ventres applied to them by the French Canadians. This has caused some to confuse them with the Hidatsa, the Gros Ventres of the Missouri. 4.) Basawunena, "Wood Lodge," or possibly, "Big Lodge People." According to tradition, they were formerly a distinct tribe and at

Washakie's camp, Wind River Mountains, Wyoming
Photo by William H. Jackson; Courtesy Museum of New Mexico, Neg. No. 58655

war with the Arapahoe but have been incorporated with them for at least 200 years. Their dialect is said to have differed considerably from the other Arapahoe dialects. There are still about 50 of this lineage among the Northern Arapahoe and perhaps a few with the other two main divisions. 5.) Hanahawunena, "Rock Men," or Aaanunhawa. These people, like the Basawunena, lived with the Northern Arapahoe but are now practically extinct.

Shoshone Business Council
P.O. Box 538
Fort Washakie, WY 82514

Shoshone (Shoshoni) (The name probably comes from the Cheyenne name Shishi-noats-hitaneo, or Snake People, without any insult intended)

Location: The Shoshone of Wyoming live on the Wind River Indian Reservation located in central Wyoming. Their agency and tribal offices are located at Fort Washakie.

Public Ceremony or Powwow Dates: The tribe conducts several powwows throughout the year, Indian Days at Fort Washakie in late June, an Indian Fair in August, and Christmas dances in December. Their Sun Dance (Offerings Lodge) is usually held in July or August. Call the tribal office for dates and times and arrangements to attend the ceremonials. At the Sun Dance, photographs, sketching, food or drink at the lodge, tape recording, and scanty clothing are prohibited. Women on their moon should not be close to the lodge.

Art Forms: The artisans of the tribe do beadwork in the traditional floral design as well as other beautiful arts and crafts. Call the tribal office for help in locating them.

Visitor Information: This tribe shares the Wind River Indian Reservation with the Northern Arapahoe, but each has its distinctive culture, language, and customs. They were traditional enemies in prereservation times. Two famous people in the history of the exploration and settlement of the West are buried in the Fort Washakie area: Sacajawea, the Shoshone Bannock woman who helped Lewis and Clark explore the West, and Chief Washakie. A monument to Chief Washakie demonstrates the respect his people hold for him.

The most northerly division of the Shoshonean family, these people formerly occupied western Wyoming, meeting the Ute on the south; the entire central and southern parts of Idaho, except the territory taken by the Bannock; northeast Nevada; and a small strip of Utah west of Great Salt Lake. The Snake River country in Idaho may be considered their stronghold. The northern bands were found by Lewis and Clark in 1805, on the headwaters of the Missouri in western Montana, but they had previously ranged farther east on the plains. They had been driven into the Rocky Mountains by the hostile Atsina and Siksika, who already possessed firearms.

The origin of the term *Shoshoni* is unknown. It apparently is not a Shoshone word, and although the name is recognized by the Shoshone as applying to themselves, it probably originated among some other tribe. The Cheyenne name for the Comanche, who speak the Shoshone language, is Shishi-noats-hitaneo, "Snake People," but they have a different name for the Shoshone. The term *Snake* seems to have no etymological connection with the designation *Shoshone*.

The more northerly and easterly Shoshone were horse and buffalo Indians. The western and southern Shoshone were very different as they lived in very barren country that did not support large game. These tribes depended largely on fish as their source of food, supplemented by rabbits, roots, nuts, and seeds. These were the Indians most frequently called "Diggers." They were also called Shoshokos, or "Walkers," which simply means that they were too poor to possess horses. This term was applied to horseless Shoshone everywhere.

None of these Shoshone were agriculturists. In general, the style of habitations corresponded to the two types of Shoshone. In the north and east, they lived in tipis; in the sagebrush country to the west, they used brush shelters entirely.

In 1909, there were 1,766 Shoshone and Bannock in Idaho under the Fort Hall School and about 200 not under official supervision; in Nevada, there were 243 under the Western Shoshone School and about 750 not under agency or school control; in Wyoming, there were 816 under the Shoshone School. The total Shoshone population was approximately 3,250.

MOUNTAIN AND PLATEAU

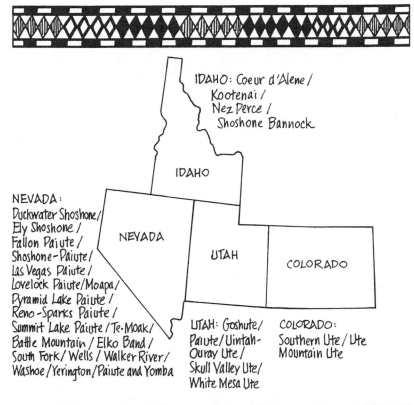

IDAHO: Coeur d'Alene /
Kootenai /
Nez Perce /
Shoshone Bannock

IDAHO

NEVADA:
Duckwater Shoshone/
Ely Shoshone /
Fallon Paiute /
Shoshone-Paiute/
Las Vegas Paiute /
Lovelock Paiute/Moapa/
Pyramid Lake Paiute /
Reno-Sparks Paiute /
Summit Lake Paiute / Te-Moak/
Battle Mountain / Elko Band /
South Fork/ Wells / Walker River/
Washoe /Yerington/Paiute and Yomba

NEVADA

UTAH

COLORADO

UTAH: Goshute/
Paiute/ Uintah-
Ouray Ute /
Skull Valley Ute/
White Mesa Ute

COLORADO:
Southern Ute / Ute
Mountain Ute

The interior of our North America is a land of basins, valleys, and great mountains. Streams rush down to the lowland river basins from springs and snow pack, and in the springtime of the year, brown cold water carries snow and ice to the warm sunlit valleys. The mountains are big. They rear their snow-capped heads above the horizons and maintain a silent vigil over all the land and all the people. And the life in the mountains and valleys and along the rivers is happy.

This is the land of the people who love the high places and the snow and winters. The mountains are their representatives to the Creator. They meet in council without demand and without being asked. The valleys that run up into the mountains are sided with steep walls and here the people have placed prayer monuments in sacred places to the Creator. The bare faces of the tall mountains are covered with prayer shrines to our ancestors and for those that have gone on before us.

Join with the tribes on the following pages to honor their ancestors and to honor our Creator, our Mother Earth, our Moon, our Sun, and the whole of all living things in the whole of all Creation. You will find that it is good. It is very, very, good.

Aho . . .

COLORADO

Koshare Indian Museum, Inc.
P.O. Box 580
La Junta, CO 81050-0580
(303) 384-4801

Location: The museum is located at 115 W. 18th Street in La Junta.

Public Ceremony or Powwow Dates: Summer ceremonials are held from mid-June to mid-August. Winter ceremonials are held the last two weeks in December. Call for dates, times, and ticket prices. No flash photography, no video cameras, and no audio recorders are allowed.

Visitor Information: The gift shop and museum hours are: summer, 9:00 a.m. to 6:00 p.m. daily; winter, noon to 5:00 p.m. Sunday through Friday, and Saturday 10:00 a.m. to 5:00 p.m. The gift shop features Southwest Indian jewelry, baskets, pottery, rugs, and Kachina statuettes.

This museum is unique in endeavoring to present the Native American Indian as an artist or as the subject of art. The Koshare organization was started fifty-five years ago by J. F. "Buck" Burshears as a Scout troop dedicated to the study of the American Indian and Indian lore. This Scout troop performs interpretive Indian dances. They are not actually Indians but members of Explorer Post 230 of the Boy Scouts of America. Woody Crumbo, the famous Indian artist who lived in Taos for so many years and has now gone to the other side, had a hand in forming the Koshare. Buck Burshears passed over to the other side last year. Hanta Yo.

Southern Ute Tribal Council
P.O. Box 737
Ignacio, CO 81137
(303) 563-4525

Ute

Location: Look for Ignacio south of Durango in southwestern Colorado.

Public Ceremony or Powwow Dates: The Bear Dance is usually held in May, the Sun Dance (Offerings Lodge) is usually held in July, and the Southern Ute Fair is held in September. Remember that no photography, no sketching, no shorts or halter tops, and no food or drink are allowed near the Sun Dance Lodge. Also, women who are on their moon are not allowed at the lodge.

Art Forms: The Sky Ute Lodge has a gift shop, the Sky Ute Gallery, which sells traditional and progressive artwork of local tribal artisans.

Visitor Information: If you like horse racing, go to Sky Ute Downs, and if you like bingo gaming, go to the Sky Ute bingo parlor. Call the tribal office for dates and times. The tribe operates the Sky Ute Country Store where you can buy supplies. RV hookups are available at the store, also. Lake Capote offers good fishing. Navajo Lake is inside the very southern edge of the reservation, and there is an Indian Museum at the state park there.

Ute Mountain
Ute Tribal Council
General Delivery
Towaoc, CO 81344
(303) 565-3751

Ute

Location: Drive south of Cortez, Colorado, on the highway to the four corners and watch for the pottery factory on your right, west of Highway 160/666, 15 miles from Cortez.

Public Ceremony or Powwow Dates: The annual Bear Dance is usually held in June. Go one mile east of the tribal offices in Towaoc.

Ute Indian, ca. 1915
Courtesy Museum of New Mexico, Neg. No. 21556

Art Forms: You can buy pottery at the Ute Mountain Pottery Factory.

Visitor Information: Don't miss the spectacular scenery of the Ute Mountain Tribal Park. The cliff dwellings and ancient Anasazi ruins are in beautiful country. There are full guided tours, hiking, camping, and backpacking trips available. All trips are arranged with the Ute Tribal Office. Stop by and see the Utes. The area is closed in the winter, so please visit from June through September.

IDAHO

Coeur D'Alene Tribal Council
Plummer, ID 83851
(208) 274-3101

Skitswish

Location: On your map of Idaho, look for Plummer just south and west of Coeur D'Alene.

Public Ceremony or Powwow Dates: The tribe has three powwows each year. Call the office above for dates and times.

The Skitswish are a Salish tribe on a river and lake of the same name in northern Idaho. Coeur d'Alene (French, "Awl-heart"), the name by which they are popularly known, was originally a nickname used by some chief of the tribe to express the size of a trader's heart. The Skitswish numbered 533 in 1909.

Fort Hall Business Council
Fort Hall, ID 83202
(208) 238-3700

Bannock (Panaiti, their own name)

Shoshone

Location: The reservation is located in southeast Idaho north of Pocatello.

Public Ceremony or Powwow Dates: The Fort Hall tribe holds its annual Fort Hall Indian Days celebration in August. The Indian Day is in September and features a total celebration. Call the tribal office for dates and times.

Art Forms: The beadwork is mostly floral in design in this area. There are also other kinds of arts and crafts to be found here. Call the office for information about the type of work you wish to buy.

Visitor Information: For more information on the Shoshone, please see Shoshone Business Council in Wyoming.

The Bannock are a Shoshonean tribe whose habitat prior to being forced onto reservations cannot be definitely outlined. There were two geographic divisions, but references to the Bannock do not always note this distinction. The home of the chief division appears to have been southeast Idaho, and they ranged into western Wyoming. The country actually claimed by the chief of this southern division, which seems to have been recognized by the treaty of Fort Bridger, July 3, 1868, lay between lat. 42 degrees and 45 degrees and between long. 113 degrees and the main chain of the Rocky Mountains. It separated the Wihinasht Shoshone of western Idaho from the so-called Washaki band of Shoshone of western Wyoming. They were found in this region in 1859, and they asserted that this had been their home in the past. Many of this division affiliated with the Washaki Shoshone and by 1859, had extensively intermarried with them. Fort Hall Reservation was set apart by Executive Order in 1869, and 600 Bannock, in addition to a large number of Shoshone, consented to remain on it. But most of them soon wandered away, and as late as 1874, an appropriation was made to enable the Bannock and Shoshone scattered in southeast Idaho to be moved to the reservation. The Bannock at Fort Hall were said to number 422 in 1885.

The north division was seen in 1853 living on the Salmon River in eastern Idaho. Lewis and Clark, who passed through their country in 1805, may have included them under the general term Shoshone, unless, as is most likely, these are the Broken Moccasin Indians they mention. In all probability, these Salmon River Bannock had recently crossed the mountains from the east because of pressure from the Siksika, as they claimed southwestern Montana, including the rich areas where Virginia City and Bozeman are situated, as their territory.

The Bannock were a widely roving tribe, a characteristic that favored their dispersal and separation into groups. Although their language is Shoshonean, in physical characters the Bannock more closely resemble the Shahaptian Nez Perces than other Shoshonean Indians.

The loss of hunting lands, the diminution of the bison herds, and the failure of the U.S. government to render timely relief led to a Bannock outbreak of 1878. During the Nez Perce war, the Bannock were forced to remain on their inhospitable reservation, to face the continued encroachments of the whites, and to subsist on goods provided from an appropriation amounting to 2-1/2 cents per capita per diem. Because of insufficient food, the Bannock left the reservation in spring 1878 and went to Camas Prairie, where they killed several settlers. A vigorous campaign under General Howard resulted in the capture of about 1,000 of them in August, and the outbreak came to an end after a fight on September 5 at Clark's ford, where 20 Bannock lodges were attacked and all the women and children killed.

About 1829, the population of the southern Bannock was estimated at 8,000. In 1901, the tribe numbered 513, but it was intermixed with the Shoshone at that time. Almost all the Bannock are now living on Fort Hall Reservation.

Kootenai Tribal Council
P.O. Box 1269
Bonners Ferry, ID 83805
(208) 267-3519

Kutenai (corrupted form, possibly by way of the language of the Siksika, of Dutonaqa, one of their names for themselves)

Visitor Information: The Kootenai hold an annual summer powwow at Fort Steele Heritage Park near Cranbrook, British Columbia, on Highway 93/95. You can call the park at (604) 489-3351 for dates and times.

These people form a distinct linguistic family who inhabited parts of southeastern British Columbia and northern Montana and Idaho, from the lakes near the source of the Columbia River to Pend d'Oreille Lake. For more information, see the Confederated Salish and Kootenai Tribal Council, Montana.

From where the sun now sets I will fight no more forever.
—Chief Joseph (Nez Perce)

Nez Perce Executive Committee
P.O. Box 305
Lapwai, ID 83540
(208) 843-2253

Nez Perces (pierced noses), a term applied by the French to a number of tribes that practiced or were supposed to practice the custom of piercing the nose for the insertion of a piece of dentalium. The term is now used exclusively to designate the main tribe of the Shahaptian family who have not, however, so far as is known, ever practiced the custom.

Location: The Nez Perce (NEZ-purse) reservation is located in northwest Idaho close to Washington and Oregon.

Public Ceremony or Powwow Dates: The Nez Perce love to powwow. There are no less than five celebrations per year, beginning with the Epethes Powwow held the first weekend in March in Lapwai. Competition war dance championships are decided at this powwow. Next comes the Mat-Al-YM'A Powwow and Root Feast at Kamiah the third weekend in May. Traditional dancing is performed there. During the third weekend in June, at Lapwai, the tribe features dances honoring Chief Joseph and his warriors at the Warriors Memorial Powwow. The next powwow held is the Looking Glass Powwow in August at Kamiah. Great dancing and drum groups celebrate the memory of Chief Looking Glass, who lost his life in the war. Last, but not least, is the Four Nations Powwow held in October. Call the tribal office for dates and times of all the above events to confirm before traveling.

Art Forms: The Nez Perce sell arts and crafts, including their exclusive corn husk bags, during their powwows.

Visitor Information: This tribe developed the Appaloosa horse, which is honored with a museum in Moscow on Highway 8 on the way to Pullman.

The Nez Perces, or Sahaptin, were found in 1805 occupying a large area in what is now western Idaho, northeastern Oregon, and southeastern Washington, on the lower Sanak River and its tributaries. They roamed between the Blue Mountains in Oregon and

Tsutlim-Mox-Mox (Yellow Bull), Nez Perce, 1912
Photo by DeLancey Gill; Courtesy Museum of New Mexico, Neg. No. 87002

the Bitter Root Mountains in Idaho and, according to Lewis and Clark, sometimes crossed the range to the headwaters of the Missouri. Certain writers have classed them under two geographic divisions, Upper Nez Perces and Lower Nez Perces. In 1834, the Lower Nez Perces lived to the north and west of the Blue Mountains on several of the branches of the Snake River, where they were neighbors of the Cayuse and Wallawalla. The Upper Nez Perces held the Salmon River country in Idaho in 1834 and probably also the Grande Ronde Valley in eastern Oregon, but by the treaty of 1855, they ceded a large part of this territory to the United States.

The reservation in which they were confined at that time included the Wallowa Valley in Oregon as well as a large district in Idaho. With the discovery of gold and the consequent influx of miners and settlers, the Nez Perces were forced out of this region by means of a new treaty that confined the tribe to the reservation at Lapwai, Idaho. The occupants of Wallowa Valley refused to recognize the treaty, and finally, under their chief, Joseph, took active measures of resistance, resulting in the Nez Perce war of 1877. Several severe defeats were inflicted on the U.S. troops sent against the Indians. Finally, when forced to give way, Joseph conducted a masterly retreat across the Bitter Root Mountains and into Montana in an attempt to reach Canadian Territory, but he and his band were surrounded and captured when within a few miles of the boundary. Joseph and his 450 followers were removed to Indian Territory (Oklahoma). Their loss from disease was so great there that in 1885 they were sent to the Colville Reservation in northern Washington, where a remnant of the tribe still resides.

The total population of the Nez Perces in 1805 was put at about 6,000. In 1885, they were estimated officially at 1,437. In 1906, the population was estimated at more than 1,600, 1,534 on the reservation in Idaho and 83 on the Colville Reservation in Washington.

At the time of Lewis and Clark's visit, the Nez Perces are reported as living in communal houses, said to contain about 50 families each. There is evidence that they used the typical underground lodge and that these seldom contained more than three or four families. A much larger dancing house was built at each permanent winter camp. Salmon constituted their most important food in early times and with roots and berries made up their entire food supply until the introduction of horses facilitated hunting expeditions to the neighboring mountains. The tribe seems to have been divided into a number of bands or villages, named according to the place where the permanent winter camp was made. Owing to the precarious nature of the food supply, the greater portion of the inhabitants of any one of these villages would often be absent for much of the year. There was no head chief of the tribe, but each band had several chiefs, one of whom was regarded as the leader. These chiefs were succeeded by their sons. Expeditions for hunting or war were led by chiefs chosen for the occasion. There are no signs of a clan system in the social organization of the Nez Perces, and marriage was apparently permitted between any couple except in the case of recognized relationship.

The spiritual beliefs of the Nez Perces, before the introduction of Christianity, were those characteristic of the Indians of the interior, the main feature being the belief in an indefinite number of spirits. An individual might procure a personal protecting spirit by rigorous training and fasting. The Nez Perces are independent and brave and have been noted for their friendliness except when acts of aggression were committed against them.

NEVADA

Paiute

The word *Paiute* properly belongs to the Corn Creek tribe of southwestern Utah but has been extended to include many other tribes. However, it is employed as a convenient divisional name for the tribes occupying southwestern Utah from around the locality of Beaver, the southwestern part of Nevada, and the northwestern part of Arizona, excluding the Chemehuevi.

With regard to the Indians of the Walker River and Pyramid Lake reservations, who constitute the main body of those commonly known as Paiute, it has been claimed that they are not Paiute at all but another tribe, the Paviotso. The Indians of this area themselves claim the Bannock as their cousins and say that they speak the same language.

The most influential chiefs among them in modern times have been Winnemucca, who died a few years before the turn of the century, and Natchez. They have been generally peaceable and friendly toward the whites, although in the early 1860s, they sometimes came into collision with miners and emigrants, the hostility frequently provoked by the whites themselves. The northern Paiute were more warlike than those of the south, and a considerable number of them took part with the Bannock in the war of 1878. The great majority of the Paiute (including the Paviotso) were not on reservations. In 1906, their population could only be estimated at between 6,500 and 7,000: approximately 486 at Walker River, 129 at Moapa, 554 at Pyramid Lake, 267 at Duck Valley, 3,500 not under a reservation, and 350 in the Western Nevada School.

Traditionally, the Paiute have been closely associated with the Shoshone.

All Indians must dance, everywhere, keep on dancing. Pretty soon in next spring Great Spirit Come. He bring back all game of every kind. The game be thick everywhere. All dead Indians come back and live again. They all be strong just like young men, be young again.

—Wovoka, the Paiute
Messiah

Duckwater Shoshone Tribal Council
P.O. Box 68
Duckwater, NV 89314
(702) 863-0227

Shoshone

Location: The reservation is located in southwestern Idaho and northeastern Nevada on State Highway 51.

Public Ceremony or Powwow Dates: There is usually a rodeo during the Fourth of July held at Owyhee, Nevada. This tribe participates in many activities of the Paiute. The *Native Nevadan* newsmagazine lists Western Shoshone events. Write to them at 98 Colony Road, Reno, NV 89502, or telephone at (702) 329-2936.

Ely Colony Council
16 Shoshone Circle
Ely, NV 89301
(702) 289-3013

Fallon Paiute-Shoshone Business Council
8955 Mission Road
Fallon, NV 89406
(702) 423-6075

Paiute-Shoshone

Location: The Fallon Indian Reservation is located north of Highway 50 (the loneliest highway in the world), northeast of Fallon.

Public Ceremony or Powwow Dates: The most well known of events for this area is Fallon Days, which features a parade where you may see Indian people in traditional clothing. The Fallon Chamber of Commerce has information and dates and times; telephone at (702) 423-2544.

Fort McDermitt Shoshone-Paiute Tribal Council
P.O. Box 457
McDermitt, NV 89421
(702) 532-8259

Shoshone-Paiute

Location: The reservation is located in northwestern Nevada on Highway 95.

1826 – PIUTE INDIAN CAMP. NEVADA.

Paiute Indians, Nevada
Courtesy Museum of New Mexico, Neg. No. 43442

Las Vegas Colony Council
No. 1 Paiute Drive
Las Vegas, NV 89106
(702) 386-3926

Lovelock Tribal Council
P.O. Box 878
Lovelock, NV 89419
(702) 273-7861

Moapa Business Council
P.O. Box 56
Moapa, NV 89025
(702) 865-2787

Moapariats (Mo-a-pa-ri-ats, "mosquito creek people")

This is a band of Paiute formerly living in or near Moapa Valley in southeastern Nevada. They numbered 64 in 1873.

Pyramid Lake Paiute Tribal Council
P.O. Box 256
Nixon, NV 89424
(702) 574-0140

Paiute

Location: The reservation is located northeast of Reno on State Highway 34.

Public Ceremony or Powwow Dates: Call the tribal office for more information.

Art Forms: The women continue to make the traditional baby cradleboards from woven baskets covered with leather. The decorations are very beautiful, and often you will find them for sale at powwows.

Visitor Information: The area around Pyramid Lake is very scenic, with various impressive geological features. Fishing permits are available from the tribe at the Tribal Enterprise Office in Sutcliffe, Abe and Sue's Store in Nixon, and Pyramid Lake Store in Nixon. The lake is known for large trout. Only Paiutes are allowed to fish for the Cui-ui, a rare fish found in the lake and still eaten by Paiute people. Camping and boating are allowed. The old Indian Trail that runs along the Truckee River between Nixon and Wadsworth can still be seen in some places.

Reno-Sparks Indian Council
98 Colony Road
Reno, NV 89502
(702) 329-2936

Paiute

Location: The Paiute and Washo people of the Reno/Sparks Indian Colony own and operate the Indian Colony Mall at 2001 E. Second Street, Reno, telephone (702) 329-2573.

Public Ceremony or Powwow Dates: The Paiute people of the area sponsor many interesting events annually. Many are held around Schurz, Reno, Sparks, and Fallon. The *Native Nevadan* lists most of these events. Subscribe by writing to 98 Colony Road, Reno, NV 89502, or calling (702) 329-2936. Besides dancing there will be hand games and crafts sales.

Visitor Information: Traditional items can be found at the Earth Window Indian Arts and Crafts Shop in the Indian Colony Mall.

Shoshone-Paiute Business Council
P.O. Box 219
Owyhee, NV 29832
(702) 757-3161

Visitor Information: Please see the general history of the Paiute at the beginning of this section.

Summit Lake Paiute Council
P.O. Box 1958
Winnemucca, NV 89445
(702) 623-5151

The Winnemucca band was a Paviotso band under Chief Winnemucca (The Giver) which formerly lived on Smoke Creek, near Honey Lake, northeastern California, and eastward to Pyramid, Winnemucca, and Humboldt lakes, Nevada. In 1859, they were said to number 155; in 1877, they were under Malheur Agency, Oregon, numbering 150.

Te-Moak Business Council
525 Sunset Street
Elko, NV 89801
(702) 738-9251

Battle Mountain Band Council
P.O. Box 578
Battle Mountain, NV 89820
(702) 835-2004

Elko Band Council
P.O. Box 748
Elko, NV 89801
(702) 738-8889

South Fork Band Council
Box B-13
Lee, NV 898209
(702) 744-4273

Wells Indian Colony Band Council
P.O. Box 809
Wells, NV 89835
(702) 752-3045

Shoshone

For more information on the Shoshone, please see the Shoshone Business Council, Wyoming.

Walker River Paiute Tribal Council
P.O. Box 220
Schurz, NV 89427
(702) 773-2306

Paiute

Location: The reservation is located east of Carson City on U.S. Highway 95.

Public Ceremony or Powwow Dates: The Walker River Paiute tribe annually holds its Pinenut Festival at Schurz in October with events including round dancing, hand games, and a barbecue. Call the tribal office for more information.

Weasaw, Shoshone, 1899
Photo by Rose & Hopkins; Courtesy Museum of New Mexico, Neg. No. 4372

Washoe Tribal Council
919 Highway 395 South
Gardnerville, NV 89410
(702) 883-1446

Carson Colony Community Council
502 Shoshone Street
Carson City, NV 89701
(702) 883-6431

Dresslerville Community Council
P.O. Box 2087
Gardnerville, NV 89410

Woodfords Community Council
Route 1, Box 102
Markleeville, CA 96120
(916) 694-2170

Washo (from washiu, "person," in their own language)

Location: All the above tribes are in the Carson City area.

Public Ceremony or Powwow Dates: There is an annual La Ka Le'l Ba powwow in Carson City put on by the Carson Colony. Call (702) 883-6431 for dates and times.

Art Forms: Arts and crafts are for sale at the powwow.

The Washo are a small tribe, but they form a distinct linguistic family, the Washoan, which, when first known to Americans, occupied Truckee River, Nevada, as far down as the Meadows. The Washo also held Carson River down to the first large canyon below Carson City, the borders of Lake Tahoe, and the Sierra and other valleys as far as the first range south of Honey Lake, California. They occupied the mountains only in summer. There is some evidence that they once were established in the valleys farther to the east, whence they had been driven by the Paiute, with whom there existed a state of chronic ill feeling. Between 1860 and 1862, the Paiute conquered the Washo in a contest over the site of Carson and forbade them to own horses. In the early 1900s, they were confined to the country from Reno on the railroad to a short distance south of Carson City. Study of their language indicates no linguistic relationship with any other people. In 1859, the Washo numbered about 900, but by 1905, they were reduced to about a third of that number.

Winnemucca Colony Council
Winnemucca, NV 89445
(702) 623-2980

Yerington Paiute Tribal Council
171 Campbell Lane
Yerington, NV 89447
(702) 463-3301

Paiute

Please see the general history of the Paiute at the beginning of this section.

Yomba Tribal Council
Route 1, Box 24
Austin, NV 89310
(702) 964-2463

Shoshone

For more information on the Shoshone, please see the Shoshone Business Council, Wyoming.

UTAH

Goshute Business Council
Ibapah, UT 87034
(801) 234-1138

Goshute (from Gossip, their chief, plus Ute)

Location: The reservation is located in western Utah south of Ibapah.

This is a Shoshonean tribe that formerly occupied Utah west of the Salt and Utah lakes and eastern Nevada.

Paiute Tribal Council
600 North 100 East
Cedar City, UT 84720
(801) 586-1111

Skull Valley Executive Committee
c/o Unitah and Ouray Agency
Fort Duchesne, UT 84026
(801) 722-2406

Uintah and Ouray Business Committee
Fort Duchesne, UT 84026
(801) 722-5141

Northern Ute (please see also Colorado, Southern Ute and Mountain Ute)

Location: The reservation is located in the northeast corner of Utah.

Public Ceremony or Powwow Dates: The Northern Ute Bear Dance is held in April or May. The Fourth of July and the fall are times of powwows. The Sun Dance (Offerings Lodge) is in July and August. Call the tribal office for dates and times. As always, the Offerings Lodge is restricted from cameras, tape recorders, sketch pads, and video equipment, and women should not wear halter tops or shorts. Women on their moon should not go near the lodge, and there is no food or drink allowed at the lodge.

Art Forms: The Utes do floral design beadwork and other arts and crafts that are Plains and Mountain in style.

Visitor Information: This is a beautiful part of Utah, particularly when you enter the northern part of the reservation toward the Uintah Mountains.

The Utes are an important Shoshonean division, related linguistically to the Paiute, Chemehuevi, Kawaiisu, and Bannock. They formerly occupied the entire central and western portions of Colorado and the eastern portion of Utah, including the east part of the Salt Lake Valley and Utah Valley. On the south they extended into New Mexico, occupying much of the upper drainage area of the San Juan. They appear to have always been a warlike people and early came into possession of horses. None of the tribes prac-

ticed agriculture. Very little is know of their social and political organization, although the seven Ute tribes of Utah were at one time
organized into a confederacy under Chief Tabby (Taiwi). There
are dialect differences in the language, but they probably presented little difficulty in communication between the several bands.
In the north part of their range, in Utah, they appear to have have
intermarried with the Shoshone, Bannock, and Paiute and in the
south, with the Jicarilla Apache.

The first peace treaty with the Ute was concluded December 30,
1849. By Executive Order of October 3, 1861, Uintah Valley was
set apart for the Uinta tribe, and the remainder of the land claimed
by them was taken without formal purchase. In a treaty of October
7, 1863, the Tabeguache band was assigned a reservation and the
remainder of their land was ceded to the United States. On May 5,
1864, various reserves, established in 1856 and 1859 by Indian
agents, were ordered vacated and sold. A treaty of March 2, 1868,
created a reservation in Colorado for the Tabeguache, Moache, Capote, Wiminuche, Yampa, Grand River, Uinta, and other bands
and the remainder of their lands relinquished; but in an agreement
of September 13, 1873, a part of this reservation was ceded to the
United States. When it was found that a portion of this last cession
was included in the Uncompahgre Valley, that part was returned
to the Ute by Executive Order of August 17, 1876. By Executive
Order of November 22, 1875, the Ute Reservation was enlarged,
but this additional tract was restored to the public domain
in 1882. In June 1878, several more tracts included in the reservations thereunder established were restored to the public domain.
Under agreement of November 9, 1878, the Moache, Capote, and
Wiminuche ceded their right to the confederated Ute Reservation
established by the 1868 treaty, and the United States agreed to es-
tablish a reservation for them on the San Juan River. In 1880, the
Southern Ute and the Uncompahgre acknowledged an agreement
to settle respectively on the La Plata River and on the Grand near
the mouth of the Gunnison, while the White River Ute agreed to
move to the Uinta Reservation in Utah. Since sufficient agricultural
land was not found at the future home of the Uncompahgre, the
president, in 1882, established a reserve for them in Utah. But in
May 1888, a part of the Uinta Reservation was restored to the public domain.

The Southern Ute lands in Colorado were in part subsequently allotted in severalty, and in April 1899, 523,079 acres were opened to settlement, with the remainder (483,750 acres) retained as a reservation for the Wiminuche. A large part of the Uinta Valley Reservation in Utah has also been allotted in severalty, more than a million acres set aside as forest and other reserves and more than a million acres more opened to homestead entry. Of the Uncompahgre Reservation in Utah in June 1897, 12,540 acres were allotted and the remainder restored to the public domain.

In 1885, official reports gave 3,391 as the population of several reservations; in 1909, 2,014.

In July 1879, about 100 men of the White River Agency, Colorado, left their reservation to hunt in southern Wyoming. During this time some forests were set on fire by railway tiemen, and the Indians were blamed. They were ordered to remain henceforth on their reservation. Orders were later issued for the arrest of the Indians charged with the recent forest fires, and Major Thornburgh was sent with a force of 190 men. Suspecting the outcome, the Indians procured ammunition from neighboring traders and informed the agent that the appearance of the troops would be regarded as an act of war. On September 20, Thornburgh's detachment was ambushed, and their leader and thirteen men were killed. The command fell back. On October 2, a company of cavalry arrived, and three days later Colonel Merritt and 600 troops reached the scene. The conflict was soon ended, mainly through the peaceful attitude and influence of Chief Ouray.

In summer 1906, about 400 Ute, chiefly of the White River band, left their allotments and the Uintah Reservation in Utah to go to the Pine Ridge Reservation, South Dakota, where they could live unrestricted. Although they committed no acts of aggression on the way, settlers became alarmed. Every peaceful effort was made to induce them to return to Utah, but only 45 returned there. Those who refused were charged with petty thefts while in Wyoming, and the matter was placed under the jurisdiction of the War Department. Troops were sent to the scene in October, and the Indians accompanied them peacefully to Fort Meade, South Dakota, in November. In the following spring (1907), arrangements were made whereby the absentee Ute were assigned four townships of the Cheyenne River Reservation, South Dakota, which was leased by the government at the expense of the Ute annuity fund, for five years. The Indians were removed in June to their new lands, where they remained until the following June (1908), when, at their own request, they were returned to their old home in Utah, arriving there in October.

White Mesa Ute Council
P.O. Box 340
Blanding, UT 84511

For more information on the Ute tribe, please see Utah, Skull Valley Executive Committee, and Colorado, Mountain Ute and Southern Ute.

NORTH

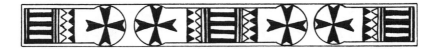

Lower Sioux /
Minnesota Chippewa /
Fond du Lac / Grand
Portage / Leech Lake /
Mille Lacs / Nett Lake /
White Earth / Prairie
Island / Red Cliff / Red
Lake / Shakopee /
Upper Sioux

MINNESOTA

The North country of North America lies in that place beyond where our plains meet the lakes and the forests of tall trees. The terrain is flat and rolling and the lakes and streams glisten and sparkle in the sun.

This is the land of the people of the wigwam; the nomadic woodland people who hunted deer and small game and lived in tune with the spirits of all living things. They gathered wild rice and collected wild herbs for food and medicine.

They have always been there and the spirits of their ancestors will always be over and in the land. From time immemorial, they have followed the streams in birch bark canoes and followed the paths worn through the forests.

They, too, have the drum. The ceremonials of the people act out their respect and their prayers for and to the Creator. They grew some tobacco and smoked it in pipes and rolled leaves with their intentions that the smoke would carry their prayers up to the Creator. And it did. And it does today.

There is no mystery or secret to Indian spirituality. There is only respect and natural praise composed into ceremony which defines the existence of the people.

Join with the tribes on the following pages to honor their ancestors and to honor our Creator, our Mother Earth, our Moon, our Sun, and the whole of all living things in the whole of all Creation. You will find that it is good. It is very, very good.

Aho . . .

MINNESOTA

Ojibwa (Chippewa)

The Ojibwa are one of the largest tribes north of Mexico. Their range was formerly along both shores of Lake Huron and Lake Superior, extending across Minnesota to the Turtle Mountains, North Dakota. Although strong in numbers and occupying an extensive territory, the Chippewa were never prominent in history, because of their remoteness from the frontier during the period of the colonial wars. According to tradition they are part of an Algonquian body, including the Ottawa and Potawatomi, that separated into divisions when it reached Mackinaw in its westward movement, having come from some point north or northeast of Mackinaw.

They were first noticed in the Jesuit Relation of 1640 under the name Baouichtigouin (probably Bawatigowininiwug, "People of the Sault") as residing at the Sault, and it is possible that Nicolet met them in 1634 or 1639. A remnant or offshoot of the tribe resided north of Lake Superior after the main body moved south to Sault Ste. Marie, or when it had reached the vicinity of the Sault. The Marameg, a tribe closely related to if not an actual division of the Ojibwa, who dwelled along the north shore of the lake, were apparently incorporated with the latter while they were at the Sault, or at any rate prior to 1670. On the north, the Ojibwa are so closely connected with the Cree and Maskegon that the three can be distinguished only by those intimately acquainted with their dialects and customs. On the south, the Chippewa (Ojibwa), Ottawa, and Potawatomi have always formed a sort of loose confederacy, frequently designated in the last century the Three Fires. It seems to be well established that some of the Chippewa have resided north of Lake Superior from time immemorial. These and the Marameg claimed the north side of the lake as their country. The

Ojibwa cultivated some maize. Another source of food was wild rice, and the possession of wild rice fields was one of the chief causes of their wars with the Dakota, Foxes, and other nations.

About 1700, the Ojibwa first came into possession of firearms and were pushing their way westward, alternately at peace and at war with the Sioux and in almost constant conflict with the Foxes. In 1692, the French reestablished a trading post at Shaugawaumi-kong, now La Pointe, Ashland County, Wisconsin, which became an important Ojibwa settlement. In the beginning of the eighteenth century the Ojibwa succeeded in driving the Foxes, already reduced by a war with the French, from northern Wisconsin, compelling them to take refuge with the Sauk. They then turned against the Sioux, driving them across the Mississippi and south to the Minnesota River, and continued their westward march across Minnesota and North Dakota until they occupied the headwaters of the Red River and established their westernmost band in the Turtle Mountains. It was not until after 1736 that they obtained a foothold west of Lake Superior. While the main divisions of the tribe were thus extending their possessions in the west, others overran the peninsula between Lake Huron and Lake Erie, which had long been claimed by the Iroquois through conquest. The Iroquois were forced to withdraw, and the whole region was occupied by the Ojibwa bands, most of whom became known as Missisauga, although they still called themselves Ojibwa. The Chippewa (Ojibwa) took part with the other tribes of the Northwest in all the wars against the frontier settlements to the close of the War of 1812. Those living within the United States made a treaty with the government in 1815 and subsequently resided on reservations or allotted lands within their original territory in Michigan, Wisconsin, Minnesota, and North Dakota, with the exception of the small band of Swan Creek and Black River Ojibwa, who sold their lands in southern Michigan in 1836 and moved to Kansas.

Their long and successful contest with the Sioux and Foxes exhibited their bravery and determination, yet they were uniformly friendly to the French. The Ojibwa are a timber people. According to tradition, the division of the tribe residing at La Pointe practiced cannibalism. (The act of eating a small particle of flesh or of an organ, such as the heart, was common practice of a victor over an enemy. This practice should not be confused with cannibalism.)

Like the Ottawa, the Ojibwa were expert in the use of the canoe and in their early history depended largely on fish for food. There is abundant evidence that polygamy was common. Their wigwams were made of birch bark or of grass mats; poles were first planed in the ground in a circle, the tops bent together and tied, and the bark or mats thrown over them, leaving a smoke hole at the top. They knew that the shade, after the death of the body, followed a wide beaten path, leading toward the west, finally arriving in the place of spirit that abounds in everything of need. The Ojibwa believed that the spirit returns to visit the body until it is reduced to dust. Like most of our people, the Ojibwa believe that all things, animate and inanimate, are alive. All objects are Manitus, which are every wakeful and quick to hear everything in the summer but in winter, after snow falls, are in a torpid state. The Ojibwa, as most of our people do, regard dreams as revelations, and some object that appears therein is often chosen as a tutelary deity. The Medewiwin, or Grand Medicine Society, is a powerful organization of the Ojibwa, which in the past controlled the movements of the tribe and was a formidable obstacle to the introduction of Christianity. The native people of this land lived in harmony with spirituality; they did not *practice* it. When an Ojibwa died, it was customary to place the body in a grave facing west, often in a sitting posture, or to scoop a shallow cavity in the earth and deposit the body therein on its back or side, covering it with earth so as to form a small mound, over which boards, poles, or birch bark were placed. According to one observer, the Ojibwa of Fond du Lac, Wisconsin, practiced scaffold burial, the body being enclosed in a box. Mourning for a lost relative usually continued for a year.

Population estimates in 1764 were about 25,000. In 1905, the estimate was 30,000, with 14,144 in the United States.

Fond du Lac Reservation Business Committee
105 University Road
Cloquet, MN 55720
(218) 879-4593

Ojibwa (to roast till puckered up)

Location: The tribal office address is listed above.

Public Ceremony or Powwow Dates: The Fond du Lac powwow is usually in July.

Art Forms: Arts and crafts can be purchased during the powwow.

Visitor Information: Wild rice harvesting takes place during September. An interesting item about wild rice can be found in the general history of the Ojibwa at the beginning of this section.

This tribe also owns its own construction company and a steel products company. The bingo enterprise is doing well in Duluth.

Grand Portage Reservation Business Committee
P.O. Box 428
Grand Portage, MN 55605
(218) 476-2279

Ojibwa (to roast till puckered up)

Location: The reservation is located in the northeastern tip of Minnesota.

Public Ceremony or Powwow Dates: Rendezvous Days is held the second weekend in August. There is traditional dancing and singing.

Art Forms: Beadwork and other arts and crafts can be found during the powwow. You can also find beadwork for sale at Crawford House in the National Monument. Also, the community arts center is an interesting place to visit.

Visitor Information: Be sure to visit Grand Portage National Monument, which is inside the reservation. Grand Portage Lodge and Conference Center on Highway 61 in Grand Portage is owned by the tribe. The marina with boat rentals, a construction company, a logging operation, a fishing company, a restaurant, an elementary school, and a cross-country skiing operation are also owned by the tribe.

Lower Sioux Indian Community Council
Rural Route 1, Box 308
Morton, MN 56270
(507) 697-6185

The Lower Sioux, as distinguished from the Upper Sioux (Sisseton and Wahpeton, are composed of the Mdewakanton and Wahpekute Sioux.

Mille Lacs Reservation Business Committee
Star Route Box 195
Onamia, MN 56359
(612) 532-4181

Ojibwa (to roast till puckered up)

Location: The museum is located twelve miles north of Onamia on U.S. Highway 169.

Public Ceremony or Powwow Dates: The powwow is held in mid-August. Call the tribal office for dates and times.

Art Forms: Artwork can be found at the museum, and arts and crafts are sold at the powwow.

Visitor Information: The bingo parlor and an assembly plant are also owned and operated by the tribe.

Minnesota Chippewa Tribal Executive Committee
Box 217
Cass Lake, MN 56633
(218) 335-2252

Leech Lake Reservation Business Committee
Route 3, Box 100
Cass Lake, MN 56633
(218) 335-2207

Ojibwa (to roast till puckered up)

Location: The powwow grounds and the convention center are located in Cass Lake.

Public Ceremony or Powwow Dates: Five annual powwows are held, on Labor Day and Memorial Day and in winter, spring, and mid-summer. Call the tribal office for dates and times.

Art Forms: Birch bark baskets, paintings, moccasins, beadwork, feather work, leather work, and more are available. The gift shop and Che-Wa-Kae-Gon Restaurant and bingo parlor show some work.

Visitor Information: This tribe owns a logging company, a construction company, the Leech Lake Wild Rice Company, and other enterprises.

Unidentified man, Chippewa, 1872
Photo by B. W. Kilburn; Courtesy Museum of New Mexico, Neg. No. 90556

Nett Lake Reservation Business Committee
(Bois Fort)
Nett Lake, MN 55772
(218) 757-3261

Ojibwa (to roast till puckered up)

Location: The location of the powwow grounds can be obtained by calling the tribal office.

Public Ceremony or Powwow Dates: The first weekend in June is powwow time with traditional dancing and drum groups. Call the tribal office for dates and times.

Art Forms: Arts and crafts are sold at the powwow. The work will include paintings, feather work, leather work, and beadwork.

Visitor Information: The Bois Fort Wild Rice Company is doing well. For interesting information on wild rice, see the general history of the Ojibwa at the beginning of this section.

Ni-Mi-Win
Spirit Mountain Sky Facility
Duluth, MN
(218) 897-1251

Ojibwa (to roast till puckered up)

Location: Call the number above for the location of the powwow.

Public Ceremony or Powwow Dates: The third weekend in August is the Ni-M-Win celebration. It is the greatest joint Ojibwa celebration and its goal is to bring everyone together. Traditional and inter-tribal dancing are performed.

Art Forms: You will find black ash basket making along with leather work, beadwork, birch bark baskets, and all kinds of arts and crafts.

Visitor Information: If you like to powwow, don't miss this one.

Prairie Island Community Council
5750 Sturgeon Lake Road
Welch, MN 55089
(612) 388-8889

Sioux

For information on the Sioux, please see the general history of the Sioux under South Dakota.

Red Lake Tribal Council
P.O. Box 550
Red Lake, MN 56671
(218) 679-3341

Ojibwa (to roast till puckered up)

For more information on the Ojibwa, please see the general history at the beginning of this section.

Shakopee Business Council
2330 Sioux Trail NW
Prior Lake, MN 55372
(612) 445-8900

Shakopee (Shakpe, "six")

Shakopee is the name of a succession of chiefs of the Mdewakanton Sioux, residing on the Minnesota River, not far from the present town of Shakopee, Scott County, Minnesota. Three men of the name are mentioned in succession. The first met Major S. H. Long at the mouth of the Minnesota in 1817, when he came up to distribute the presents that Lt. Z. M. Pike had contracted to send them twelve years earlier. Long found him very offensive. This Shakopee was succeeded by his son, who was known as Eaglehead Shakopee, and he by his son Little Six (Shakopeela), who was a leader in the Minnesota raids of 1862.

Grey Eagle and his lodge, Sioux
Photo by Keystone View Co.; Courtesy Museum of New Mexico, Neg. No. 91500

Upper Sioux Board of Trustees
P.O. Box 147
Granite Falls, MN 56241
(612) 564-4504

The Upper Sioux are the Sisseton and Wahpeton Sioux, on the upper Minnesota River, as distinguished from the Lower Sioux (Mdewakanton and Wahpekute).

White Earth Chippewa
P.O. Box 418
White Earth, MN 56591
(218) 983-3285

Ojibway

Location: The location of the tribal offices is in northwestern Minnesota, north of Detroit Lakes on Highway 59.

Public Ceremony or Powwow Dates: The official powwow date is June 14, and the powwow takes place on the weekend of or before the 14th.

Art Forms: Members of the tribe do beautiful floral design beadwork and basket weaving.

Visitor Information: The nearest airport served by a charter airline is in Detroit Lakes, 12 miles from the reservation. A variety of lodging, restaurants, and travel services are also available there. As for gift shops and museums on the reservation, there are very few. There are many resorts and campsites on the reservation, because of the numerous lakes and forest areas. Hunting and fishing are quite prominent, and wildlife is abundant, once again because of the landscape.

Tribal Council headquarters are located right in White Earth, and the largest employer on the reservation is the White Earth Reservation Tribal Council, supporting an average of 225 employees currently through state and federal grants and contracts. The Tribal Council also owns the White Earth Garment Manufacturing Company, Inc., the Ojibwa Forest Products, Inc., the Ojibwa Building Supplies, Inc., and owns and operates the Golden Eagle Bingo Lodge. These enterprises employ approximately 49 people full-time and 20 part-time. The surrounding area is predominantly dependent on the agricultural and tourism industries. The main recreational areas of interest are the resorts and hunting and fishing. Both draw large numbers of tourists/vacationers to the area.

Even though the current Bureau of Indian Affairs labor force report lists unemployment at 71 percent, the outlook of the people is positive, primarily because of the improvements in education.

There are two churches in White Earth which are open to the public. These are St. Benedict's Catholic Church and St. Columba's Episcopal Church.

The White Earth Band of Chippewa is the official name of the tribe, and they are of Ojibwa Indian origin. Their reservation was formed through a treaty with the government in 1867, in which 837,120 acres of land was allotted to them. Today, only 7 percent, 57,000 acres, of that land remains, which is held in trust by the Bureau of Indian Affairs.

The Chippewa were nomadic timber people, traveling in small bands, engaging primarily in hunting and fishing, sometimes settling to carry on a crude form of agriculture. Although social organization was loose, the powerful Grand Medicine Society controlled the tribe's movements and was a formidable obstacle to Christianizing attempts of missionaries. The Chippewa today are largely of mixed blood, including French and English.

NORTHEAST

MAINE: Houlton Maliseet/ Passamaquoddy/ Penobscot

MAINE

WISCONSIN

MICHIGAN

MASSACHUSETTS

RHODE ISLAND

NEW YORK

CONNECTICUT

WISCONSIN: Chippewa/ Potawatomi/ Menominee/Oneida/ Mahican/Winnebago

MICHIGAN: Chippewa

NEW YORK: Cayuga/Oneida/Onondago/ Seneca/Mohawk/Tuscarora

MASSACHUSETTS-RHODE ISLAND – CONNECTICUT: Mashantucket/Pequot/ Narragansett/Wampanoag/Paugussett/ Mohegan/Schaghticoke/Paucatuck/

The Northeast of our North America lies above the Great Plains and east of the Great Waters we call the Great Lakes. The trees are pines and broadleafs that bring colors bright and warm in the fall. When the winds of winter come from the north, the leaves flutter and fall in great piles below the bare branches reaching for the sky in silent prayer. Black water, turned dark by the leaves, winds in little streams through the woods. And, on the coast, the winds and waves roar on the rocks leaving mists of colored rainbows in the air.

This is the land of the longhouse people and the people of the sacred fire. They kept the land good and respectfully administered their responsibility as guardians.

They wore the masks of their societies, and when they prayed the drum of the heartbeat of our Mother Earth, the songs sent the message to the Creator that all life is to be praised and that all life is good and beautiful and more than mere chance. Whoever considers himself more beautiful than the whole of life has no heart. They chant prayed in the interiors of their sacred longhouses, and life was in tune with the heartbeat of the drum.

All of life remained in constant prayer to the Creator then. All of the people remained in always respecting the whole of all living things.

Join with the tribes on the following pages to honor their ancestors and to honor our Creator, our Mother Earth, our Moon, our Sun, and the whole of all living things in the whole of all Creation. You will find that it is good. It is very, very good.

Aho . . .

All the Indian Nations from the Sun Rise to these beyond the Lakes, as far as the Sun sets, have heard what has passed between you and me and are pleased with it . . .
—Teedyuscung
(Delaware)

You must lift the hatchet against them.
—Pontiac (Ottawa)

Father, be strong and take pity on us, your children, as our former father did.
—Pontiac (Ottawa)

Listen to me, fathers of the thirteen fires . . .
—Cornplanter (Seneca)

Brother, the Great Spirit has made us all . . .
—Red Jacket (Seneca)

We have borne everything patiently for this long time.
—Joseph Brant
(Mohawk)

Brothers, these people never told us they wished to purchase our lands from us.
—Little Turtle

Sleep not longer, O Choctaws and Chickasaws.
—Tecumseh (Shawnee)

Father, listen! The Americans have not yet defeated us by land.
—Tecumseh (Shawnee)

For more than a hundred winters our nation was a powerful, happy, and united people.

—Black Hawk (Sauk)

Let the Sioux keep from our lands, and there will be peace.

—Keokuk (Sauk)

CONNECTICUT

Golden Hill Paugusset
427 Shelton Road
Trumbull, CT 06611

Paugusset ("where the narrows open out")

This Algonquian tribe was a part of the Wappinger Confederacy.

Mashantucket Pequot Tribal Council
P.O. Box 160
Ledyard, CT 06339
(203) 536-2681

Mashantucket Pequot

Location: The reservation is located in southern New England in the state of Connecticut. The main entrance to the reservation is located just off Route 214 and is centrally located between New Haven, Hartford, and Providence in Rhode Island. The Mashantucket Pequot live within the town of Ledyard.

Public Ceremony or Powwow Dates: None are being held at this time in the community.

Art Forms: The art forms of the tribe were lost when the tribe was dispersed as a result of the massacre of 1637, which killed most of the men, women, and children.

Visitor Information: The tribe is presently selling crafts at their bingo hall and are in the process of expanding into a small gift shop. In the future, there will also be a shop in the museum which is in the planning stages.

The tribal enterprises at this time are High Stakes Bingo, the Owl's Nest Restaurant (Ohomowauke), Mashantucket Sand and Gravel, and the Indian Health Service, which provides service to all federally recognized Indians in New London County.

The name of the tribe means "many wooded lands" in their own language. The Pequot were known as the Fox People. The tribe's logo is a mix of four symbols reflecting the tribe's last few hundred years: the fox, which recalls their former name; the sign of Cassassinamon, the first leader of the Pequot to spring up after the devastating attack by John Mason against the Pequot's fort in Mystic, Connecticut, in 1637, which nearly wiped out the tribe; and the tree and rocky knoll represent "Mashantucket, the much wooded land" in Ledyard, given as a reservation to the remnants of the tribe in 1667.

The outlook for the future of the people of the Mashantucket Pequot is to become more self-sufficient and to be able to provide housing, jobs, and services so the people can come back to the reservation to live and bring back their traditions that have been lost.

Mohegan Nation
Box 105
Uncasville, CT 06382

Mohegan (from Maingan, "Wolf")

Visitor Information: The Mohegan Indian Fort and Indian Cemetery are on Highway 32 in Fort Shantock State Park four miles south of Norwich, Connecticut.

James Fenimore Cooper was wrong. There are Mohegans surviving today.

Paucatuck Pequot
935 Lantern Hill Road, RFD 7
Ledyard, CT 06339

Pawcatuck (the village name)
Pequot (Paquatauog, "destroyers")

This Algonquian tribe is an ally of the Mohegan.

Schaghticoke Nation
34 Constance Lane
Bristol, CT 06010

(P ska tikuk, "at the river fork")

More information on this Indian Nation will be in the revised edition of *Indian America*. The Schaghticoke are in the process of reorganizing.

DELAWARE

Nanticoke Indian Association
Route 4, Box 170B
Millsboro, DE 19966

Nanticoke (from Nentego, variation of Delaware Unechtgo, Unalachtgo, "tidewater people")

This tribe is connected linguistically and ethnically with the Delaware and the Conoy.

MAINE

Houlton Maliseet Band Council
P.O. Box 576
Houlton, ME 04730
(207) 523-7339

Malecite (Malisit, "broken talkers")
(Mahnesheets, "slow tongues")

Location: The tribal office is in Houlton.

Public Ceremony or Powwow Dates: Traditional dancing is done on occasion at Tobique and Kingsclear, New Brunswick.

Art Forms: Ash basketry is produced for sale. The tribal office can help with names and places.

Visitor Information: The Maliseet of Maine are related to the neighboring Passamaquoddy tribe. The Passamaquoddy-Maliseet Bilingual Program is trying to preserve the culture and educate the young people.

The Malecite belong to the Abnaki group of the Algonquian group. Their closest linguistic affinity is with the Passamaquoddy, the language of the two being almost identical. In 1884, they numbered 767, of whom 584 were in New Brunswick and the others in Quebec province. According to the 1904 report of Canadian Indian Affairs, their number was 805, 702 in New Brunswick and 103 in Quebec province.

Indian Township Passamaquoddy Reservation
P.O. Box 301
Princeton, ME 04668
(207) 796-2301

Pleasant Point Passamaquoddy Reservation
P.O. Box 343
Perry, ME 04667
(207) 853-2551

Peskedemakddi, "plenty of pollock"

Location: The tribal offices can be located by calling their respective numbers listed above.

Public Ceremony or Powwow Dates: There are still celebrations today which are traditional Passamaquoddy. The Ceremonial Day on the reservation is held between Perry and Eastport, Maine. Take Highway 1 to Perry, and go toward Eastport on Highway 190. The reservation is about two miles from Perry, five miles before Eastport. Call (207) 853-2551 for more information on dates and times.

Art Forms: The artisans of the tribe still do the traditional splint and sweetgrass baskets.

Visitor Information: The Ceremonial Day Celebration should not be missed. Generally held on August 1, it features canoe races, a pageant that shows the history of the Passamaquoddy, traditional dancing and singing, the chiefs' welcome dance, the greeting dance, the peace pipe ceremonial, and social dances. The bilingual program is developing a textbook in Passamaquoddy which will teach traditional culture and history. One that is for sale currently is *Chipmunk,* a novel for young people.

The Indian Township Passamaquoddy also sponsor an Indian pageant in the summer. Be sure to call their tribal office for dates and times.

The tribe belongs to the Abnaki Confederacy but speaks nearly the same dialect as the Malecite. They formerly occupied all the region around Passamaquoddy Bay and on the St. Croix River and Schoodic Lake, on the boundary between Maine and New Brunswick. Their principal village was Gunasquamekook, on the site of St. Andrews, N.B. They were restricted by the pressure of the white settlements and in 1866 were settled chiefly at Sebaik, near Perry, on the south side of the bay, and on Lewis Island. They had other villages at Calais, on Schoodic Lake in Washington County, Maine, and on St. Croix River in New Brunswick. They were estimated at about 150 in 1726, 130 in 1804, 379 in 1825, and from 400 to 500 in 1859. In 1904, the Passamaquoddy and Penobscot tribes sent to the Maine legislature a representative permitted to speak only on matters connected with the affairs of the Indian reservations.

Penobscot Tribe
Six River Road Indian Island Reservation
Old Town, ME 04468
(207) 827-7776

(Penobscot, derived from Pannawanbskek, "it forks on the white rocks," or Penaubsket, "it flows on rocks"; the name applying directly to the falls at Old Town, but it has also been rendered "rock land" from penops (penopsc), "rock," and cot (ot) locative, applied to the bluff at the mouth of the river near Castine. The aboriginal form is Penobskat, "plenty stones.")

Location: The tribe is located on the river at Indian Island just north by bridge from Old Town.

Public Ceremony or Powwow Dates: Call the tribal office for dates and times of their annual pageant.

Art Forms: Some of the arts and crafts stores on the island will have the baskets, moccasins, quill work, beadwork, fish spears, carved canes, bows, war clubs, and other items that you will want to purchase.

Visitor Information: Visit the museum weekdays from noon to 4:00 p.m. for exhibits on traditional arts of the Penobscot. The museum telephone number is (207) 827-6544.

This tribe is one of the Abnaki Confederacy, closely related in language and customs to the Norridgewock. They are not in the Malecite group. They were encountered where they are today by the French as early as 1555. In 1904, the membership was down to about 410.

Nipmuck Tribal Council
Hassanamico Indian Reservation
Grafton, MA 01519

Nipmuc (from Nipamaug, "freshwater fishing place")

Location: The Longhouse Museum, Hassanamico Indian Reservation, is located in Grafton. Their displays relate to the Nipmuck Nation.

The New England missionaries had seven villages of Christian converts among the Nipmuck in 1674. But on the outbreak of King Philip's war in the next year, almost all of them joined the hostile tribes and at its close fled to Canada or westward to the Mahican and other tribes on the Hudson.

Wampanoag Tribal Council of Gay Head, Inc.
State Road, RFD Box 137
Gay Head, MA 02535
(617) 645-9265

Wampanoag ("eastern people")

Location: The people of the Wampanoag still live in this area.

Art Forms: The artisans of the tribe make pottery in colorful styles. Shops on the island have their work for sale.

This is one of the principal tribes of New England. Their proper territory appears to have been the peninsula on the east shore of Narragansett Bay now included in Bristol County, Rhode Island, and the adjacent parts in Bristol County, Massachusetts. The Wampanoag chiefs ruled all the country extending east from Narragansett Bay and the Pawtucket River to the Atlantic coast, including the islands of Nantucket and Martha's Vineyard. The Nauset of Cape Cod and the Saconnet near Compton, Rhode Island, although belonging to the group, seem to have been somewhat independent. Before the pilgrims, explorers visited the region and provoked the natives by ill treatment. Champlain found those of Cape Cod unfriendly, on account of previous ill treatment, and had an encounter with them. In 1620, there were about 30 villages, and they must have been much stronger before the great pestilence of 1617 nearly depopulated the whole southern New England coast.

Their chief was Massasoit, who made a treaty of friendship with the colonists, which he faithfully observed until his death, when he was succeeded by his son, known to the English as King Philip. The bad treatment by the whites and their encroachment on the lands of the Indians led this chief, then the head of 500 warriors of his own tribe, to join with all the Indians from the Merrimac River to the Thames for the purpose of driving out or exterminating the whites. The war, which began in 1675 and lasted two years, was the most destructive in the history of New England and was most disastrous to the Indians. Philip and the leading chiefs were killed, the Wampanoag and Narraganset were practically exterminated, and the survivors fled to the interior tribes. Many of those who surrendered were sold into slavery, and others joined the various Praying villages in southern Massachusetts. The greater part of the Wampanoag who remained in the country joined the Saconnet. The Indians of Cape Cod and Martha's Vineyard generally remained faithful to the whites, the latter persistently refusing to comply with Philip's solicitations to join him in the contest.

MICHIGAN

Bay Mills Executive Council
Route 1
Brimley, MI 49715
(906) 248-3241

Ojibwa, "to roast till puckered up," referring to the puckered seam on their moccasins; from Ojib "to pucker up," Ub-way "to roast."

The Ojibwa are one of the largest tribes north of Mexico. Their range was formerly along both shores of Lake Huron and Lake Superior, extending across Minnesota to the Turtle Mountains, North Dakota. For more information, please see Minnesota, Ojibwa.

Grand Traverse Band
Route 1, Box 135
Suttons Bay, MI 49682
(616) 271-3538

The Grand Traverse settlement of the Chippewa near the site of Flint, Genesee County, Michigan, was so named because this point was the great ford of the Flint River on the Indian trail from the Saginaw to Detroit. French traders were fond of the hunting, camping, game, and fishing available in the area.

Hannahville Indian Community Council
Route 1, Community Center
Wilson, MI 49896
(906) 466-2342

Keweenaw Bay Tribal Council
Center Building
Route 1, Box 45
Baraga, MI 49908
(906) 353-6623

Ojibwa, "to roast till puckered up," referring to the puckered seam on their moccasins; from Ojib "to pucker up," Ub-way "to roast."

For more information on the Ojibwa, please see Minnesota.

Saginaw Chippewa Tribal Council
7070 East Broadway Road
Mt. Pleasant, MI 48858
(517) 772-5700

Ojibwa, "to roast till puckered up," referring to the puckered seam on their moccasins; from Ojib "to pucker up," Ub-way "to roast."

Visitor Information: This Chippewa village is situated near the present Saginaw, Michigan. It was first occupied by the Sauk and when deserted by that tribe, it was settled by a band of Ottawa and Chippewa, known as Saginaw, who continued to live there until 1837, when they removed beyond the Mississippi. The term was also officially employed to designate all the Chippewa of eastern lower Michigan from Thunder Bay southward.

For more information on the Ojibwa, please see Minnesota.

Sault Ste. Marie Chippewa Tribal Council
206 Greenough Street
Sault Ste. Marie, MI 49783
(906) 635-6050

Ojibwa, "to roast till puckered up," referring to the puckered seam on their moccasins; from Ojib "to pucker up," Ub-way "to roast."

For more information on the Ojibwa, please see Minnesota.

NEW YORK

Cayuga Nation
P.O. Box 11
Versailles, NY 14168
(716) 532-4847

Kwenio gwe n ("the place where locusts were taken out")

Visitor Information: The Iroquois, or Six Nations, comprise the Cayuga, Mohawk, Oneida, Onondaga, Seneca, and Tuscarora tribes. These six nations joined together centuries ago and formed the well-known Iroquois Confederacy. Our U.S. Constitution was probably modeled after the organization of this unit. The Iroquois have done well to maintain their culture, arts, dances and songs, and spirituality within this encroaching society. Today, people from this confederacy live in New York, Wisconsin, Oklahoma, Ontario, and Quebec. They still hold special events and there are several reconstructed villages, culture centers, and museums devoted to Iroquoian culture.

This tribe of the Iroquois Confederacy formerly occupied the shores of Cayuga Lake, New York. Its local council was composed of four clan phratries, and this form became the pattern, tradition says, of that of the confederation of the Five Nations of the Iroquois, in which the Cayuga had ten delegates. In 1660, they were estimated to number 1,500, and in 1778, 1,100. At the beginning of the American Revolution, a large part of the tribe removed to Canada and never returned, while the rest of the people were scattered among the other tribes of the confederacy. Soon after the revolution, the latter sold their lands in New York; some went to Ohio, where they joined other Iroquois and became known as the Seneca of the Sandusky. These subsequently moved to Indian Territory. Others joined the Oneida in Wisconsin; 175 joined the Iroquois in New York; and the majority, numbering 700 or 800, moved to the Grand River Reservation in Ontario.

Iroquois Nation of Cobleskill, Fonda, and Hunter, New York

Location: All the above towns in New York have interesting Iroquois Indian events. The annual Iroquois Indian Festival is held Labor Day weekend at the State University of New York in Cobleskill. Authentic Iroquois dancing, art exhibits, food, games, and more, are presented.

The Kateri Indian Festival in Fonda and the Mountain Eagle Indian Festival in Hunter are also events not to be missed. Call the Schoharie Museum of the Iroquois at (518) 295–855, or write to them at Box 158, Schoharie, NY 12157, for more information.

Oneida Nation of New York
Oneida, NY 13421

Oneida (Anglicized compressed form of the common Iroquois term *tüonen iote*, "a boulder standing up")

Visitor Information: Please see New York, Cayuga Nation.

This tribe is of the Iroquois Confederacy, formerly occupying the country south of Oneida Lake, Oneida County, New York. According to authentic tradition, the Oneida was the second tribe to accept the proposition of Dekanawida and Hiawatha to form a defensive and offensive league of all the tribes of men for the promotion of mutual welfare and security. Like the Mohawk, the Oneida have only three clans, the Turtle, the Wolf, and the Bear.

Onondaga Nation
P.O. Box 270A
Nedrow, NY 13120
(315) 469-8507

Onondaga

Visitor Information: Please see New York, Cayuga Nation.

This is the former chief Onondaga town of central New York, whose site and name were shifted from time to time and from place to place. Within its limits formerly lay the unquenched brands of the Great Council Fire of the League of the Iroquois.

Seneca Nation
1490 Route 438
Irving, NY 14081
(716) 532-4900

Seneca ("place of the stone," the Anglicized form of the Dutch enunciation of the Mohegan rendering of the Iroquoian *Oneniute a ka*, and with a different ethnic suffix, *Oneniute ron non*, meaning people of the standing or projecting rock or stone)

Visitor Information: Please see New York, Cayuga Nation.

This is a prominent and influential tribe of the Iroquois. When first known, they occupied that part of western New York between Seneca Lake and the Geneva River. They had their council fire at Tsonontowan, near Naples, in Ontario County.

Shinnecock Reservation
Route 27A, Montauk Highway
Southampton, NY 11968
(516) 283-9266

Shinnecock

Location: The people of Shinnecock welcome you to Long Island, New York.

Public Ceremony or Powwow Dates: The powwow is held over Labor Day weekend.

Art Forms: Traditional arts and crafts from native people all over the east will be featured at the powwow.

Visitor Information: The Shinnecock Community Center is raising funds to benefit the tribe and the church.

Seneca Iroquois National Museum
Broad Street Extension
Salamanca, NY 14779
(716) 945-1738

Location: This museum is located on the Allegany Indian Reservation and shows modern as well as traditional art. The museum shop has horn rattles, corn husk dolls, baskets, carved wooden false face masks, woven corn husk masks, and other traditional arts and crafts for sale. Many displays of wampum belts, clothing, games, and masks are shown for informative purposes. This is owned and operated by the Seneca Indian Nation, so I can recommend it.

St. Regis Mohawk Council Chiefs
St. Regis Reservation
Hogansburg, NY 13655
(518) 358-2272

Mohowauuck ("they eat animate things")

Visitor Information: Please see New York, Cayuga Nation.

This is the most easterly tribe of the Iroquois Confederacy and they called themselves Kaniengehage, "people of the place of the flint."

Tonawanda Band of Senecas Council of Chiefs
7027 Meadville Road
Basom, NY 14013
(716) 542-4244

Tonawanda ("confluent stream")

Visitor Information: Please see New York, Cayuga Nation.

This is a Seneca settlement on Tonawanda Creek in Niagara County, New York. In 1890, there were 517 Seneca and a few Iroquois on the reservation.

Please see New York, Seneca, for more information on this Nation.

Tuscarora Nation
5616 Walmore Road
Lewiston, NY 14092
(716) 297-9279

Skaru ren ("hemp gatherers," the Apocynum cannabinum, or Indian hemp, a plant of many uses among the Carolina Tuscarora)

Visitor Information: Please see New York, Cayuga Nation.

The Tuscarora are formerly an important confederation of tribes, speaking languages related to those of the Iroquoian linguistic group. When first encountered, they lived on the Roanoke, Neuse, Taw, and Pamlico rivers, in North Carolina. The evidence drawn from writers contemporary with them, confirmed in part by tradition, makes it appear that while occupying this primitive habitat, the Tuscarora league was composed of at least three tribal constituent members, each bearing an independent and exclusive name. The names of these component members still survive in the traditions of the Tuscarora now living in western New York and southern Ontario, Canada.

RHODE ISLAND

Narragansett Indian Tribe
P.O. Box 268
Charlestown, RI 02813
(401) 792-9700

Naragansett ("people of the small point," from *naiagans*, diminutive of *naiag*, "small point of land")

Location: The Narragansett and other Algonquin people can be found right here in Charlestown.

Public Ceremony or Powwow Dates: The powwow and annual meeting of the tribe is in August. Call for dates and times.

Visitor Information: The *Eagle Wing Press* is a good Indian events newspaper. You can subscribe by writing P.O. Box 579, Naugatuck, CT 06770. Events of this area will be listed in the paper.

The Narragansett are an Algonquian group and were formerly one of the leading tribes of New England. They occupied Rhode Island west of Narragansett Bay, including the Niantic Territory, from Providence River on the northeast to Pawcatuck River on the southwest. On the northwest they claimed control over a part of the country of the Coweset and Nipmuc, and on the southwest they claimed by conquest of the Pequot a strip extending to the Connecticut line. In 1633, they lost 700 to smallpox, but in 1674, they still numbered about 5,000.

VIRGINIA

Chickahominy Indian Tribe
RFD 1, Box 226
Providence Forge, VA 23140

K'chick-aham-min-nough, "hominy people"

Visitor Information: The Chickahominy tribe holds a fall festival with many activities including dancing.

The state of Virginia has jurisdiction over Indian reservations instead of the federal government.

Mattaponi Indian Reservation
RFD 1, Box 667
West Point, VA 23181
(804) 769-2229

Mattapony

Location: The museum is about 13 miles west of West Point on Highway 30.

Public Ceremony or Powwow Dates: Call the tribal office for details on public ceremonies. Traditional dances are done within the membership of the tribe, and on occasion the public will be invited.

Art Forms: Traditional arts and crafts including pottery, beadwork, and miniatures are sold by the museum.

Pamunkey
Box 217-AA
King William, VA 23086

Pamunkey (from pam, "sloping," slanting; anki, "hill," or "rising upland," referring to a tract of land in what is now King William County, Virginia, beginning at the junction of the Pamunkey and Mattapony rivers)

WISCONSIN

Bad River Tribal Council
P.O. Box 39
Odanah, WI 54861
(715) 682-4212

Ojibwa, "to roast until puckered up," referring to the puckered seam on their moccasins; from Ojib "to pucker up," Ub-way, "to roast."

Location: The reservation is fourteen miles east of Ashland on U.S. Highway 2.

Public Ceremony or Powwow Dates: The Manomin (wild rice) Celebration is usually the weekend before Labor Day. There is feasting, dancing, and activities traditional to the Ojibwa.

Visitor Information: The history center shows the arts and crafts of this band of the Ojibwa.

The Ojibwa are one of the largest tribes north of Mexico. Their range was formerly along both shores of Lake Huron and Lake Superior, extending across Minnesota to the Turtle Mountains, North Dakota. For more information, please see North, Minnesota.

Forest County Potawatomi General Council
P.O. Box 346
Crandon, WI 54520
(715) 478-2087

Potawatomi (Potawatamink or Potawaganink, "People of the Fire")

In 1616, written record places the Potawatomi on the west shores of Lake Huron. The Potawatomi, Chippewa, and Ottawa were originally one people. About 1838, the tribe was moved south toward Indian Territory. The Oklahoma Potawatomi recall this event as the "Trail of Death" due to the trail of ones lost on the way.
    A few remained in their homeland. This is one of those bands.

Lac Courte Oreilles Tribal Council
Tribal Office
Route 2, Box 2700
Hayward, WI 54843
(715) 634-8934

Ojibwa, "to roast till puckered up," referring to the puckered seam on their moccasins; from Ojib "to pucker up," Ub-way "to roast."

Public Ceremony or Powwow Dates: The Honor the Earth Powwow is held here in July. Call the tribal office for dates and times.

Visitor Information: The Ojibwa Indian Museum, Historyland, is on Highway 27 and is open during the summer.

This band of Ojibwa received their name from the lake on which they lived, at the headwaters of Chippewa River, in Sawyer County, Wisconsin. In 1852, they formed a part of the Betonukeengainubejig division of the Chippewa and in 1854, were assigned a reservation. In 1905 they were officially reported to number 1,214, to whom lands had been allotted in severalty.

Lac du Flambeau Tribal Council
Tribal Office
P.O. Box 67
Lac du Flambeau, WI 54538
(715) 588-3303

Ojibwa, "to roast till puckered up," referring to the puckered seam on their moccasins; from Ojib "to pucker up," Ub-way "to roast."

Location: The tribal office is on Main Street in Lac du Flambeau.

Public Ceremony or Powwow Dates: The Indian Bowl shows Indian dancing during July and August on Tuesday and Thursday nights at 8:30. Drive to the lakeshore in the center of the reservation. Wonderful drumming and singing can be heard there. The Bear River Powwow is in July.

Visitor Information: To see Ojibwa Indian exhibits, visit the Museum Cultural Center.

Menominee Indian Tribe of Wisconsin
P.O. Box 397
Keshena, WI 54135
(715) 799-5100

O-Maeh-No-Min-Ni-Wuk

Location: The reservation is located seven miles north of Shawano, Wisconsin, which is in the northeast part of the state.

Public Ceremony or Powwow Dates: The Land of the Menominee Powwow is held annually on the first weekend in August . It is considered one of the main cultural events of the year in the Midwest. No drugs or alcohol are allowed on the powwow grounds. The powwow is held in the Woodland Bowl, which is amid giant white pines.

Art Forms: You can find embroidery work on clothing and all other forms of art of Eastern Woodland culture.

Visitor Information: Shawano, Wisconsin, provides a fine assortment of retail outlets, hotels/motels, and restaurants.

The reservation has two privately owned gift shops that sell Menominee-made crafts as well as other genuine Native American crafts. The Menominee Reservation is the home of one of the largest and most modern sawmills in the Midwest, Menominee Tribal

Enterprises, Inc. There are also two privately owned raft rental outlets along the Wolf River. There is no hunting, fishing, or food gathering allowed by any nontribal members. The tribe also operates a bingo hall and gaming casino.

Early reservation days for the Menominee do not afford a pleasant story to relate. The people survived under the most trying conditions. Sickness, winters that were hard with deep snow and below-freezing temperatures, moving here and there to fuel their bodies with food all contributed to the misery the people endured. The Menominee are proud to have survived. Each spring, those who were lucky enough to live through the winter greeted one another with "We made it to another spring."

Summers were a little easier, but still each family worked. They planted large gardens, picked berries, and canned everything. Each family had a root cellar where they stored food to be used in the winter months. A government warehouse in Keshena issued rations (coffee, sugar, tea, and salt pork) to the elderly once a month.

Transportation, along with mail delivery, was by horse and buggy and in winter by sleigh and cutter. Roads were cleared, and ruts were made by the lumber wagons. When it rained, travel was slow, but teams of horses were sure and dependable.

There was a hospital in Keshena, but most people treated themselves with herbs, which were gathered in the fall of the year.

Education was furnished by the Franciscan Fathers and the St. Joseph Sisters in Keshena and by the Franciscan Sisters in Neopit. A government school in Keshena and a day school in Neopit provided education for those who did not want to attend a Christian school. Boys and girls also went to Tomah Indian School in Wisconsin, Flandreau Indian School in South Dakota, Pipestone Indian School in Minnesota, and Haskell Institute in Kansas where the Menominee pupils learned the three Rs and a trade.

For recreation, the Menominee played baseball and lacrosse. In the winter they ice-skated and sleighed. Those who did not have sleds made staves from hardwood barrels and used them on steep hills. Once a year, the Bureau of Indian Affairs Agency put on a fair. A merry-go-round pulled by a tractor was the only entertainment provided. The fair was mostly a time for visiting. Pony races and baseball games took up most of the afternoon.

Perhaps the people would have preferred the old life. Maybe

they were slow in their endeavors, but the Menominee people have always taken their time deciding their way of life. Again today, Menominees have to think of their young people's education. Maybe they will prefer the Waupiskayit life (white way of life); going back to the blanket is not what they prefer. The young people have tasted the Waupiskayit way of life and they do not want to look back.

The Menominee are an Algonquian-speaking tribe (meaning wild rice gatherers) and are Wisconsin's oldest continuing residents. The original Menominee land once stretched across 9.5 million acres from the Great Lakes to the Mississippi River. A century before the Menominee were visited by Nicolet, who reached Wisconsin in 1634, the continent had already been visited by Spaniards from the south, European fishermen from the east, and French explorers and fur traders from the St. Lawrence area. The dress of Menominee men was breechclout and leggings, and blouses and skirts were worn by the women. Ornamentation consisted of quills, plant and earth colors, and beads of natural materials. Footwear consisted of soft-soled moccasins.

The Menominee lived by hunting, fishing, and gathering. The abundant wild rice was a staple food, augmented by corn, beans, and squash grown in small gardens. Part of the food supply was dried in the sun for winter use. Boiling and roasting were common methods of cooking. The land that now comprises the Menominee Reservation established by the 1854 Treaty is densely forested, dotted with clear streams, lakes, rivers, and waterfalls and rich in four kinds of resources: land, timber, water, and wildlife. There are 234,000 acres of the finest old stands of hardwood, virgin pine, and hemlock in the Great Lakes states. All of Wisconsin's timber species grow on the reservation—approximately 46 varieties of trees. The Wolf River is the reservation's largest waterway, winding its way through 59 miles of Menominee land.

The present Menominee land holdings, once much more extensive, were chipped away through numerous government treaties and bargaining with the tribe. Emigrant bands of Stockbridge-Munsee and Oneida Indians from the east were the recipients of over one-half million acres of Menominee land.

"We accepted our present reservation when it was considered to be of no value by our white friends. All we ask now is that we are permitted to keep it as a home." Chief Neopit, Menominee, said these words in 1882.

This is a story about Kaku'ene, the Jumper, and the origin of tobacco. One day Ma'nabush passed by a high mountain and he detected a delightful odor coming from a crevice in the cliffs. Going to the mouth of the cavern he followed the passage that led into the very center of the mountain, where he found a large chamber occupied by a giant known as the keeper of tobacco.

The giant asked him gruffly what he wanted. Ma'nabush replied that he had come for tobacco. The giant replied that the ma'nidos had already been there for their annual smoke.

Ma'nabush saw there were many bags filled with tobacco in the cavern. He snatched one of these and darted out pursued by the irate giant. Ma'nabush ran to the mountaintop and leaped from peak to peak with the giant in pursuit. When Ma'nabush reached a high peak, he dropped flat on the rocks. The giant leaped over him and fell into the chasm below. The giant was badly bruised, but he struggled up the face of the cliff where he hung.

Ma'nabush grasped the giant and, drawing him upward, dashed him to the ground and said, "For your meanness you shall become Kaku'ene (the Jumper Grasshopper) and you shall be known by your stained mouth. You shall become the pest of those who raise tobacco."

Then Ma'nabush took the tobacco and divided it among his brothers. He gave each some of the seed that they might never be without this plant for their use and enjoyment.

Throughout their history animals have played an important role in the lives of the people. During early times, they served as food, clothing, tools, and shelter.

Early Menominee kinship divisions were based on five major totemic groups, each with subgroups named for various animals and birds. These animals were also the main subjects of each clan's creation myth.

When Menominee came in contact with whites and other Indians they depended on animal pelts as a main item of trade. Without these animals, early encounters with other people might have been more hostile. Even today, as noted in their legends, the Menominee hold in high respect the wildlife on their reservation.

Originally, temporary Menominee dwellings were made of saplings bent to form a dome-shaped structure covered with bark or mats. These dwellings were later replaced by log houses. Some of them are still standing today. The early 1900s saw Menominee progressing toward the use of modern homes as they began to build with lumber from the tribal sawmill. Recently, monies have been allocated to renovate these homes and in some cases, build new ones where the old home is irreparable. In the mid-1960s, Housing and Urban Development allocated funding to build 64 new homes on the reservation. In addition, there are Menominee training programs on the reservation such as the Home Improvement Program and the Indian Technical Assistance Center where trainees are provided with valuable on-the-job training and marketable skills in carpentry, masonry, and electrical and plumbing trades in connection with home renovation and construction.

Oneida Executive Committee
P.O. Box 365
Oneida, WI 54155-0365
(414) 869-2214

Oneida (Anglicized compressed form of the common Iroquois term *tiionen iote,* a boulder standing up)

Location: The Oneida Nation Museum is on Road EE, west of Highway E between Oneida and Freedom, Wisconsin.

Public Ceremony or Powwow Dates: There is an annual powwow during the Fourth of July weekend and the Nation has a traditional Iroquoian dance group that performs periodically. Call the tribal office for dates and times.

Art forms: The museum preserves the culture with moccasins, baskets, clothing, quill work, and gustoweh hats. Arts and crafts are also sold at the powwow.

Visitor Information: The herb garden, where medicinal herbs that are used by the Oneida are shown, is a fascinating place to visit.

This tribe is of the Iroquois Confederacy, formerly occupying the country south of Oneida Lake, Oneida County, New York. According to authentic tradition, the Oneida was the second tribe to accept the proposition of Dekanawida and Hiawatha to form a defensive and offensive league of all the tribes of men for the promotion of mutual welfare and security. Like the Mohawk, the Oneida have only three clans, the Turtle, the Wolf, and the Bear.

Red Cliff Tribal Council
P.O. Box 529
Bayfield, WI 54814
(715) 779-5805

Ojibwa, "to roast till puckered up," referring to the puckered seam on their moccasins; from Ojib "to pucker up," Ub-way "to roast."

Location: Three miles north of Bayfield, Wisconsin, on Highway 13 is the location of the Buffalo Arts Center, Red Cliff Cultural Institute, and Red Cliff Indian Reservation.

Public Ceremony or Powwow Dates: The annual powwow is in August or September. Check with the tribal office for exact dates and times.

Art Forms: The Red Cliff Festival of the Arts and crafts demonstrations vary from stone pipe making to birch bark canoe building. Bark baskets, beadwork, and other arts can be found in the museum shop.

Visitor Information: The Buffalo Arts Center shows the culture and the history of the Ojibwa people with emphasis on the Lake Superior Chippewa. The exhibits show traditional Ojibwa settings such as figures in full outfits around the drum. Others show the daily life of the people. May through September is the normal season. Call for times when the center is open.

For more information please see Minnesota, the general history of the Ojibwa.

St. Croix Council Tribal Office
P.O. Box 287
Hertel, WI 54845
(715) 349-2195

Ojibwa, "to roast till puckered up," referring to the puckered seams on their moccasins; from Ojib, "to pucker up," Ub-way, "to roast."

For more information please see Minnesota, the general history of the Ojibwa.

Sokaogon Chippewa Tribal Council
Route 1, Box 328
Crandon, WI 54520
(715) 478-2604

Ojibwa, "to roast till puckered up," referring to the puckered seams on their moccasins; from Ojib, "to pucker up," Ub-way, "to roast."

For more information, please see Minnesota, the general history of the Ojibwa.

Stockbridge-Munsee Tribal Council
Route 1
Bowler, WI 54416
(715) 793-4111

Stockbridge are really Mahican ("Wolf")
Munsee are a branch of the Delaware (Min-asin-ink, "at the place where stones are gathered together")

Location: The reservation is located west of Green Bay on Highway 29, through Shawano, to Bowler. When you see the turnoff on County Road J, you will find Bowler. Then take County Road J three miles to Mohheconnuck Road. Go two miles north on Mohhecconnuck Road to the log tribal office.

Public Ceremony or Powwow Dates: The powwow is held in the summer. Call the tribal office for dates and times. The powwow will be held two miles north of the library on Mohheconnuck Road in the vicinity of the campground and picnic area along the Red River.

Art Forms: Baskets and other old forms of art are displayed in the museum.

Visitor Information: The museum and library hold a fund raising auction the second Saturday in October. Also, the tribe operates a bingo parlor.

The Mahican are an Algonquian tribe that occupied both banks of the upper Hudson River, in New York, extending north almost to Lake Champlain.

The Munsee originally occupied the headwaters of Delaware River in New York, New Jersey, and Pennsylvania, extending south

Chief Blackhawk, wife, and child, Winnebago, ca. 1899
Photo by T. W. Ingersoll; Courtesy Museum of New Mexico, Neg. No. 91494

to the Lehigh River, and also held the west bank of the Hudson from the Catskill Mountains nearly to the New Jersey line. They had the Mahican and Wappinger on the north and east and the Delaware on the south and southeast and were regarded as the protecting barrier between the latter tribe and the Iroquois.

Wisconsin Winnebago Business Council
P.O. Box 311
Tomah, WI 54660
(608) 372-4147

Winnebago (winnipig, "filthy water" [Chippewa]; winipyagohagi, "people of the filthy water" [Sauk and Fox])

Location: The Wisconsin Dells Stand Rock Ceremonials are located four miles north of the Wisconsin Dells on Stand Rock Road.

Public Ceremony or Powwow Dates: The Ceremonials are presented every night from mid-June through Labor Day and start about 8:45 p.m. The dancers and performers of the pageant are mostly Winnebago people.

Art Forms: Dance forms from various tribes are likely to be presented at the pageant.

Visitor Information: You can get to the pageant by boat. Call the tribal office for more information.

The Winnebago have been known to the whites since 1634 when the Frenchman Nicolet encountered them in Wisconsin, on Green Bay, at which time they probably extended to Lake Winnebago.

NORTHWEST

WASHINGTON: Chehalis / Colville / Hoh / Klallam / Kalispel /
Lower Elwha / Lummi / Makah / Muckleshoot / Nisqually / Nooksack /
Port Gamble / Puyallup / Quileute /
Quinault / Tulalip / Sauk-Suiattle /
Shoalwater Bay / Skokomish /
Spokane / Squaxin / Stillaguamish /
Suquamish / Swinomish /
Upper Skagit and Yakima

OREGON: Burns-Paiute / Coos,
Lower Umpqua and Siuslaw /
Grande Ronde / Umpqua Cow Creek /
Klamath / Siletz / Umatilla /
Warm Springs

The Northwest of the continental United States lies in, and west of, that place where the great Rocky Mountains rise up out of the great water, the Pacific Ocean. It is the place of the great high trees. There are mysterious fogs and clouds over the inlets of water that invade the edge of the land and small islands jut up out of the great water to form mazes off the shore. And the mountains that are inland are snow-capped and high between inland deserts, trees, and lakes fed by fast-moving crystal clear streams.

This is the land of the People of the Totem and Longhouse and Potlatch. They are descendants of a great and proud culture that lived in the rugged areas where land meets water in tune with their environment and with respect for the whole of Creation.

The art of the Northwest People was, and is, steeped in symbolism, as all Indian art is. The symbol is not a mere sign for the visual satisfaction of the eye but a disguise, a mask, within which a living agent lives. It is a talisman, a charm, a key, and a revelation incorporating the wisdom of being the original inhabitants of the wilderness. Only the original people have the "medicine power" to incorporate innocence with significance into their art forms. It is through this naive, innocent, primitive art form that the Indian of the Northwest, as with all Indian people, both acts and speaks and even realizes to himself the justification of his existence. When the Northwest People masked themselves, they became no longer the natural man. They became mythic beings, embodied powers, with emblems expressing whole groups of kinships—with the animal kind, with the thunder and lightning, with the spirits of our ancestors—so that they became sacred entities, closer in touch with the Creator.

So, when we must consider that each and every movement and act was in the name of art, then all existence was in the name of the Creation and for the good of all living things. The masks of the ceremonials of the people of the Northwest act out the reality of the necessity of ceremony and project the realization that with ceremony we can become in tune with the whole of all living things and we can learn the respect necessary for the survival of the race of man in the universe. How can we respect all life without ceremony?

When you obtain an art object such as a basket or carving from the People of the Northwest, remember that the spirit of the ancestors and the spirit of the artist are embodied with it and within it. They are inseparable and always alive.

The People of the Northwest have always been there. Ask the elders of the people; they know. The legends and stories passed down from generation to generation by the oral traditions of the people say "We have always been here." When you go to the ceremonies of the Northwest People, show the respect and courtesy you would show to any sacred ceremony. If there is any question of proper etiquette, always ask an elder or tribal official for proper behavior. The original people of the Northwest deserve our respect for their culture and ceremonies.

The tribes on the following pages are found in Washington and Oregon. Join with them to honor their ancestors and to honor our Creator, our Mother Earth, our Moon, our Sun, and the whole of all living things in the whole of all Creation. You will find that it is good. It is very, very good.

Aho . . .

OREGON

Burns-Paiute General Council
P.O. Box 71
Burns, OR 97720
(503) 573-2088

The Paiute people lived from the gifts the Creator provided from the fish of the lakes, jackrabbits and small game of the sage plains and mountains, and from piñon nuts and other seeds, which they grind into flour for bread. Their ordinary dwelling is the wikiup, or small rounded hut of tule rushes over a framework of poles, with the ground for a floor and the fire in the center, and almost entirely open at the top.

For more information on the Paiute, please see Nevada, the general history of the Paiute.

Confederated Tribes of Coos, Lower Umpqua, and Siuslaw Indians
338 Wallace Street
Coos Bay, OR 97420
(503) 888-3536

Coos
Umpqua
Siuslaw

Location: The tribal offices are located in Coos Bay, Oregon.

Public Ceremony or Powwow Dates: There are no ceremonies at this time.

Art Forms: Basketry has reached a particularly fine degree of quality with these native artisans.

The Confederated Tribes of Coos, Lower Umpqua, and Siuslaw Indians are the aboriginal inhabitants of the central and south central coast of Oregon. Their homeland includes the estuaries of Coos Bay, Umpqua, and Siuslaw, a region of vast stands of forest and stretches of open beaches. The tribes, which have operated under a confederated government since the signing of the treaty of August 1855, possess a 6.1-acre reservation and tribal hall, erected for them by the Bureau of Indian Affairs in 1938 in Coos Bay, Oregon.

The Confederated Tribes were in a regular and continuous government to government relationship with the United States from 1853 until their termination by Congress in 1956. Initially, they were under the jurisdiction of the Umpqua subagency. In 1856, because of the exigencies of the Rogue River Indian War (in which they inclined to participate), the majority of the members of the Coos, Lower Umpqua, and Siuslaw Indians were removed from their aboriginal homelands and held on a windswept spit at the mouth of the Umpqua River at Fort Umpqua.

Thus began the breakup of these large Indian families. If the women were married to white men, they were allowed to remain in their homeland while their children and other Indian relatives were taken away. Some Indians hid from the soldiers who had been commissioned to lead the infamous march to Fort Umpqua. A feeling of great hopelessness settled on these people who had been forcibly removed from all that was familiar and dear to them.

In 1859, the Coos, Lower Umpqua, and Siuslaw Indians were moved from Fort Umpqua and taken to the Yachats Agency on the Siletz Reservation, where an effort was made to turn these gatherers into farmers. After clearing the land, the Indians were given simple farm tools and seed. After many of the people of these tribes died of starvation and ill treatment, the U.S. government decided to close the Yachats Agency and opened this part of the reservation to non-Indian settlement. The tribal members thus returned to their aboriginal homelands only to find that this territory was settled by non-Indians too. So the members of the Coos, Lower Umpqua, and Siuslaw tribes had no home to return to. Again, these people were wanderers, settling wherever they could find a place.

Family, pride, homeland, and life-style were all taken away and/

or changed for the members of these tribes. The subsequent feelings of low self-esteem and hopelessness set the stage for alcoholism and, later, drug addiction.

The road back was long and, indeed, seemed endless for the Coos, Lower Umpqua, and Siuslaw Indians. Some members of these tribes left the area permanently. Others stayed and found menial employment as domestics or in the fields, as harvesters of cranberries, for example. The tribal members who stayed in their aboriginal homeland kept their sense of tribalism. They held monthly meetings and observed special celebrations throughout the years.

Then fell what appeared to many as the final blow. The federal government announced it had a new plan. It would "terminate" the Indians of western Oregon. All Indians in the area would be made American citizens. They would have all the "privileges" afforded non-Indians. They would be first-class citizens. The Indians did not fully understand that termination would deprive them of the few services they had been given because of their special status as Indians. There would be no more education in Indian boarding schools, no more Indian Health Service, no more reservations.

Some of the tribes in western Oregon approved of termination. The Confederated Tribes of Coos, Lower Umpqua, and Siuslaw, however, did not. Their protests were of no avail. In 1956, Congress passed Public Law 588, which became known as the "Termination Act." To the federal government, this meant that no Indians existed in western Oregon.

The aim of the termination act was to assimilate the Indian people into the "dominant society." It did not work. The people of the Confederated Tribes of Coos, Lower Umpqua, and Siuslaw still maintained their "Indian-ness." They continued to hold meetings and celebrations.

Early in the termination years, the tribes of western Oregon began to look for a way out of the travesty of termination. They learned that because Congress had "terminated" them, it would take an act of Congress to "restore" them if they were once again to become federally "recognized" tribes.

In 1981, bouyed by the award of a modest Campaign for Human Development (CHD) grant, the Confederated Tribes of Coos, Lower Umpqua,and Siuslaw Indians began in earnest the arduous trail leading to restoration. The restoration project was launched from donated office space in a private home with volunteer labor. There were no salaries or rents paid. All of the money from the CHD grant was used for telephone services and for essential trips to Washington, D.C.

Finally, on October 17, 1984, after setbacks, tears, frustration, and the supreme effort of tribal members, President Reagan signed Public Law 98–481, which became known as the "Restoration Act." The members of these tribes were once again "federally recognized" Indians.

With the restoration of the tribes in 1984, the relationship with the Bureau of Indian Affairs was reestablished. The tribal council began the implementation of education and housing programs. The tribal constitution was approved, and the tribes are electing council members again.

The name Coos is employed to denote the villages or tribes of the Kusan family formerly on Coos Bay, Oregon. Lewis and Clark estimated their population at 1,500 in 1805.

The Umpqua are an Athapascan tribe formerly settled on upper Umpqua River, Oregon, east of the Kuitsh. They lived in houses of boards and mats and derived their sustenance mainly from the river. In 1902, there were 84 on Grande Ronde Reservation, Oregon. Their chief village was Hewut. A part of them, the Nahank-huotana, lived along Cow Creek.

The Siuslaw are a small Yakonan tribe formerly living on and near the Siuslaw River in western Oregon.

Confederated Tribes of the Grande Ronde Tribal Council
P.O. Box 38
Grande Ronde, OR 97347
(503) 879-5215

Visitor Information: The people of this reservation comprise several tribes. They were terminated as members of Indian tribes by the federal government in 1954. As of 1974, they have reorganized as a nonprofit organization and are in the process of rebuilding an economy and rebuilding their feeling of belonging to the community as a tribe.

In 1908, the tribes placed on this reservation were the Kalapuya, Clackamas, Cow Creek, Lakmiut, Mary's River, Molala, Nestucca,

Rogue River, Santiam, Shasta, Tumwater, Umpqua, Wapato and Yamhill.

Confederated Tribes of Siletz Indians of Oregon
P.O. Box 549
Siletz, OR 97380
(503) 444-2532
Within Oregon 1-800-922-1399

Siletz

Location: The Confederated Tribes are located in the town of Siletz, approximately fifteen miles inland from the central Oregon coast town of Newport. The tribal center is located on Government Hill. The remaining reservation occupies small parcels of timberland scattered within Lincoln County.

Public Ceremony or Powwow Dates: The Nesika Illahee Powwow is held the second weekend in August of each year. Restoration Day is November 18 of each year, but sometimes the celebration is moved to the Saturday following the 18th for ease of attendance. Everyone is welcome. It is good to ask permission prior to taking pictures. No pictures are allowed during traditional ceremonies, for example, the Eagle Feather Ceremony.

Art Forms: You will find traditional design work in beading and basketry. Call the tribal office for details on where to purchase artwork.

Visitor Information: There are many motels, restaurants, and services located in the nearby town of Newport, Oregon.

The close proximity to the Pacific Ocean draws many people to the Newport area (15 miles away) each year. Several local events occur. The Siletz tribe sits among some of the best sport fishing rivers and streams for steelhead, salmon, and trout. The ocean provides opportunities for clam digging, crabbing, and ocean fishing.

The Siletz tribe is actually a confederation of tribes, comprised of 24 separate tribes and bands. A terminated tribe from 1954 to 1977, the Siletz, through an act of Congress, was restored to federal recognition in 1977.

The Siletz Tribal Council established the Siletz Tribal Economic

Development Corporation (STEDCO), which is responsible for economic development enterprises on and off the Siletz Reservation. Because the Siletz tribe only received approximately 3,600 acres of reservation land back in 1980, most of which is timberland and not suitable for development or housing, an eight-county service area was established. Recently, the service area was increased to include eleven counties in the state of Oregon. STEDCO is working currently on building an evergreen management building. They plan to market fern, salal, and other evergreen products.

Possible future development for the Siletz tribe includes a health clinic in Siletz to service both tribal and nontribal members, a mini-mall in the city of Siletz, and possibly, office buildings for rent.

Cow Creek Band of Umpqua Indians
1376 NE Walnut, Suite 1
Roseburg, OR 97470-2027
(503) 672-9696

Umpqua

Please see Oregon, Confederated Tribes of Coos, Lower Umpqua, and Siuslaw Indians, for more information. This is the Nahankhuotana group of the Umpqua Indian Tribe.

Klamath General Council
Box 436
Chiloquin, OR 97624
(503) 783-2219

Klamath (possibly from Maklaks, the Lutuami term for Indians, "people," "community," the encamped)

Location: Look on your atlas in southern Oregon for the location of the Klamath Indian Reservation north of Klamath Falls.

Public Ceremony or Powwow Dates: Memorial Day weekend is the holiday for celebrating in Klamath Falls, Oregon, with the Chief Schonchin Days Powwow. Just find the fairgrounds, and you will find a powwow, Indian rodeo, parade, and arts and crafts.

Art Forms: The tribe is restoring the art of basket making from tule. These and other arts and crafts will be found at the powwow.

Visitor Information: This reservation was "terminated" in 1954, and with the land base gone, the people were in a state of culture shock. Cash payments cannot replace the feeling of belonging to a tribe when it has been that way for hundreds of years. Many people became alcoholics, and as a result, death rates were on the rise. The government treaties guaranteed health and education benefits in exchange for the tribe's land; with "termination" these benefits were lost. In August 1986, the Klamath tribe was restored to full federal recognition as a result of years of work by the people. It is good to be a tribe again.

The Klamath call themselves Eukshikni or Auksni, "people of the lake," referring to the fact that their principal residences were on Upper Klamath Lake. There were also important settlements on the Williamson and Sprague rivers. The Klamath, unlike the other branch of the family, the Modoc, have always lived at peace with the encroaching whites. In 1864, they joined the Modoc in ceding the greater part of their territory to the United States and settled on the Klamath Reservation, where they numbered 755 in 1905. This included, however, many members of other tribes who had become more or less assimilated with the Klamath since the establishment of the reservation.

Umatilla Board of Trustees
P.O. Box 638
Pendleton, OR 97801
(503) 276-3165

Umatilla

Location: Look on your map of Oregon in the northeast corner for Pendleton.

Public Ceremony or Powwow Dates: Local celebrations are held here occasionally. Call the tribal office for dates and times.

Art Forms: The tribe offers arts and crafts that include beadwork, moccasins, cradleboards, and traditional clothing, all at Mission Market.

Visitor Information: The Umatilla, Walla Walla, and Cayuse tribes share this reservation.

Umatilla: This Shahaptian tribe formerly lived on Umatilla River and the adjacent banks of the Columbia in Oregon. They were included under the Walla Walla by Lewis and Clark in 1805, though their language is distinct. In 1855, they joined in a treaty with the United States and settled on Umatilla Reservation in eastern Oregon.

Wallawalla ("Little River"): This Shahaptian tribe formerly lived on the lower Wallawalla River and along the east bank of the Columbia from Snake River nearly to the Umatilla in Washington and Oregon. While a distinct dialect, their language is closely related to the Nez Perce. Their number was estimated by Lewis and Clark as 1,600 in 1805, but it is certain this figure included other bands now recognized as independent. By treaty of 1855, they were removed to the Umatilla Reservation in Oregon.

Cayuse: This Waiilatpuan tribe formerly occupied the territory around the heads of the Wallawalla, Umatilla, and Grande Ronde rivers and from the Blue Mountains to Deschutes River in Washington and Oregon. The tribe was closely associated with the neighboring Nez Perces and Wallawalla and was regarded by the early explorers and writers as belonging to the same stock. So far as the available evidence goes, however, they must be considered linguistically independent.

Warm Springs Tribal Council
P.O. Box C
Warm Springs, OR 97761
(503) 553-1161

Des Chutes
John Day
Paiute
Tenino
Warm Springs (Tilkuni)
Wasco

Location: The reservation is located in north central Oregon.

Public Ceremony or Powwow Dates: The biggest powwow here is probably the one held in June, but there are dances during the Fourth of July also. The traditional Root Festival is held in mid-April. Call the tribal office for dates and times. Also, dances are held Sundays, May through October.

Art Forms: Some arts and crafts are sold during the celebrations. The gift shop at the Warm Springs Information Center is on Highway 26 at the east end of Warm Springs. The cradleboards, baskets, beadwork, feather work, and tule mats are all of good quality.

Visitor Information: You can rent tipis from the tribe at their nice campground. Also, visit the Kah-Nee-Tah Resort for swimming, hot springs, tennis, saunas, and other enjoyable activities.

Des Chutes: This Shahaptian group lived formerly on and around the Deschutes River, Oregon. The term probably included remnants of several tribes.

John Day: This Shahaptian tribe, speaking the Tenino language, formerly lived on John Day River, Oregon, and had their principal village four miles above the mouth. In 1909, there were 50 survivors of the tribe at Warm Springs, Oregon.

Paiute: Please see the general history of the Paiute in the Nevada section of *Indian America.*

Tenino: This Shahaptian tribe formerly occupied the valley of Des Chutes River, Oregon. The Tenino dialect was spoken on both sides of the Columbia from The Dalles to the mouth of the Umatilla. In 1855, they joined in the Wasco treaty and were placed on the Warm Springs Reservation, since which time they have usually been called Warm Springs Indians, a term embracing a number of tribes of other groups that were included in the treaty. In 1909, there were 30 survivors on this reservation.

Tilkuni (Warm Springs): This Shahaptian tribe is said to have spoken the Tenino language and to have claimed the territory between Tygh and Warm Springs rivers in Wasco County, Oregon. They were classed Warm Springs Indians by the U.S. government.

Wasco (from the Wasco word wadalo, "cup or small bowl of horn," the reference being to a cup-shaped rock a short distance from the main village of the tribe; from the tribal name Galasq!o, "those that belong to Wasco," or "those that have the cup"): This is a Chinookan tribe formerly living on the south side of the Columbia River, in the neighborhood of The Dalles, in Wasco County, Oregon. This tribe, with the Wishram, on the north side of the river, were the easternmost branches of the Chinookan family. These two tribes were practically identical in language and culture, though they were removed to different reservations. On the north, east, and south they bordered the Shahaptian tribes, on the west, closely related Chinkookan tribes (White Salmon and Hood River Indians, Chiluktkwa and Kwikwulit). In 1822, the population estimate was 900. About 200 joined in the Warm Springs Reservation treaty in 1855.

It is interesting to note that Coyote is a transformer and hero in this culture.

Wishram

See this section, Warm Springs Indian Reservation.

WASHINGTON

Hoh Indian Tribe
HC 80, Box 917
Forks, WA 98331
(206) 374-6582

Hoh

Location: The boundary of the reservation is determined by the Hoh River on two sides and the Pacific Ocean on the other—with a total of one square mile in area. Look on your map in northwest Washington State where Federal Highway 101 connects with the Pacific Ocean south of Forks.

Art Forms: Some members of the tribe still do basket weaving.

Visitor Information: There is a camping spot at the lower village.

Some of the members of this tribe participate in the motorized canoe races using traditional canoes outfitted with high-powered engines. They race in the rivers, which can be dangerous because of snags and boulders. The Hoh can be seen racing at Chief Taholah Days against the Quinault and Quileute on Fourth of July weekend.

Chehalis Community Council
P.O. Box 536
Oakville, WA 98568
(296) 273-5911

StsEe lis

Location: Please look on your map of Washington State, in the southwest corner, on Interstate 5 for Chehalis.

Public Ceremony or Powwow Dates: The tribe has its Tribal Day Celebration in late May. Call the office for dates and times.

The Chehalis are a Salishan tribe on the Chehalis River and its affluents and on Grays Harbor, Washington. There were five principal villages on the river and seven on the north and eight on the south side of the bay; there were also a few villages on the north end of Shoalwater Bay. Many historians divided the tribe into Upper Chehalis or Kwaiailk, dwelling above Satsop River, and the Lower Chehalis from that point down. In 1806, Lewis and Clark assigned to them a population of 700 in thirty-eight lodges. In 1904, there were 147 Chehalis and 21 Humptulips under the Puyallup School Superintendent, Washington.

Colville Business Committee
P.O. Box 150
Nespelem, WA 99155
(509) 634-4711

Colville (etymology doubtful)
Skitswish (Coeur D'Alene [French, Awl-heart])
Kalispel (popularly known as Pend d'Oreilles, "ear drops")
Okinagan (etymology doubtful)
Senijextee (etymology unknown)
Methow (Met-how, etymology unknown)
Nespelim, (etymology unknown)
Pend d'Oreille ("ear drops")
Sanpoil (etymology unknown)
Spokan (etymology doubtful)

Location: The Colville Reservation is located in northeast Washington state, northwest of Spokane.

Coleville Indians, 1914
Photo by Paul Standar; Courtesy Museum of New Mexico, Neg. No. 121219

Public Ceremony or Powwow Dates: The joint tribes of the Colville Reservation hold powwows, Indian fairs, and other varied activities during the late spring, summer, and fall. During Stampede Days in Omak, Washington, you can see the great tipi encampment. Call the tribal office for dates and times.

Art Forms: There are varied art forms to be found here. Call the tribal office for the names of individuals who do the kind of work you want to buy.

The following is a short synopsis of each tribe listed above.

Colville: A division of the Salish between Kettle Falls and the Spokane River, eastern Washington; it is said to have been one of the largest of Salish tribes. Lewis and Clark estimated their number at 2,500 in 130 houses in 1806. There were 321 under the Colville Agency in 1904.

Skitswish: This is a Salish Tribe on a river and lake of the same name in northern Idaho. The name Coeur d'Alene (French "Awlheart"), by which they are popularly known, was originally a nickname used by some chief of the tribe to express the size of a trader's heart.

Kalispel (popularly known as Pend d'Oreilles, "ear drops"): This is a Salish tribe around the lake and along the river of the same name in the extreme north part of Idaho and northeast Washington. The Lewis and Clark expedition found three divisions: Upper Pend d'Oreilles, Lower Pend d'Oreilles, and Micksucksealton. Lewis and Clark estimated their number at 1,600 in 30 lodges in 1805. In 1905, there were 640 Upper Pend d'Oreilles and 197 Kalispel under the Flathead Agency, Montana, and 98 Kalispel under the Colville Agency, Washington.

Okinagan: This name originally applied to the confluence of the Similkameen and Okanogan rivers but extended first to include a small band and afterward to a large and important division of the Salishan family. They formerly inhabited the west side of the Okanogan River, Washington, from Old Ft. Okanogan to the Canadian border, and in British Columbia the shores of Okanagan Lake and the surrounding country. Later they displaced an Athapascan tribe from the valley of the Similkameen. In 1906, there were 527 Okinagan on Colville Reservation, Washington, and 824 under the Kamloops-Okanagan Agency, British Columbia.

Senijextee: This is a Salish tribe formerly residing on both sides of the Columbia River from Kettle Falls to the Canadian boundary; they also occupied the valley of the Kettle River, the Kootenay River from its mouth to the first falls, and the region of the Arrow Lakes, British Columbia. In 1909, those in the United States numbered 342, on the Colville Reservation, Washington.

Methow: This Salishan tribe of eastern Washington was formerly living in the area of the Methow River and Chelan Lake. As of 1909, they were mostly living on the Colville Reservation and their population was not recorded.

Nespelim: This Salish tribe is from a creek of the same name, a north tributary of the Columbia River, about 40 miles above Ft. Okinakane, Washington. As of 1906, they numbered 653 on Colville Reservation, Washington.

Pend d'Oreille: See Kalispel.

Sanpoil: This body of Salish people on Sans Poil River and on the Columbia below Big Bend, Washington, are classed as one of the eight bands of Spokan and also as one of the six bands of Okinagan. No treaty was ever made with these Indians for their lands; the government simply took possession of their country except for those portions set apart by executive order for their occupancy.

Spokan: This name has been applied to several small bodies of Salish on and near the Spokane River in northeastern Washington. The name was originally employed by the Skitswish to designate a band at the forks of the river, called also Smahoomenaish. The whites extended the name to cover eight other groups. The population was estimated by Lewis and Clark in 1805 at 600 in thirty houses. In 1908, the entire number of Spokan on Coeur d'Alene Reservation, Idaho, was 634. In 1909, the entire number of Spokan in Washington was 509, while those in Idaho numbered 104.

Jamestown Klallam Tribal Council
305 Old Blyn Highway
Sequim, WA 98382
(206) 683-1109

Clallam ("strong people")

This Salish tribe lived on the south side of Puget Sound, Washington, formerly extending from Port Discovery to the Hoko River, bounded at each end by the Chimakum and Makah. Subsequently, they occupied Chimakum Territory and established a village at Port Townsend. A comparatively small number found their way across to the south end of Vancouver Island, and there was a large village on Victoria harbor. They are said to be more closely related to the Songish than to any other tribe. The population was 800 in 1854 and 336 in 1904.

Kalispel Business Committee
Box 39
Usk, WA 99180
(509) 445-1147

Kalispel Pend d'Oreilles (popularly known as "ear drops")

Location: The reservation is located north of Spokane near Usk.

Public Ceremony or Powwow Dates: The tribe sponsors an annual powwow and potlatch. Call the office above for dates and times.

Art Forms: The arts and crafts of the people can be found by calling the tribal office and by attending the powwow.

Please see Washington, Colville, for more information on the Kalispel.

Lower Elwha Community Council
1666 Lower Elwha Road
Port Angeles, WA 98362
(206) 452-8471

Elwha (a Clallam village at the mouth of the river of the same name in Washington state)

Please see Washington, Jamestown Klallam Tribal Council, for more information on the Clallam people.

Lummi Indian Business Council
2616 Kwina Road
Bellingham, WA 98226-9298
(206) 734-8180

Ca-Choo-Sen
Nuh-Lummis

Location: The 12,000-acre Lummi Indian Reservation is located 12 miles south of the Canadian/U.S. border on a peninsula with water to the west, south, and east. The reservation begins 3 miles to the west of Interstate Highway 5, which connects Vancouver, British Columbia, one hour away, and Seattle, Washington, which is an hour and a half away.

Public Ceremony or Powwow Dates: During the month of June, the annual Stommish Festival is held at the reservation (Stommish means warrior or veteran). The celebration is patterned after the old potlatches, still fresh in the memories of tribal elders. Activities include exciting war canoe races, the Princess contest, Sla-hal bone games (gambling), authentic Indian music, and Lummi Spirit dances. Genuine Indian art and craft booths, traditional Indian foods, and the world-famous Lummi barbecued salmon, cooked slowly in front of alder-fired pits, add to this once-in-a-lifetime experience. Call the tribal office for exact dates. No drugs or alcohol are allowed. No fireworks are allowed. Any eagle or prayer feather that is found is not to be picked up; instead, you should inform the closest elder for proper retrieval.

Art Forms: The art of basketry has been reintroduced to the younger generation recently through the Heritage Program in conjunction with Lummi Community College. The students are taught all phases of gathering and preparing traditional materials that go into the Lummi baskets. Students are encouraged to do only the style of work that was traditionally done by their ancestors. The types of baskets the students make include clam baskets, cooking baskets, and food storage baskets. The Heritage Program produced a lot of fine new artists in a number of areas.

The Lummi Indians were known for knitting Indian sweaters made of wools. These sweaters are known around the world for their fine quality, warmth, and durability. In the past few years, the art of Salish weaving has been revived, and a few people are doing this type of work. Some women knit ski socks and hats for the local shops using only the natural colored wools and spin their yarns by hand.

Carving is another art being taught to a few people by the elders of the tribe. There are those who do small carvings for retail sale. These carvings include canoe paddles, canoes, masks, feast bowls, totem poles, and rattles, in cedar. A select few artists carve in the mediums of soapstone, antler, and bone. There are some who specialize in two-dimensional paint design.

Visitor Information: Fisherman's Cove Restaurant is located at the southern tip of the Lummi Reservation. Tribally owned and operated, it provides a spectacular view of Lummi Island and Hales Pass. The restaurant specializes in seafood that is obtained fresh daily, locally. One of the specialties of the house is their well-known oyster omelet. Delicious salmon dishes are prepared in many different ways.

Adjacent to the restaurant is the Hyas Gift Shop, which features articles made by Lummi and other Indian artists and craftspersons. The wide variety of handicrafts includes wood carvings, leather work, beadwork, silverwork, and different kinds of sketches and paintings.

The tribe operates a charter boat that visitors can use to take a cruise through the surrounding waters for an unforgettable experience. The boat is operated by personnel with wide experience in the local waters. The sunsets are magnificent and can only be appreciated fully when seen reflecting on the crystal clear waters.

Overwhelming views of Lummi Bay, Hales Pass, Lummi Island, Bellingham Bay, and the majestic 10,000-foot-high snowcapped Mount Baker await the visitor to the Lummi Reservation. The breathtaking multicolored sunsets cannot be found elsewhere due to the unique combination of latitude and local geography. For those who enjoy strolls along the beach, certain areas have been retained in their natural state so that visitors can enjoy these simple pleasures from the past.

When the white man arrived, the Lummi Chief was Chow-Its-Hoot. In 1875, he was succeeded by Chief Kwina, who ruled the Lummis for over 50 years. Kwina was succeeded in 1926 by August Martin who was followed by Norbert James in 1960 and by the present chief, James McKay, in 1958.

In 1855, Isaac I. Stevens, Governor and Superintendent of Indian Affairs for the.Territory of Washington, negotiated the Point Elliott Treaty with Western Washington Tribes north of the present city of Seattle. In this treaty, the Indians ceded land between Olympia and the Canadian border for annual payments of money, protection of certain hunting and fishing rights, for implements, smithies, carpenters, doctors, and schools. The island called Ca-Choo-Sen (the home of the Lummis) became the home of the Huh-Lummis or the combined tribes of Lummi, Samish, Skagit, Semiahmoo, and Nooksack.

The Lummi people, along with many others, lived in this territory from the beginning of time. They lived in huge buildings made from ancient cedar trees, carved into beams and planks. These homes were known as longhouses.

There were up to ten families living in these homes. An average compartment inside the longhouse and lining the walls would be 6 fathoms by 6 fathoms square (1 fathom equals 6 feet). These homes were occupied in the winter. The longhouses were built to provide the warmth needed during the cold winter months.

There were many social gatherings in one of these longhouses. One of these is known as the potlatch. During the potlatch, large meals were prepared. Many people gathered from all parts of the country. Gifts were exchanged. The people at this time were very generous. It was the ability to give that determined a wealthy man, village, clan, or tribe. At these gatherings, beautiful handwoven blankets were given away. These blankets were made from the split roots and from other parts of the young cedar tree. There were different kinds of animal furs and bird feathers mixed into this material to make it soft and colorful.

The Lummis have always depended on fishing as their main source of subsistence. In warm weather, they moved from place to place, camping along riverbanks and beaches, fishing and gathering clams, oysters, berries, and wild roots. The men hunted extensively and caught wild fowl in nets. In the winter, the people settled into their cedar-built longhouses. The tribal knowledge required that no overharvesting take place; thus, the harvest site of the tribes was always rotated.

The Lummi fishing fleet is the largest in the Northwest and employs over 600 Lummis. Approximately 500 make their sole source of income from fishing. There are 447 fishing boats in the Lummi fleet: 32 seine boats, 165 gill net boats, and 250 skiffs. Total annual harvest value of the fleet exceeds $13,000,000. Lummi fishermen landed 5.8 million pounds of seafood in 1986. Salmon species dominate the landings.

The largest employer on the reservation is the Lummi Indian Business Council, which has 167 people on its payroll. The Indian Health Service employs 37, the Tribal Agriculture Program employs 21, and the Lummi Water and Sewer Department employs 8. The Fishermen's Cove employs over 30 people in the summer and 15 in the winter; the Lummi Seafood Processing Venture employs over 45 in the summer and 15 in the winter. Other economic development plans include entry into the recreational field through the operation of card and bingo games. The Lummis have been approved to operate a Foreign Trade Zone. They are currently seeking businesses to locate in this zone. Development of a commercial marina is being planned. The salmon enhancement program has been a tremendous success, with millions of salmon added to the fishery catch that is enjoyed by both Indian and non-Indian fishermen alike.

The overriding mission of the Lummi Indian Business Council is to realize economic self-sufficiency for its tribal members, tribal government, and tribal institutions. In the pursuit of having new business and industry locate on the reservation, it is also a goal of the tribe to assist and train members to be capable of owning and managing them. The Lummi Community College has established a training program to assure that the businesses and industries have the trained personnel they require.

Makah Tribal Council
P.O. Box 115
Neah Bay, WA 98357
(206) 645-2205

Makah ("cape people")

Location: The Makah Cultural Center and Museum are on the east side of Highway 112 in Neah Bay, Washington.

Public Ceremony or Powwow Dates: In late August, you will find the Makah people participating in one of the best celebrations in the Northwest with dancing and other activities.

Art Forms: The artwork of this area includes woodcarvings and baskets. Other types of artwork will also be found at the powwow.

Visitor Information: The museum is operated by the Makah Nation and includes some artifacts from a village buried by a mudslide some 500 years ago.

The Makah are the southernmost tribe of the Wakashan group, the only one within the United States. They belong to the Nootka branch. In 1905, there were two reservations, Makah and Ozette, Washington, on which there were, respectively, 399 and 36 people. In 1806, they were estimated by Lewis and Clark to number 2,000. By treaty of January 31, 1855, the Makah ceded all their lands at the mouth of the Strait of Juan de Fuca except the immediate area. This reservation was enlarged by Executive Order of October 26, 1872, superseded by Executive Order of January 2, 1873, and in turn revoked by Executive Order of October 12 of the same year, by which the Makah Reservation was established and defined. The Ozette Reservation was established by order of April 12, 1893. It's no wonder that Indian people were confused.

Muckleshoot Tribal Council
39015 172nd Street SE
Auburn, WA 98002
(206) 939-3311

Nisqually Indian Community Council
4820 She-Nah-Num Drive SE
Olympia, WA 98503
(206) 456-5221

This Salish tribe lived on and around the river of the Salish River, which flowed into the south extension of Puget Sound, Washington. The Nisqualli Reservation is on the Nisqualli River between Pierce and Thurston counties. The name has also been extended to apply to those tribes of the east side of Puget Sound speaking the same dialect. The Nisqualli made a treaty with the United States at Medicine Creek, Washington, December 26, 1854, ceding certain lands and reserving others. The Executive Order of January 20, 1857, defined the present Nisqualli Reservation.

Nooksack Tribal Council
P.O. Box 157
Deming, WA 98244
(206) 592-5176

Nooksak ("mountain men")

This name was given to a Salish tribe, said to be divided into three small bands, on the Salish River in Whatcom County, Washington, About 200 Nooksak were officially counted in 1906, but they speak the same dialect as the Squawmish, from whom they are said to have separated.

Port Gamble Community Council
P.O. Box 280
Kingston, WA 98346
(206) 297-2646

Puyallup Tribal Council
2002 East 28th Street
Tacoma, WA 98404
(206) 597-6200

Puyallup ("shadow," from the forest shade)

This important Salish tribe is of the Puyallup River and Commencement Bay. By treaty of December 26, 1854, the Puyallup and other tribes at the head of Puget Sound ceded their lands to the United States and agreed to go to a reservation set apart for them on the sound near Shenahnam Creek, Washington. In 1901, there were 536 on Puyallup Reservation, Washington; in 1909, 469.

Quileute Tribal Council
P.O. Box 279
LaPush, WA 98350
(206) 374-6163

Visitor Information: The Quileute compete in the racing at Chief Taholah Days at Quinault Nation, Taholah, Washington, on the Fourth of July. These power motorboats are exciting to watch.

This is a Chimakuan tribe, now the only representatives of this linguistic group. The main seat of the reservation is at LaPush at the mouth of the Quillayute River, about 35 miles south of C. Flattery, on the west coast of Washington state. A small division of the tribe, the Hoh, live at the mouth of the river of the same name, 15 miles south of LaPush. Although the Quileute have always been few in number, they successfully resisted all the attempts of neighboring tribes to dislodge them. Their most active enemies have been the Makah, of Neah Bay, and until they came under the control of the United States, petty warfare between the two tribes was constant. The Quileute were noted for their skill in pelagic sealing and were the most successful in that pursuit of all the tribes of the coast. They were also daring whalers. Salmon constituted an important food, and roots and berries of various kinds were also relied on for sustenance. Although the woods in their vicinity abounded with deer, elk, and bear, the Quileute seem to have hunted little, confining themselves to a seafaring life. There is some evidence that a clan system of some sort formerly existed among them. Their customs as well as their mythology indicate a possible connection with the tribes of Vancouver Island. The Quileute, together with the Quinaielt, by treaty at Olympia, July 1, 1855, and January 25, 1856, ceded all their lands to the United States and agreed to remove to a reserve to be provided for them in Washington Territory. The tribe gradually diminished, until in 1909, it numbered slightly more than 200.

Quinault Business Committee
P.O. Box 189
Taholah, WA 98587
(206) 276-8211

Quinaielt

Location: This reservation borders the Pacific Ocean and is located north of Aberdeen.

Public Ceremony or Powwow Dates: Chief Taholah Days is the event to attend during the Fourth of July weekend in Taholah.

Art Forms: A few arts and crafts will be offered for sale during the celebration. If you consider delicious salmon cooked over an open fire art, then you are in the right place, also.

Visitor Information: The tribe operates a cannery on the Quinault River.

Lewis and Clark found this Salish tribe along the coast between the Quileute and the Quaitso on the north and the Chehalis on the south. They described them in two divisions, the Calasthocle and the Quiniilt, with 200 and 1,000 in population, respectively. In 1909, they numbered 156, under the Puyallup School Superintendency. For their treaty with the United States, see Washington, Quileute.

Sauk-Suiattle Tribal Council
5318 Chief Brown Lane
Carrington, WA 98241
(206) 435-8366

Shoalwater Bay Tribal Council
P.O. Box 579
Tokeland, WA 98590
(206) 267-6766

Skokomish Tribal Council
N. 80 Tribal Center Road
Shelton, WA 98584
(206) 426-4232

Skokomish ("river people")

This body of the Salish form one of three subdivisions of the Twana. They lived at the mouth of the Skokomish River, which flows into the upper end of Hoods Canal, Washington, where a reservation of the same name was set aside for them. They officially numbered 203 in 1909, but this figure included the two other subdivisions of the Twana.

Spokane Business Council
P.O. Box 100
Wellpinit, WA 99040
(509) 258-4581

Spokan

Location: This reservation is located north and west of Spokane, Washington.

Public Ceremony or Powwow Dates: The tribe holds its annual Labor Day Celebration at Wellpinit each year. There is war dance competition and intertribal dances of all kinds.

Art Forms: There are many arts and crafts and other kinds of booths featured at the powwow. Food is an art, also, and there are many Indian food booths there. We found fresh sweetgrass braids, too. The stick game players were there in force and continued their play all night.

Visitor Information: Contact the Spokane Community Center for other arts and crafts that might be available on a daily basis.

Spokan has been applied to several small tribes of Salish on and near the Spokane River in Washington. The name was originally employed by the Skitswish to designate a band at the forks of the river, called also Smahoomenaish. The population in 1805 was 600 in 30 houses, and in 1853 the population was 450. In 1909 the Spokan in Washington numbered 509, while those in Idaho numbered 104.

Squaxin Island Tribal Council
W. 81 Highway 108
Shelton, WA 98584
(206) 426-9781

Squaxon

This is a division of the Salish on the peninsula between Hoods Canal and Case Inlet, Washington. The population in 1909 was 98.

Stillaquamish Board of Directors
2439 Stoluckquamish Lane
Arlington, WA 98223
(206) 652-7362

Stillaquamish

This division of Salish formerly lived on a river of the same name in northwest Washington. They are a branch of, or closely related to, the Snohomish and were moved to the Tulalip Reservation.

Suquamish Tribal Council
P.O. Box 498
Suquamish, WA 98392
(206) 598-3311

Suquamish

Location: The Port Madison Indian Reservation is located west of Seattle, at Suquamish.

Public Ceremony or Powwow Dates: Chief Seattle Days is held August 18–20, or the third weekend in August. The Native American Art Fair is held in mid-April. Call the tribal office for exact dates and times. No alcohol or drugs are allowed on the reservation.

Art Forms: Basketry and carving are the main art forms on the reservation today.

Visitor Information: The Suquamish Museum is located forty minutes from downtown Seattle, via the Winslow ferry. For visitors to the Olympic Peninsula, the Suquamish Museum is located on Highway 305, the gateway to and from the peninsula.

The museum staff will be happy to assist you in making arrangements for transportation and tours. Picnics, traditional salmon dinners, and special luncheons at nearby Kiana Lodge are available to museum visitors. For information, call (206) 598-3311. Hours are 10:00 a.m. to 5:00 p.m. daily, April through September; Tuesday-Friday, 11:00 a.m. to 4:00 p.m., and Saturday and Sunday, 10:00 a.m. to 5:00 p.m., October through March.

Quotes from tribal elders give a powerful voice to the Suquamish Museum experience: "It was my grandmother that taught me how to make the baskets. She used to make clam baskets. She used to make me sit down and do it. She says 'You got to learn how. You're going to get old, too, like I am, so you better learn how to make this.'" (Ethel Sam)

"My earliest recollection of living in the village first five or six years of my life . . . the children were always playing there and the village run for about a mile along the shore of Suquamish. There's where we always seemed to gather, elders and children, sometime through the day . . . and the life of the people at that time wasn't too complicated . . . get up and do whatever chores or work they had to." (Lawrence Webster)

Chief Sealth (or Seattle), Dwamish, 1865
Photo by E. M. Sammis; Courtesy Museum of New Mexico, Neg. No. 88464

Here you can experience the history of the Pacific Northwest from the perspective of Chief Seattle and his descendants, the Suquamish people. In a forested setting on the shores of Agate Passage, the Suquamish Museum reveals the world of Puget Sound's original inhabitants. Sights and sounds from the past bring life to the museum's premier exhibition, The Eyes of Chief Seattle, which received international acclaim when it traveled to Nantes, France, as part of Seattle's Sister City exchange. The museum's award-winning media production, Come Forth Laughing: Voices of the Suquamish People, provides a firsthand account of life over the past one hundred years.

Spend time at the museum, and then walk along their beautiful beach, have a picnic lunch overlooking Agate Pass, stop in the gift shop, and tour the nature trail. Their guides can direct you to other spots on the Port Madison Indian Reservation, including Chief Seattle's grave, Old Man House, the site of the original Suquamish village and the largest longhouse in the Pacific Northwest, and the Suquamish Fish Hatchery.

Chief Seattle, head of the Suquamish and Duwamish tribes, has been given honors that few other Indians have received. The City of Seattle, Washington, was named for him; there is a bronze statue in Seattle commemorating this. Each year, the Boy Scouts of America hold a memorial ceremony at his tomb at Suquamish.

Seattle and his father before him were both friendly to the white settlers and eagerly helped them. After Seattle became a Catholic in the 1830s, he demonstrated his beliefs in the way he lived. He was the first to sign the Port Elliott Treaty in 1855 whereby the Suquamish and other Washington tribes received reservations. Seattle was born in 1786 and died June 7, 1866.

The speech that follows on these pages was taken down by Dr. Henry Smith, a man who mastered the Suwamish language in about two years. Dr. Smith did us a great service in preserving this address, which may cause some present-day citizens to wonder at his predictions. The Washington Territory was organized in 1853. A plat for the town of Seattle was filed, and the first post office was put into use. Governor Stevens soon visited Seattle and on the occasion, made an address to the settlers and Indians gathered in the small community. After his talk, Seattle made his reply, which was delivered through an interpreter. Dr. Smith carefully wrote it down on the spot.

Angelina, Chief Seattle's daughter, Dwamish
Courtesy Museum of New Mexico, Neg. No. 73091

Yonder sky that has wept tears of compassion upon my people for centuries untold, and which to us appears changeless and eternal, may change. Today is fair. Tomorrow it may be overcast with clouds. My words are like the stars that never change. Whatever Seattle says the great Chief at Washington can rely upon with as much certainty as he can upon the return of the sun or the seasons. The White Chief says that Big Chief at Washington sends us greetings of friendship and goodwill. This is kind of him for we know he has little need of our friendship in return. His people are many. They are like the grass that covers vast prairies. My people are few. They resemble the scattering trees of a storm swept plain. The great, and I presume, good White Chief sends us word that he wishes to buy our lands but is willing to allow us enough to live comfortably. This indeed appears just, even generous, for the Red Man no longer has rights that he need respect, and the offer may be wise also, as we are no longer in need of an extensive country.

There was a time when our people covered the land as the waves of a wind ruffled sea cover its shell paved floor, but that time long since passed away with the greatness of tribes that are now but a mournful memory. I will not dwell on, nor mourn over, our untimely decay, nor reproach my paleface brothers with hastening it as we too may have been somewhat to blame.

Youth is impulsive. When our young men grow angry at some real or imaginary wrong, and disfigure their faces with black paint, it denotes that their hearts are black, and that they are often cruel and relentless, and our old men and old women are unable to restrain them. Thus it has ever been. Thus it was when the white man first began to push our forefathers westward. But let us hope that the hostilities between us may never return. We would have everything to lose and nothing to gain. Revenge by young men is considered gain, even at the cost of their own lives, but old men who stay at home in times of war, and mothers who have sons to lose, know better.

Our good father at Washington, for I presume he is our father as well as yours, since King George has moved his boundaries further north, our great and good father, I say, sends us word that if we do as he desires he will protect us. His brave warriors will be to us a bristling wall of strength, and his wonderful ships of war will fill our harbors so that our ancient enemies far to the northward, the Hydas and Tsimpsians, will cease to frighten our women, children and old men. Then in reality will he be our father and we his children. But can that ever be? Your God is not our God! Your God loves your people and hates mine. He folds his strong protecting arms lovingly

about the paleface and leads him by the hand as a father leads his
infant son, but He has forsaken His red children, if they really are
His. Our God, the Great Spirit, seems also to have forsaken us. Your
God makes your people wax strong every day. Soon they will fill all
the land. Our people are ebbing away like a rapidly receding tide
that will never return. The white man's God cannot love our people
or He would protect them. They seem to be orphans who can look
nowhere for help. How then can we be brothers? How can your God
become our God and renew our prosperity and awaken in us dreams
of returning greatness. If we have a common heavenly father He
must be partial, for He came to His paleface children. We never saw
Him. He gave you laws but had no word for his red children whose
teeming multitudes once filled this vast continent as stars fill the fir-
mament. No; we are two distinct races with separate origins and
separate destinies. There is little in common between us.

To us the ashes of our ancestors are sacred and their resting place
is hallowed ground. You wander far from the graves of your ancestors and seemingly without regret. Your religion was written upon
tables of stone by the iron finger of your God so that you could not
forget. The Red Man could never comprehend nor remember it.
Our religion is the traditions of our ancestors, the dreams of our old
men, given them in the solemn hours of night by the Great Spirit;
and the visions of our sachems, and is written in the hearts of our
people.

Your dead cease to love you and the land of their nativity as soon
as they pass the portals of the tomb and wander way beyond the
stars. They are soon forgotten and never return. Our dead never
forget the beautiful world that gave them being. They still love its
verdant valleys, its murmuring rivers, its magnificent mountains, se-
questered vales and verdant lined lakes and bay, and ever yearn in
tender, fond affection over the lonely hearted living, and often return from the Happy Hunting Ground to visit, guide, console and
comfort them.

Day and night cannot dwell together. The Red Man has ever fled
the approach of the White Man, as the morning mist flees before the
morning sun.

However, your proposition seems fair and I think that my people
will accept it and will retire to the reservation you offer them. Then
we will dwell in peace, for the words of the Great White Chief seem
to be the words of nature speaking to my people out of dense
darkness.

It matters little where we pass the remnant of our days. They will
not be many. The Indians' night promises to be dark. Not a single
star of hope hovers above his horizon. Sad voiced winds moan in the

distance. Grim fate seems to be on the Red Man's trail, and wherever he goes he will hear the approaching footsteps of his fell destroyer and prepare stolidly to meet his doom, as does the wounded doe that hears the approaching footsteps of the hunter.

A few more moons. A few more winters, and not one of the descendants of the mighty hosts that once moved over this broad land or lived in happy homes, protected by the Great Spirit, will remain to mourn over the graves of a people, once more powerful and hopeful than yours. But why should I mourn at the untimely fate of my people? Tribe follows tribe, and nation follows nation, like the waves of the sea. It is the order of nature, and regret is useless. Your time of decay may be distant, but it will surely come, for even the White Man whose God walked and talked with him as friend with friend, cannot be exempt from the common destiny. We may be brothers after all. We will see.

We will ponder your proposition and when we decide we will let you know. But should we accept it, I here and now make this condition that we will not be denied the privilege without molestation of visiting at any time the tombs of our ancestors, friends, and children. Every part of this soil is sacred in the estimation of my people. Every hillside, every valley, every plain and grove, has been hallowed by some sad or happy event in days long vanished. Even the rocks, which seem to be dumb and dead as they swelter in the sun along the silent shore, thrill with memories of stirring events connected with the lives of my people, and the very dust upon which you now stand responds more lovingly to their footsteps than to yours, because it is rich with the blood of our ancestors and our bare feet are conscious of the sympathetic touch. Our departed braves, fond mothers, glad, happy hearted maidens, and even our little children who lived here and rejoiced here for a brief season, will love these somber solitudes and at eventide they greet shadowy returning spirits. *And when the last Red Man shall have perished, and the memory of my tribe shall have become a myth among the White Men, these shores will swarm with the invisible dead of my tribe,* and when your children's children think themselves alone in the field, the store, the shop, upon the highway, or in the silence of the pathless woods, they will not be alone. In all the earth there is no place dedicated to solitude. At night when the streets of your cities and villages are silent and you think them deserted, they will throng with the returning hosts that once filled them and still love this beautiful land. The White Man will never be alone.

Let him be just and deal kindly with my people, for the dead are not powerless. Dead, did I say? There is no death, only a change of worlds.

Suquamish Tribal Council
P.O. Box 498
Suquamish, WA 98392
(206) 598-3311

Suquamish

This Salish division claimed their homeland on the west side of Puget Sound. According to records, they claimed the land from Appletree Cove in the north to Gig Harbor in the south. Seattle, who gave his name to the city, was chief of this tribe and the Suwamish in 1853. The population was 441 in 1857, 180 in 1909.

Please see the previous listing of the Suquamish for more information.

Swinomish Indian Senate
P.O. Box 817
La Conner, WA 98257
(206) 466-3163

This tribe is a subdivision of the Skagit, formerly on Whidbey Island, northwest Washington. The Skagit and Swinomish together numbered 268 in 1909.

Tulalip Board of Directors
6700 Totem Beach Road
Marysville, WA 98270
(206) 653-4585

Visitor Information: The Tulalip today live north and west of Everett, Washington. They operate a bingo parlor and have other economic development programs.

The Tulalip are one of three divisions of the Twana, a Salish tribe on the west side of Hoods Canal, Washington. This branch lived on a small stream, near the head of the canal, called Dulaylip. In 1909, the name was also given to a reservation on the west side of Puget Sound.

Upper Skagit Tribal Council
2284 Community Plaza
Sedro Woolley, WA 98284
(206) 856-5501

Skagit

This body of the Salish lived on a river of the same name in Washington. In 1853, the population of the Skagit proper was about 300. They moved to the Swinomish Reservation, Washington, in 1909.

Yakima Tribal Council
P.O. Box 151
Toppenish, WA 98948
(509) 865-5121

Yakima (Ya-ki-ma, "runaway")
Waptailmin ("people of the narrow river")
Pa kiut lema ("people of the gap")

Location: Look on your map of Washington, near Yakima, for the location of the Yakima Reservation.

Public Ceremony or Powwow Dates: The Yakima Nation Summer Encampment and the Toppenish Powwow are both held over the Fourth of July weekend. Traditional dancing and a powwow competition are featured along with intertribal dancing. The common name of this area's celebrations is White Swan. The Yakima Powwow is usually held in September. Call the tribal office for dates and times.

Art Forms: Arts and crafts of many kinds are offered during the powwows. There are also hand games.

Visitor Information: The Cultural Center at Highway 97 and Fort Road, Toppenish, is preserving some of the most important aspects of Yakima culture. Arts and crafts—beadwork, silverwork, and other interesting items—are offered for sale at the gift shop. The Heritage Inn Restaurant has ordinary food as well as Indian food.

This important Shahaptian tribe, formerly living on both sides of the Columbia River and on the northerly branches of the Yakima (formerly Tapteal) and the Wenatchee, in Washington, are mentioned by Lewis and Clark in 1806 under the name Cutsahnim and estimated as 1,200 in number. In 1855, the United States made a treaty with the Yakima and thirteen other tribes of Shahaptian, Salishan, and Chinookan groups, by which they ceded the territory from the Cascade Mountains to the Palouse and Snake rivers and from Lake Chelan to the Columbia. The Yakima Reservation was established, on which all the participating tribes and bands were to be confederated as the Yakima Nation under the leadership of Kamiakan, a distinguished Yakima chief. Before this treaty could be ratified, the Yakima war broke out, and it was not until 1859 that the provisions of the treaty went into effect. The Paloos and certain other tribes never recognized the treaty or moved to the reservation. In 1909, the total population on the reservation was 1,900. There is little reason to believe that the customs of this tribe differed from the Nez Perces and other Shahaptian people. Please see Idaho, Nez Perces, for more information.

SOUTH

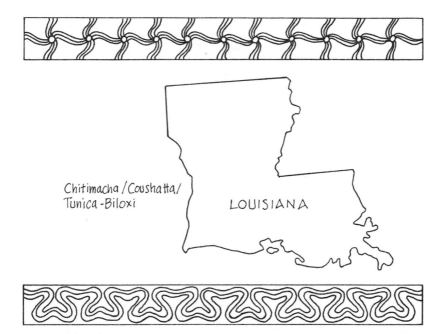

Chitimacha / Coushatta /
Tunica -Biloxi

LOUISIANA

The South of North America is above that place where the waters of the Gulf of Mexico meet the great river, the Mississippi, from the north. The terrain is largely flat and rolling, with some swamps and bogs and trees and streams. There are grasses and the land is green.

This is the land of the people of the towns; the houses lined the rivers. Often, houses lined both sides of the river for miles. In the larger towns, there were squares like plazas in the center. This is where the people gathered to dance pray the ceremony of keeping tradition alive.

The sacred fire was always kept alive and burning and the people danced around it with dedication and steadfastness. Then, the seasons brought the greater ceremonies of hope and thanks. The dances around the fire always culminated in the seasonal blessings.

Join with the tribes on the following pages to honor their ancestors and to honor our Creator, our Mother Earth, our Moon, our Sun, and the whole of all living things in the whole of all Creation. You will find that it is good. It is very, very good.

Aho . . .

LOUISIANA

Chitimacha Tribal Council
P.O. Box 661
Charenton, LA 70523
(318) 923-4973

chuti masha (they have cooking vessels)

Location: The tribal office is in Charenton.

Art Forms: The Chitimacha are known for their fine baskets made of cane.

This tribe is of the Chitimachan linguistic family, whose earliest known residence was the shores of Grand Lake, formerly Lake of the Shetimasha, and the banks of Grand River, Louisiana. Some 16 or 18 of the tribe were living on the Grand River in 1881, but the majority, about 35, lived at Charenton, on the south side of Bayou Teche, in St. Mary's Parish, about ten miles from the Gulf of Mexico. This tribe's name for itself is Pantch-pinunkansh, "men altogether red," a designation apparently applied after they came into contact with white people. The Chitimacha were known soon after the French settled Louisiana, through the death by one of their men of St. Cosme, a missionary, on the Mississippi in 1706. This was followed by protracted war with the French, who compelled them to sue for peace. It was granted on condition that the head of the Indian be brought to him; this was done and peace was made. It is believed the tribe was then reduced to a small number of warriors.

Little is known about their traditional customs. Fish and the roots of native plants constituted their food, but later they planted maize and sweet potatoes. They were strict monogamists, and women appear to have had considerable authority in their government. The men wore their hair long, with a piece of lead at the end of the queue, and tattooed their arms, legs, and faces. The noonday sun is said to have been their principal celebration representative. The dead of the tribe were buried in graves, and after the flesh had decayed, the bones were taken up and reinterred.

Coushatta Tribal Council
P.O. Box 818
Elton, LA 70532
(318) 584-2261

Koasati

This is an upper Creek tribe that speaks a dialect almost identical with the Alibamu. The name contains the word for "cane" or "reed," and it may signify "white cane."

During the middle and latter part of the eighteenth century, the Koasati lived, apparently in one principal village, on the right bank of the Alabama River, three miles below the confluence of the Coosa and Tallapoosa, where the modern town of Coosada, Alabama, perpetuates their name; but soon after west Florida was ceded to Great Britain, in 1763, "two villages of Kosati" moved over to the Tombigbee and settled below the mouth of Sukenatcha Creek. A "Coosawda" village existed on the Tennessee River, near the site of Langston, Jackson County, Alabama, in the early part of the nineteenth century, but it is uncertain whether its occupants were true Koasati. In 1805, some members of the tribe settled in Louisiana. From there, they spread over much of east Texas as far as Trinity River, while a portion, or perhaps some of those who had remained in Alabama, obtained permission from the Caddo to settle on the Red River. Those who stayed in their original homes and subsequently moved to Indian Territory also largely remained near the Alibamu, although they are found in several places in the Creek Nation, Oklahoma. Two towns in the Creek Nation are named after them.

Houma Nation
Star Route Box 95A
Golden Meadow, LA 70357

Visitor Information: There is an Indian Crafts Coop based in Dulac, Louisiana, for the Houma Nation. Call the tribal office for more details.

Tunica-Biloxi Indian Tribe
P.O. Box 2182
Mansura, LA 71350
(318) 253-9767

Tunica (article people)
Biloxi (Taneks haya, "first people")

Location: The tribal office is in Marksville, Louisiana.

Tunica

This tribe is from a distinct linguistic family known as Tonikan that formerly dwelled on the lower Mississippi. The Tunica are prominent in the early history of the lower Mississippi region because of their attachment to the French and their service as allies in fights with neighboring tribes. When first visited by the whites, they lived in Mississippi on the lower Yazoo River. In 1699, the number of their cabins was estimated at 260, scattered over four leagues of countryside. At that time, they lived entirely on Indian corn and did no hunting. In 1700, they occupied seven hamlets containing 50 or 60 small cabins. In 1706, the Tunica were driven from their villages by the Chickasaw and Alibamu and joined the Huma; it is said that subsequently they killed more than half that tribe and occupied its territory. In 1730, the Natchez, who had taken refuge among the Chickasaw, burned their village and a large number of them were killed. In 1760, they occupied three villages, the largest of which was on a lake at Tunica Bayou. In 1802, the population was estimated at 120 men, a total of about 450 people altogether.

In 1908, the Tunica consisted of about thirty people and were in east and southeast Marksville, the parish seat, on what is called Marksville Prairie. At that time, they spoke Tunica, Creole, and English.

A description of the Tunica in 1700 indicates that the women made an excellent fabric of mulberry cloth; there was fair division of labor between the sexes; the men cultivated the soil, planted and harvested the crops, cut the wood and brought it to the cabin, and dressed the deer and buffalo skins; the women performed the indoor work and made pottery and clothing.

Biloxi

This is a tribe of Siouan origin which formerly lived in southern Mississippi. The first direct notice of the Biloxi was in 1699 around

Biloxi Bay, on the gulf coast of the Mississippi area, in connection with two other small tribes, the Paskagula and Moctobi, the three altogether numbering only about 20 cabins. In 1828, there were 20 families of the tribe on the east bank of the Neches River, Texas. In 1829, approximately 65 were living with the Caddo, Paskagula, and other small tribes on the Red River, near the Texas frontier, and in 1846, a Biloxi camp was seen on Little River, a tributary of the Brazos in Texas. After this, little was heard of them until 1886, when a few Biloxi were seen among the Choctaw and Caddo. Prior to the coming of the whites, the men wore breechcloths, belts, leggings, moccasins, and garters and wrapped skin robes around their bodies. Feather headdresses and necklaces of bone and the bills of a long-legged redbird (flamingo?) were worn, as were nose rings and earrings. The dwellings of the people resembled those found among the northern tribes of the same family, one kind similar to the low tent of the Osage and Winnebago, the other like the high tent of the Dakota and Omaha. It is said they formerly made pottery, wooden bowls, horn and bone implements, and baskets. Tattooing was practiced to a limited extent. Descent was through the female line, and there was an elaborate system of kinship.

SOUTHEAST

NORTH CAROLINA
Cherokee

SOUTH
CAROLINA

ALABAMA

MISSISSIPPI
Choctaw

Creek

GEORGIA

FLORIDA

Seminole
Miccosukee

The Southeast of our North America lies in that place toward where the sun rises and all the days of men begin. It is a land of rolling hills, valleys, mountains rounded by time, streams and coastlines with bright sands. There are forests of broadleaf trees and pine. There are swamps and bogs and rivers running to the Great Water, the Gulf of Mexico.

This is the land of the people of the thatched houses. The floors are raised above the often-rising water from storms from the coast. The people lived by the gifts from deer, small animals, herbs, and vegetable gardens and the corn.

There was beauty in the path of the people and they acted out the goodness of the gift from the Creator with sacred ceremonies. The most perfect time of Creation was the time of the people living in harmony with all living and natural things. There was no need for machines. No need for things that polluted and ruined the earth. There was no need to live in unnatural ways. Man had reached the best of his culture.

Join with the tribes on the following pages to honor their ancestors and to honor our Creator, our Mother Earth, our Moon, our Sun, and the whole of all living things in the whole of all Creation. You will find that it is good. It is very, very good.

Aho . . .

We do not take up the warpath without a just cause and honest purpose.

—Pushmataha
(Choctaw)

ALABAMA

Poarch Band of Creek Indians
Route 3, Box 243A
Atmore, AL 36502
(205) 368-9136

Muscogee

This confederacy forms the largest division of the Muskhogean family. They received their name from the English on account of the numerous streams in their country. During early historic times, the Creeks occupied the greater portion of Alabama and Georgia, residing chiefly on the Coosa and Tallapoosa rivers, the two largest tributaries of the Alabama River, and on the Flint and Chattahoochee rivers. The tribes at the time of the confederation were Abihka (or Kusa), Kasihta, Kawita, and Oakfuskee. Before 1540, there may have been another tribe at the Coosa and Tallapoosa rivers. In the last quarter of the eighteenth century, the Creek population may have been about 20,000, occupying from 40 to 60 towns. In 1789, there were 6,000 warriors and 24,000 inhabitants in 100 towns. In 1775, the whole confederacy, without the Seminole, was 11,000 in 55 towns. In 1785, there were 5,400 men with a total of 19,000. In 1904, after removal to Indian Territory, the population was 9,905.

TO-CHA-KA-JO. or DRUNKEN TERRAPIN.   CREEK.

Lo-cha-ha-jo (The Drunken Terrapin), Treaty-making chief of the Creeks, pre-1877
Courtesy Museum of New Mexico, Neg. No. 87530

FLORIDA

Bobby Henry's Seminole Indian Village
5221 N. Orient Road
Tampa, FL 33610
(813) 626-3948

Seminole ("Runaways," from the Creek language)

Location: Leave Interstate 4 on the eastern outskirts of Tampa at Orient Road (Exit 5). Drive north on Orient Road a quarter mile to the Seminole Cultural Center, which is now Bobby Henry's Seminole Indian Village.

Visitor Information: The Seminoles fought for their homeland in one of history's most lethal guerrilla wars in the nineteenth century. The swamps and forests of Florida were their home after being forced out of their native Georgia and Alabama by the encroaching white settlers. General Andrew Jackson with 3,000 federal troops invaded Florida in 1818. His victory not only claimed the land for the United States but also confined the Seminoles to Florida's swamps. Then, in May 1830, President Jackson signed into law the Indian Removal Act. It called for the removal of all the Indians of the so-called Five Civilized Tribes from their southeastern homelands to Indian Territory (what we know as Oklahoma today). The Seminoles proudly refused to move, and thousands were killed in the second Seminole War of 1835–1842. Medicine Man Bobby Henry has preserved the arts, crafts, history, and way of life of the Seminole in this traditional village. Hours are Monday through Saturday, 9:00 a.m. to 5:00 p.m.; Sunday, noon to 5:00 p.m.

Miccosukee Business Committee
P.O. Box 440021
Tamiami Station
Miami, FL 33144
(305) 223-8380

Mikasuki

Location: The tribal complex is 25 miles west of Miami on the Tamiami Trail which is Highway 41.

Public Ceremony or Powwow Dates: Call for the dates of the Green Corn Ceremonies and stomp dances. The Arts Festival featuring dancing, arts, and crafts is held the week after Christmas.

Art Forms: The Miccosukee museum shows traditional Miccosukee life in exhibits, films, photos, and paintings. There is a reconstructed village with open-sided Miccosukee "chickees," the old-fashioned houses of the tribe. Here you can find traditional colorful Miccosukee clothing, dugout canoes, and arts and crafts demonstrations and sales.

Visitor Information: Don't miss the alligator wrestling. I made friends with one member of the tribe during Denver Indian Market and I would imagine he handles the alligators very well! Across the street from the village is the Miccosukee restaurant serving Miccosukee and regular fare. Adjacent to the restaurant are the Miccosukee airboat rides, which fly you through the Everglades. Your guides will be happy to take you to a small tree-covered island to show you a real oldtime Miccosukee camp that is still in use.

The Mikasuki are a former Seminole division. They spoke the Hitchiti dialect and were partly emigrants from the Sawokli towns on the lower Chattahoochee River, Alabama. At this time, they had 300 houses, which were burned by General Jackson. There were then several villages near the lake, known also as Mikasuki towns, which were occupied almost wholly by blacks. In the Seminole War of 1835–1842, the people of this town became noted for their courage and audacity.

Seminole Tribal Council
6073 Stirling Road
Hollywood, FL 33024
(305) 583-7112

Sim a no le or Isti simanole, "separatist," "runaway" from the Creek language.

Location: The Seminole Okalee Village is on the Seminole Reservation west of Dania, near Hollywood, Florida.

Public Ceremony or Powwow Dates: The annual powwow is usually held in February. The Seminole Fair is generally held the fourth weekend in December.

Cora Osceola Seminole Indian Camp, Tamiami Trail
Photo by Doubleday; Courtesy Museum of New Mexico, Neg. No. 88478

Art Forms: The Arts and Crafts Center, 6073 Sterling Road, in Hollywood, is at Highway 441 and Sterling Road, four miles west of Dania, telephone (305) 583-3590. Many traditional arts and crafts are sold. There are beautiful patchwork clothes, baskets, and carvings for sale.

Visitor Information: The Florida Seminole are very traditional in some aspects of their life-style in the Everglades of Florida. They wear colorful clothing and practice traditional ceremonial ways. For a tour of the area, call the tribal office.

This is a Muskhogean tribe of Florida, originally made up of immigrants from the lower Creek towns on the Chattahoochee River, who moved down into Florida following the destruction of the Apalachee and other native tribes. They were at first classed with the lower Creeks but began to be known under their present name about 1775. Those still residing in Florida call themselves Ikaniuksalgi, "peninsula people."

Before the removal of the main body of this tribe to Indian Territory, the Seminole consisted chiefly of descendants of Muscogee (Creeks) and Hitchiti from the lower Creek towns, with a considerable number of refugees from the upper Creeks after the Creek war, together with remnants of Yamasee and other conquered tribes, Yuchi, and many blacks who were runaway slaves. While still under Spanish rule, the Seminole became involved in hostility with the United States, particularly in the War of 1812 and again in 1817–18, the first Seminole war. This war was quelled by General Andrew Jackson, who invaded Florida with a force exceeding 3,000 men, as the result of which Spain ceded the territory to the United States in 1819. By the treaty of Ft. Moultrie in 1823, the Seminole ceded most of their lands, except for a central reservation. Because of pressure from the border population for their complete removal, another treaty was negotiated at Paynes Landing in 1832, by which they were bound to move beyond the Mississippi within three years. The treaty was repudiated by a large proportion of the tribe who, under the leadership of the great Osceola, at once prepared to resist. Thus began the second Seminole War in 1835, with the killing of Emathla, the principal signer of the removal treaty, and of General A. R. Thompson, who had been instrumental in applying pressure to those who opposed the arrangement. The war lasted nearly eight years, ending in August 1842 with the practical expatriation of the tribe from Florida for the west, but at the cost of the lives of nearly 1,500 American troops and the expenditure of $20 million. Blacks took an active part throughout the war on the side of the Seminole. Those removed to Oklahoma were subsequently organized into the "Seminole Nation," as one of the so-called Five Civilized Tribes. With the other tribes, they signed the agreement for the opening of their lands in Oklahoma, Indian Territory, to settlement. In 1908, they were officially reported as numbering 2,138, largely mixed with blacks in addition to 986 "Seminole Freedmen." At this time, a refugee band of Seminole lived on the Mexican side of the Rio Grande in Eagle Pass, Texas. The Seminole still residing in the southern part of Florida were officially estimated at 275.

MISSISSIPPI

Mississippi Band of Choctaw Indians
Route 7, Box 21
Philadelphia, MS 39350
(601) 656-5251

Chata Hapia Hoke

Location: Tribal headquarters are located in the Pearl River Community, which is also the site of the bustling Choctaw Industrial Park, east of Philadelphia, Mississippi. Visitors will find the Choctaw Museum, Arts and Crafts Shop, and the Choctaw Indian Fair in Pearl River. Nanih Waiyah, Mother Mound of the Choctaws, is near Bogue Chitto. Bogue Homa is the southernmost community.

Public Ceremony or Powwow Dates: The annual four-day Choctaw Indian Fair begins in the early morning of the first Wednesday after the Fourth of July. In olden times, it was the Green Corn Ceremony. Now, as traditionally, it is the grand gathering of the Okla, the people. Here you can participate in the world of the Indian: dances, crafts, entertainers, and pageantry. You can also see the incomparable granddaddy of games, the Choctaw Stickball World Series, the oldest field sport in America.

Art Forms: Members of the tribe do basket weaving, beadwork, and needlepoint on traditional styles of clothing.

Visitor Information: Every year in midsummer since 1949, the Mississippi Band of Choctaw Indians has presented the Choctaw Indian Fair as a major social gathering to revive and preserve Choctaw heritage and to promote public relations with surrounding communities. It has grown into a major tourist attraction. The fair attracts over 20,000 people a year in four days. These visitors come from nearby and faraway, even Europe, where there is considerable interest in Indian cultures.

The Choctaw were once one of the largest of tribes in what is now the southeastern United States, with strong democratic governmental institutions and a productive, agriculture-based community. The colonial powers vying for Choctaw Country (Britain, France, Spain, and later the United States) destroyed the tribal economy and forced the tribal government into a series of treaties making economic and land cessions. Although the tribe had developed sophisticated educational and law enforcement systems on the lands it administered, the last 10,423,130 acres of Choctaw Country were ceded to the United States under the Treaty of Dancing Rabbit Creek (1830), a treaty endorsed by only a minority of tribal members.

The members of the Choctaw tribe now living on a 21,000-acre reservation in east central Mississippi are the descendants of those tribal members who elected to remain in the original homeland when faced with removal to Indian Territory in the nineteenth century and who struggled with poverty and segregation in their homeland in order to preserve and enhance their traditional culture.

With the establishment of the tenant farming system after the Civil War, the Choctaw became sharecroppers. In the late nineteenth century, the Catholic Church established a mission and school in the Tucker community. In 1918, the Congress, reacting to hearings that revealed the dire living conditions endured by the members of the tribe, established a Bureau of Indian Affairs agency at Philadelphia and schools in each of the seven Choctaw communities and began buying the land that today forms the reservation.

In 1945, the tribe adopted a Constitution and By-laws that provided for establishment of a Tribal Council. In the 1960s, the council and other tribal governmental institutions began to develop rapidly under the tribal goal of "Choctaw Self-Determination." Resources for social programs to improve the tribal standard of living and health status were obtained, and an effort to develop the reservation economy was begun. This effort paid off in 1979, when, under the aegis of Chief Phillip Martin, the first tribal enterprise opened its doors. Since then, five additional industrial plants have been built. The Mississippi Band of Choctaw Indians is now the largest employer in Neshoba County and one of the largest in the state.

Choctaw people have been on their land so long that their origin is known only through legends. These legends focus on Nanih Waiya, the Mother Mound, located near Preston, Mississippi. This mound is connected by legend with both the creation and migration of the tribe. The center of the Choctaw before advent of the white man, it was considered by Indians to be the birthplace of their race. Out of the mound ages ago, they believe, came first the Creeks, Cherokees, and Chickasaws, who sunned themselves until dry to settle around the mound, their Great Mother, who told them that if ever they left her side they would die.

Another legend relates Nanih Waiya to Choctaw migration in the tribe's search for a new homeland. A tribal elder gives one account:

"Many years ago, the ancestors of our people lived in the northwest. In time their population became so large that it was difficult to exist there. The prophets of the tribe announced that a land of fertile soil and abundant game lay in the southeast and that the people could live there in peace and prosperity forever. Under the leadership of Chahta, our people set forth.

"At the end of each day's journey, a sacred pole was planted erect in front of the camp. The next morning the pole would be found to be leaning one way or another; in that direction the tribesmen were to travel for that day. For months our people followed the sacred staff. One day when the tribe stopped on the west side of a creek, Chahta planted the pole; heavy rain began to fall. The next day, the staff which had burrowed itself deeper in the ground stood straight and tall for all to see. Chahta proclaimed that the long sought land of Nanih Waiya had been found. Here, we would build our homes and a mound as the sacred burial spot for our ancestors."

Today Nanih Waiya is surrounded by fields and pasture. Nature's wind and water erosion and man's farming have reduced the mound to a fraction of its former size. Several years ago, the state of Mississippi developed a small state park at the site which included a trail to the legendary Nanih Waiya cave, a picnic area, and a small meeting hall. Although figuring in the Choctaw legends, Nanih Waiya as it exists today is not under the ownership or control of the Mississippi Band of Choctaw Indians.

Gold seekers were the first Europeans to come to Choctaw Country. The Choctaw lands stretched from offshore islands in the Gulf of Mexico to north central Alabama and central Mississippi and from the Mississippi River to eastern Alabama. A Spaniard, Alonzo Pineda, was the first known European to enter Choctaw territory, although before his arrival in 1519, the coastline had been charted by an unknown cartographer.

In 1540, Hernando de Soto, a cruel and powerful man, came to the Choctaw land. He brought about 600 well-armed men, 200 of them on horseback. They enslaved, looted, and killed Indian people as they traveled through the Southeast. Thousands were killed, but finally the Choctaw drove the Spanish from the territory. They left behind their booty stolen from the Indians.

About 1700, the French came and were soon followed by the Spanish and English. Choctaw Country became pivotal in the struggle of the three powers to gain eçonomic and political control of the vast Mississippi Valley. For over 100 years, the Choctaw were caught up in the struggle for occupation of their lands by the three powers. Finally, the Choctaw were recognized as an independent nation by the United States and a treaty was signed in 1786. This treaty aligned the Choctaw with the United States against the other nations. But their determined efforts to gain friendship and fair treatment from the United States eventually failed.

Thomas Jefferson's 1803 message to Congress urging that the huge Louisiana Territory be purchased from France included the proposal that Indian nations be moved to less desirable lands west of the Mississippi. Accordingly, the Louisiana Territorial Act of 1804 empowered the president to move tribes off their land to make way for American settlers. But removal was delayed for a generation during which Choctaw people sought to accept non-Indian customs. For thirty years, the Choctaw people made an effort to please the United States by adapting their governmental and social institutions and were successful, until the tragedy at Dancing Rabbit Creek.

The succession of treaty agreements had restricted Choctaw land to east central Mississippi. In 1829, encouraged by President Andrew Jackson, the State of Mississippi declared all members of the tribe to be citizens of the state and attempted to obliterate the tribal government through laws that imposed severe punishment on any Choctaw who accepted tribal office. Spokesmen for Jackson claimed the federal government, in spite of treaties, could not prevent the State of Mississippi from enforcing its new laws. In 1830, the Choctaw were coerced into accepting the terms of the Treaty of Dancing Rabbit Creek. The treaty was signed, however, only after many of the tribal negotiators had left in disgust. The last of the Choctaw land was lost. Provision was made for individuals to stay and claim the land, but strong inducement was given the tribe to move to lands set aside for them in Oklahoma. The trek to Oklahoma was marked with hardship, heartbreak, and disease. Many died.

Over 8,000 Choctaw remained in Mississippi, relying on the promise of allotments of land and other considerations. For them, treachery came soon and hope died fast. Those few who acquired allotted land were forced out with the approval, often with the active support, of state and federal governments. In the years after 1830, harsh, constant pressure was placed upon Mississippi Choctaw to move west. From a preremoval population of 19,200, 1,253 remained in 1910. During this period, concerted federal efforts to remove the tribe to Oklahoma took place in 1831, 1846, 1849, 1853, 1854, 1890, and 1903.

From the beginning of removal until after the American Civil War, Choctaw lived as squatters and sharecroppers on the land that was once theirs. Finally in 1918, the U.S. government acknowledged that this tribe was not going to leave Mississippi.

It is ironic that the Choctaw had allied themselves with the young United States, seeing their future as part of the new experiment in democracy. Indeed, Benjamin Franklin and others of the founding fathers drew heavily on the Native American confederacy pattern as they shaped the Union. Franklin said, in effect, if the Indians can do it, so can we. A great confederacy in the South, the Choctaws were composed of many subtribes, allies, and satellite groups.

In 1824, Pushmataha and other chiefs journeyed to Washington City to call on the president. His opening speech was to the Secretary of War. At that time, the Indian Service was in the War Department. This speech was to be his last. In it, he reaffirmed the alliance of the Choctaw Nation with the United States: "I can boast and say, and tell the truth, that none of my fathers, or grandfathers, nor any Choctaw, ever drew bows against the United States. They have always been friendly. We have held the hands of the United States so long that our nails are long like the talons of a bird and there is no danger of their slipping out."

Pushmataha was buried in the Old Congressional Cemetery in Washington, D.C. He was a warrior of great distinction. He was wise in council, eloquent in an extraordinary degree; and on all occasions, and under all circumstances, the white man's friend.

NORTH CAROLINA

Eastern Band of Cherokee Indians
Cherokee Council House
P.O. Box 455
Cherokee, NC 28719
(704) 497-2771

Cherokee

Location: The Cherokee Reservation is in western North Carolina, south of Interstate 40, with State Highway 19 running through it.

Public Ceremony or Powwow Dates: Many festivals are held from April through December, including the ongoing festival "Unto These Hills." Please call or write Cherokee Tribal Travel and Promotion at P.O. Box 465, Cherokee, NC 28719, (704) 497-9195 or 1-800-438-1601, for a beautiful full-color kit with *everything* you need to know for a great travel experience with the whole family in Cherokee country.

Art Forms: Nearly all the people spend some of their time doing arts and crafts, producing some of the very finest Native American baskets, pottery, beadwork, finger weavings, stone carvings, and wood carvings.

Visitor Information: Your visit to the Cherokee Indian Reservation will be an adventure in fun and learning. Visit the Oconaluftee Indian Village, a replica of a 1700s Cherokee community featuring guided tours, demonstrations by craftworkers, and the traditional seven-sided Council House. The Museum of the Cherokee Indian tells the story of the Cherokee through the magic of electronics, audiovisual displays, and priceless artifacts. The Qualla Arts and Crafts Mutual next door is nationally known for handmade quality arts and crafts.

Other popular Cherokee attractions include the Cherokee Heritage Museum and Gallery located in Saunooke's Village, the Cyclorama Cherokee Indian Wax Museum, the Museum of the American Indian, and the Pioneer Farmstead Visitor Center located at the Cherokee entrance to the Great Smoky Mountains National Park. A guided visit into the back roads and contemporary life of the Cherokee is available through Smoky Mountain Tours.

In addition, the Cherokee have Santa's Land theme park as well as one of the largest trout farms in the Southeast. They also stock three huge ponds and 30 miles of mountain streams with over a quarter of a million trout per year. Horseback riding, rafting, tubing, and miniature golf are also available.

At night from mid-June through late August, the outdoor drama, "Unto These Hills," portraying the history of the Eastern Band of Cherokee Indians, is presented.

Cherokee forefathers had a very thought-provoking way of looking at life. They believed that the universe was made up of three separate worlds, the Upper World, the Lower World, and the world we live in. This world, a round island resting on the surface of the waters, was suspended from the sky by four cords attached to the island at the four cardinal points of the compass.

Each direction of this world was identified by its own color. According to Cherokee doctrine, east was associated with the color red because it was the direction of the sun, the greatest deity of all. Red was also the color of sacred fire, believed to be directly connected with the sun, with blood, and, therefore, with life. Finally, red was the color of success.

The west was the moon segment. It provided no warmth and was not life-giving as the sun way. So its color was black, which also stood for the region of the souls of the dead and for death itself. North was the direction of cold, and so its color was blue, representing trouble and defeat. South was the direction of warmth. Its color, white, was associated with peace and happiness.

This world hovered somewhere between the perfect order and predictability of the Upper World and the total disorder and instability of the Lower World. Mankind's goal, according to the Cherokees, was to find some kind of halfway path, or balance, between the Upper World and the Lower World while living in this world today. It is not surprising that many Cherokees still believe in an Upper World and a Lower World. The Upper World is called Heaven, the religion is called Christianity, and many denominations are very active on this reservation, both Protestant and Catholic. If you are visiting the reservation on a Sunday, you are welcome to join the Cherokee for Sunday worship at any of their many churches.

Years ago, around the campfires, men and women took their turn telling stories and entertaining the whole tribe. Some stories had serious meanings and others were just for fun. For instance, if you were a young Cherokee boy you would learn that the bears in the Great Smokies were once men, who were transformed into bears by the Great Spirit because they were so lazy. You would learn that the Buzzard is a highly respected bird and that a huge Buzzard formed the Great Smoky Mountains by flying too close to the ground. The valleys of the mountains are where the giant Buzzard's wings hit, pushing the ground down and the mountains up.

If you were sick, your Cherokee Indian mother would explain why. "Man made the animals of the woods angry by killing them. One day, the bears, fishes, deer, reptiles, and birds got together for a meeting and decided to punish man by giving him diseases. When the plants, who were friendly to Man, heard what had been done by the animals, the plants decided to defeat the animal's evil diseases. Each tree, shrub, and herb agreed to furnish a cure for one of the diseases for man. Man had only to figure out which type of plant cured which diseases."

Because the early Cherokee really believed this story, they discovered many, many useful medicines. In fact, some modern-day doctors believe that many of these long-lost Cherokee remedies would be just as effective as, and in some cases more effective than, modern medicines commonly used today.

The Cherokees were once a mighty and powerful nation. At the time when the Cherokee first came into contact with the white man (DeSoto in 1540), they claimed 135,000 square miles of territory covering parts of eight states: North Carolina, South Carolina,

Georgia, Alabama, Tennessee, Kentucky, Virginia, and West Virginia. By the end of the revolution, the Cherokees had lost about half their land. Between 1785 and 1835, the Cherokee lands had shrunk to a few million acres. By the Treaty of New Echota in 1835, all lands east of the Mississippi were ceded to the federal government. (Of the 40 treaties executed with the Cherokees, the federal government chose to break each and every one.) Article 12 of this treaty, as amended, provided that Cherokees who were adverse to removal (about 1,200) could become citizens and remain in the state of North Carolina.

The status of those who remained in the state was anomalous. Their connection with the main body of the Cherokee Nation, which had removed to lands west of the Mississippi, were severed. They became subject to the laws of the state of North Carolina although they were not admitted to the rights of citizenship. Any interest in the lands formerly held by the Nation in North Carolina had been divested by the treaty, and even their right to self-government had ended. North Carolina later granted a charter to the Cherokees authorizing them to exercise limited powers of self-government.

Pressure to force removal of this remnant of Cherokees continued. Funds due them were withheld by the U.S. government unless they would remove to the Indian Territory or would secure an act of the Legislature of North Carolina permitting them to remain permanently within the state. A statute was passed in 1866 granting this permission.

Through purchase by an agent, the Eastern Band of Cherokee Indians acquired the right to possession of tracts of land in North Carolina, and by a North Carolina statute of 1866, they acquired, with the approval of the U.S. government, permission to remain in the state. Cherokee possession of their lands was conveyed to the United States to be held in trust for the Eastern Band. Taking the land into trust status had the effect of establishing Cherokee lands as an Indian reservation and recognizing them as such by the federal government. Although the manner in which the Cherokee Reservation was established is different from the ways in which other reservations were established, the Cherokee Reservation is subject to the same general federal laws and regulations that apply on other Indian reservations.

The lands now held in trust by the U.S. government for the Eastern Band of Cherokee Indians comprise 56,572.8 acres scattered over five counties. It consists of 52 tracts or boundaries, which are contained in 30 completely separated bodies of land. All of the land is held in common by the tribe; possessory holdings are issued to individuals. The Council of the Eastern Band of Cherokee Indians determines the management and control of all real and personal property belonging to the Band, subject to the trust responsibility of the United States.

For the most part, the lands are mountainous with small valleys along the rivers and streams suitable for farming, business, and recreational sites. The elevation varies from 1,718 feet to over 5,000 feet.

The latest official enrollment was conducted in 1982. There were 8,822 enrolled members, with 5,971 living on Eastern Band of Cherokee Indians lands and 2,851 residing off the reservation.

As a federally recognized tribe, the Eastern Band of Cherokee Indians possesses sovereignty over its territory and its members. Like other tribes, the Eastern Band is a sovereign unit of government in its own right. It is neither an instrumentality of the federal government nor a political subdivision of the state government.

Much of the old culture remains, consisting principally of nonmaterial elements. Most, if not all, Cherokees speak or understand English, but the Cherokee language is taught in the homes and elementary schools. Sequoyah's syllabary, which uses symbols of sounds instead of letters or words, has made it possible for this language to be written and taught from text.

Bean dumplings, bean bread, chestnut bread, and ramps are a few native foods that are still commonly eaten in Cherokee homes. Many still cling to the ancient lore and customs. They sing old hymns in their own musical language. Some of the older women wear long full dresses and a bright kerchief tied on their heads. Occasionally, one can see a baby tied on the back of a Cherokee woman.

In earlier times, Cherokees had their own set of laws, they farmed, and they lived in log houses. They made clothing from a type of cloth and did not wear feather headdresses. They introduced corn and tobacco to the white man and used salicylic acid (aspirin) for headaches and had caffeine in their drinks for a "pick-me-up" before Bayer or Coca-Cola was even thought of.

Haliwa-Saponi Tribal Office
P.O. Box 99
Hollister, NC 27844
(919) 584-4017

Location: The Tribal Pottery and Arts is located on Highway 561, twenty miles west of Hollister. Call for hours they will be open.

Art Forms: Pottery, quilts, beadwork, and stonework are offered for sale.

The Saponi are one of the eastern Siouan tribes, formerly living in North Carolina and Virginia. The Saponi were at war with Virginia settlers as early as 1654–1656, the time of the attack by the Cherokee, probably in alliance with them.

SOUTH CAROLINA

Catawba Indian Community
Route 3, Box 324
Rock Hill, SC 29730

Catawba (probably from the Choctaw language Katapa, "divided," "separated," "a division")

Visitor Information: The artisans of this tribe still make pottery and welcome inquiries at their address above.

SOUTHWEST

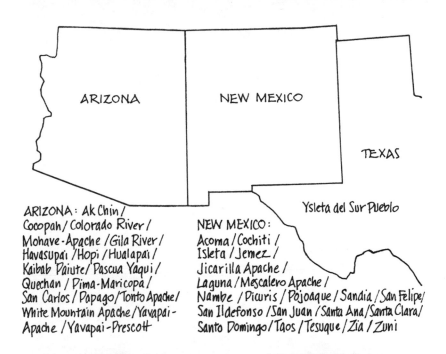

ARIZONA

NEW MEXICO

TEXAS

ARIZONA: Ak Chin / Cocopah / Colorado River / Mohave-Apache / Gila River / Havasupai / Hopi / Hualapai / Kaibab Paiute / Pascua Yaqui / Quechan / Pima-Maricopa / San Carlos / Papago / Tonto Apache / White Mountain Apache / Yavapai-Apache / Yavapai-Prescott

NEW MEXICO: Acoma / Cochiti / Isleta / Jemez / Jicarilla Apache / Laguna / Mescalero Apache / Nambe / Picuris / Pojoaque / Sandia / San Felipe / San Ildefonso / San Juan / Santa Ana / Santa Clara / Santo Domingo / Taos / Tesuque / Zia / Zuni

Ysleta del Sur Pueblo

The Southwest of North America lies in, and south of, that place where the great Rocky Mountains slope down to meet the mesas and deserts. The terrain is rugged and the combination of plains, valleys, mesas, and mountains create breathtaking visual experiences while the sunsets and cloud formations often combine to create indescribable beauty.

This is the land of the People of the Villages, the Pueblo People. And it is the land of the nomadic and mysterious Apache. And it is the land of those people who live in hogans in the desolate and isolated deserts and mesas, the Navajo.

The Southwest People are descendants of a proud and great culture. The ruins of villages can be found throughout the area, and sacred prayer sites are found in the mountains, valleys, and mesas. These people are now, as they have always been, spiritually attuned with their environment and respectful of the natural ways of life.

You can feel the spirit of the old ones in this land. Stand on a mesa and lift up your arms and your heart to the Creator and a feeling of awe for the Creation will overwhelm your being. This is the land of original life.

Before the coming of the European, this land was unspoiled and untouched by pollution. The Southwest People planted their crops with prayers and respect for the Creator of all life. They hunted for food with prayers and respect for the spirits of the animals that gave their lives for food. And they gathered food and herbs for medicine with offerings and thanks for these blessings from the Creator. Religion was not a part of their life; spirituality was their whole life. The old ones taught the young ones in ceremony, in the deserts, in the village kivas, and in the mountains by sacred lakes and streams, the wisdom of the goodness of life and that life is valuable only when it is good.

They developed one of the greatest cultures ever to exist on our Mother Earth. Their art forms were beautiful and functional. Pottery, turkey feather quilts, cotton cloth and buckskin for clothing, weavings, and stone jewelry were all refined to a fine degree. They utilized their resources without waste and gave thanks with every breath for the goodness provided to them by the Creator. They traded their artworks with the Plains People for buffalo meat and horses.

And they played the drum, the heartbeat of our Mother Earth, in their ceremonies while the people danced in honor of the Creator and all living things. They danced in thanks for good crops and good harvest and all the things the Creator provides through respect and love.

The sacred winds blow even today in the Southwest. The Southwest People still celebrate life in ceremony and praise of the Creator and the Creation.

You are welcome to join with the Southwest People and attend sacred ceremonies. As visitors, you are asked to stay in public areas only. Photographing, videotaping, tape recording, and sketching are not allowed unless specifically permitted by the people you are visiting. Navajo families determine etiquette of the particular ceremony you are attending, but be sure you obtain permission before invading their privacy. The Apaches also frown on photography or recording of their rituals. The Hopi ban any photography, recording, sketching, or videotaping on their reservation unless express permission is given. Always ask tribal officials before ceremonies begin for the proper etiquette to follow.

Shorts, halter tops, and short skirts are not proper attire at ceremonials, and spectators should remain silent and respectful. Women who are on their moon should also refrain from attending ceremonies.

Join with the tribes on the following pages to honor their ancestors and to honor our Creator, our Mother Earth, our Moon, our Sun, and the whole of all living things in the whole of all Creation. You will find that it is good. It is very, very good.

Aho . . .

You must speak straight so that your words may go as sunlight to our hearts.

—Cochise (Apache)

There is one God looking down upon us all.

—Geronimo (Apache)

ARIZONA

Ak Chin Indian Community
Route 2, Box 27
Maricopa, AZ 85239
(602) 568-2227

Pima
Maricopa

Location: The Ak Chin community is located straight south of Phoenix at Maricopa.

Public Ceremony or Powwow Dates: The Feast of St. Francis is held October 4th each year, and it is a major holiday on many reservations because it honors St. Francis, who loved nature. There will be chile stew, flour tortillas, beans, fry bread, corn, and kool-aid served. The afternoon and evening will be filled with traditional dances, in which more than 500 dancers usually participate.

Art Forms: The Pima are outstanding basket weavers, and the pottery of the Maricopa is ranked with the best in the Southwest. Look for their work at the Gila River Arts and Crafts Museum at Sacaton, Arizona. Take Interstate 10 and exit at Casa Blanca at Exit 175; telephone (602) 963-3981.

Visitor Information: Don't miss the dances. It is a moving celebration.

Cocopah Tribal Council
P.O. Box Bin "G"
Somerton, AZ 85350
(602) 627-2102

Cocopah

Location: The reservation is located south of Yuma at Somerton.

Unidentified man and woman, Pima, ca. 1883
Photo by Ben Wittick; Courtesy Museum of New Mexico, Neg. No. 102058

Public Ceremony or Powwow Dates: The annual Cocopah Festivities Day is held in March or April. There is traditional dancing and singing, including the Rabbit Dance and Round Dances.

Art Forms: You can find good beadwork and fine gourd rattles at the festival. Also, the Cocopah Elderly Center on Cedar Street on the reservation has a small gift shop that sells ribbon shirts, beadwork, and other arts and crafts. Telephone 627-2632 for more details. The traditional singers from this community often sing at memorial services, but there are also occasions when they do sing for the public.

Visitor Information: There are plans for a museum at the Yuma Territorial Mall.

Colorado River Tribal Council
Route 1, Box 23B
Parker, AZ 85344
(602) 669-9211

Mojave
Chemehuevi
Navajo
Hopi

Location: To find the museum, go two miles south of Parker, and at 2nd and Mojave streets turn off toward the hospital.

Art Forms: Baskets and modern arts and crafts are offered for sale in the gift shop.

Visitor Information: The first two tribes, the Mojave and Chemehuevi, are the original people of this area. The museum offers a collection of ancient and modern arts and crafts, a library, a gift shop, and cultural collections.

These tribes are in the process of developing commercial enterprises and currently are operating the Blue Water Marine Park, a mobile home park, a charter air service, and large-scale farming.

Big Frank (Frank Tehanna), Cocopa, 1900
Photo by DeLancey Gill; Courtesy Museum of New Mexico, Neg. No. 59448

Fort McDowell Mohave-Apache Council
P.O. Box 17779
Fountain Hills, AZ 85268
(602) 990-0995

Mohave-Apache

Location: This reservation is a suburb of the city of Phoenix and is located in the northeast part of the city.

Gila River Indian Community Council
P.O. Box 97
Sacaton, AZ 85247
(602) 562-3311

Pima
Maricopa

Location: This reservation is located south of Phoenix. Take Interstate 10 south and exit the freeway at Casa Blanca. Take Exit 175 and drive to Sacaton.

Public Ceremony or Powwow Dates: There is usually a festival held the second weekend in March. There is traditional Pima dancing with crafts demonstrations, foods, and other interesting events. Call the Gila River Arts and Crafts Museum at (602) 963-3981 for dates and times.

Art Forms: The Pima make fine baskets, and the Maricopa make some of the best pottery to be found in the Southwest. The gift shop at the Gila Arts and Crafts Museum sells arts and crafts from over 30 tribes in the Southwest, California, and Mexico.

Visitor Information: There is a great restaurant here which serves Indian food. The outdoor museum displays reconstructed houses of the Pima, Maricopa, Apache, and Papago.

Havasupai Tribal Council
P.O. Box 10
Supai, AZ 86435
(602) 448-2961

Havasupai

Location: The tribal offices are in Supai, which is located in the bottom of the Grand Canyon. Drive from Peach Springs to the canyon rim and leave your vehicle. Hike the eight miles down to the reservation or call from the phone at the rim to make arrangements for mules or horses available for rent from the tribe. This is the most advisable way because the hike back up and out of the canyon can be a challenge.

Public Ceremony or Powwow Dates: The Peach Festival is held in August, and dances are often held on Memorial Day. Call the tribal office for dates and times.

Visitor Information: This is an unusual opportunity to experience a place that is not accessible by modern means. Arrange your visit ahead of time with the tribally owned Havasupai Tourist Enterprise in Supai. You will enjoy the beauty of the area. If you've seen the Grand Canyon and liked it, you will love the trip to Havasupai country.

Hopi Tribal Council
P.O. Box 123
Kykotsmovi, AZ 86039
(602) 734-2445

Hopi

Location: The mesa villages are located on State Highway 264 in northeast Arizona.

Public Ceremony or Powwow Dates: Kachina dances are held from late winter to midsummer, but the dates are usually not set more than two or three weeks in advance. Inquiries about dates and places may be addressed to the Hopi Cultural Center, P.O. Box 67, Second Mesa, AZ 86043; telephone (602) 734-2401. Remember, no alcohol, no drugs, and no photographs or tape-recordings can be made without the approval of the tribal office. Be respectful of the ceremonies and the people.

Art Forms: The Hopi have never faltered in their respect for the arts. They create pottery, baskets, jewelry, paintings (both traditional subject matter and very progressive), and cottonwood root carvings of Kachina dolls. Traditional Hopi people do not approve of the sale of Kachina dolls, so you may not wish to purchase any yourself. However, the artists feel that they are preserving the culture and they need the income so it is a matter of your own heart.

Da-wa-uni-ci, Mishongnovi Pueblo, Hopi, Arizona, 1901
Photo by Carl N. Werntz; Courtesy Museum of New Mexico, Neg. No. 37536

Visitor Information: I recommend that you stay with the tribe in their Cultural Center Motel and Restaurant. There is traditional Indian food, and the lodging is excellent. A guide is required to visit Walpi, on First Mesa, along State Route 264 at Polacca. Drive to the top of the mesa (leave motor homes and buses) and arrange for a guide at the Village Information Office, at the entrance to Walpi village (9:00 a.m. to 5:00 p.m. daily, no telephone). No fee will be charged to enter the reservation, but a donation is always appreciated.

The Hopi have lived in the Southwest for more than 2,000 years; their ancestors were called the Anasazi. When Coronado entered the Southwest in 1540, the might of the Spanish with their guns and horses enslaved the Hopi and their spiritual ceremonial life was altered.

They were forced to close their kivas (circular underground ceremonial chambers), and their sacred Kachina dances were prohibited. The Hopi, normally pacifist in nature, then joined with the other New Mexico pueblos in a successful revolt in 1680 that drove the Spanish from the country. About twenty years later the mission at Awatovi was rebuilt by the Spanish, but, as before, the mission was ultimately destroyed by tribal members. During the next two hundred years, serious droughts diminished their crops. Raids by the Navajo, Apache, and Ute slowly reduced the membership of the tribe. Then smallpox, brought by the Europeans in the 1800s, almost destroyed them entirely.

Today, the tribe has over 9,000 members and the reservation covers over one and a half million acres of high plateau country. Completely surrounded by the gigantic Navajo Reservation, most of the people of the tribe live on three mesas near the center of the reservation. Three long fingers of land several miles apart stick up from the valley floor, and they are named from east to west, First Mesa, Second Mesa, and Third Mesa. On the top of each one are the three ancient Hopi villages and at the base of each one are the three modern communities.

The people are friendly and courteous, but please contact the tribe for a guide before entering. The Hopi Mesa villages are constructed of stone, not adobe as most of the New Mexico Pueblos. Many Hopi prefer to live in the traditional villages despite the inconveniences. The people still use wood and coal for cooking and heating, but some homes have electricity. Many Hopi still farm the valleys below by hand with a planting stick as did their ancestors. Corn can be seen growing out of sand along hillsides and along dry creek beds. The power of prayers and ceremony cannot be overlooked. The corn is typical "Indian corn" in shades of blue, gold, maroon, and yellow. It is dried in the sun and ground into meal. Some of the fields are irrigated from springs, but most Hopi farmers practice dry farming. Small fields of corn, melons, beans, and squash flourish in almost impossible places. Again, the power of prayer and ceremony is the power of growth.

While they retain many ancient traditions, the Hopi have faced many changes over the years, as have all Indian people. Arts and crafts provide more personal income than any other source on the reservation. Jobs are hard to find and the young people often move to urban areas to obtain work or more education. Many return to Hopiland to take part in ceremonies or to stay. The HUD houses below the mesas are typical of housing in rural communities.

The old stone pueblo villages on the mesas endure the passage of time and sacred places are undisturbed. Prayer feathers and eagle feathers awaiting some upcoming ceremonial are tied in crevices among the dwellings. Stacks of gray dry cedar from juniper trees are waiting to be burned in outside ovens to bake traditional Indian bread.

Hopi ceremonials are intertwined with the everyday life of the people. One will not exist without the other. Kachina ceremonies are conducted to maintain the harmony of the world and satisfy the spirits of man, animals, rocks, trees, and all living things in the whole of all the Creation. The Kachinas are the embodiment of the spirits and all Hopi life revolves around the proper performance and completeness of these spiritual ceremonies. The dancers who portray the Kachinas do ancient rituals after days of fasting and secret ceremony in the Kiva. The dances, in the end, are always offered to the Creator in praise and thanks and celebration for good crops, good health, well-being, and the welfare of all living things.

The Kachinas live in the San Francisco peaks near Flagstaff and only come to Hopiland for the ceremonials. The Hopi, being among the most spiritually oriented of the people, celebrate in a regular fashion. The Wuwuchim, or New Year, is held on the eve of the new moon in November. It is among the most important of rituals because it establishes the rhythms for the year to come. For four days, prayers, songs, and dances for a prosperous and safe new year are led by the priests (Hopi Medicine People) before the Kivas in their respective villages. The men of the tribe dance bare-chested, dressed in embroidered Hopi cotton kilts. Priests, from the Bear Clan, chant about the time before there were Hopi people, the time of Creation. It is a re-creation of the Creation; the time of the Creator's introduction of Hopi into the world.

The winter solstice celebration, December 21 and 22, is in ceremonial fashion the creation of the Hopi universe. The priests of the Bear Clan bless prayer feathers for the protection of the people. Traditionally, eagle feathers were used, but now, to protect the endangered species, turkey feathers are used.

The Hopi people follow a matrilineal society. The Basket Dances are held from late October through November. These dances remember the time when all the men were gone from the villages and the women kept the spiritual life of the people whole.

There are three different societies, each with their own dance and outfits. The Mamzaw is the group that represents the Hopi Spirituality. The women wear the headdress and costume, but not the mask of the Kachinas, representing various spirits that are in Hopi ceremonies. These ceremonies that take place in the plazas of the villages are the most popular of the year because the women throw little gifts from the baskets when they dance. People scramble for the houseware items, groceries, and baskets because it is close to the new year and it is time to renew and forget the old year.

Each individual village sponsors the dances that are called social dances. They are held from August to mid-October, to celebrate the good harvest and to give the young people the opportunity to mingle. The dances are open to young women, as long as they are not married and have no children, and even young children of both sexes. Among the most popular of the dances is the Butterfly, for which the men are outfitted in embroidered kilts and velvet shirts with ribbons. The dances usually take place on weekends, from about 10:00 a.m. until about 6:00 p.m. Competition dancers from neighboring villages often drop by and the dancing can be fierce.

Enjoy your visit in Hopiland.

Hualapai Tribal Council
P.O. Box 168
Peach Springs, AZ 86434
(602) 769-2216

Walapai

Location: Peach Springs is located northeast of Kingman on old Route 66.

Public Ceremony or Powwow Dates: There are traditional dances held, but you must check with the tribal office for dates and times. The women are beautiful as they dance to Bird Songs. There is also a powwow in August.

Art Forms: The women wear long traditional dresses with beaded collars.

Visitor Information: The tribe is engaged in cattle raising and lumbering, and they operate Hualapai Grand Canyon Outfitters, which will take you on an exciting rafting trip down the Grand Canyon. Call the number above for more details.

Kaibab-Paiute Tribal Council
Tribal Affairs Building
Pipe Springs, AZ 86022
(602) 643-7245

Kaibab Paiute

Location: The Kaibab Indian Reservation is in the northwest corner of Arizona, 14 miles west of Freedonia.

Visitor Information: The tribe owns and operates an RV park for visitors to the reservation. It is a modern facility that includes a laundromat and a store. Pipe Springs National Monument is located on the reservation. It is the site of a fort from the days of the Indian wars.

The tribe plans to build a museum of Paiute culture and history.

Sam Yazzie, Navajo, Pine Springs, Arizona, 1938
Courtesy Museum of New Mexico, Neg. No. 29934

Navajo Tribal Council
P.O. Box 308
Window Rock, AZ 86515
(602) 871-4941

Dene

Location: The Navajo Indian Reservation is in the four corners area of the United States (where Utah, Arizona, Colorado, and New Mexico have a common corner). Tribal headquarters are located in Window Rock. Navajo Community College is located in Tsaile. Monument Valley Navajo Tribal Park is north of Kayenta. Navajo Nation Visitor Centers are located in Cameron, Chinle, and Monument Valley. Kinlichee Navajo Tribal Park is eight miles east of Gando.

Public Ceremony or Powwow Dates: The Northern Navajo Fair in Shiprock, New Mexico, is one of three major Navajo fairs that take place during the year. Indians from all over the whole of Turtle Island gather for this powwow, which features competitions in traditional song and dance. This one is usually the first weekend in October. Other powwows are held throughout the year and you can find one somewhere on this huge reservation almost any weekend. Call the tribal office for places and times.

Traditional dances are also held regularly all over this reservation. Most are healing ceremony dances, and visitors may be allowed with the family's permission. Again, no pictures or sketching or tape recordings are allowed without the express permission of the medicine people or family involved in the ceremony.

Art Forms: Of course, the Navajo are famous for their fine rugs and jewelry and sand paintings, but they also do fine pottery and other traditional forms of functional arts. The Navajo Nation Arts and Crafts Enterprise is just east of Window Rock, at the junction of Highway 264 and Navajo Highway 12. Owned by the Navajo Nation, this is the home of authentic Indian arts and crafts. Also, the people sell their fine arts at the four corners area and along the highways throughout the reservation.

Visitor Information: Contact the Navajo Tourism Office, P.O. Box 308, Window Rock, AZ 86515, (602) 871-6436, for more information about lodging, restaurants, arts and crafts, dances, powwows, and other activities.

When I worked with Nelson Lewis, a fine sand painter from Shiprock, on a sand painting for the film *The Primal Mind* at the Ghost Ranch near Abiquiu, New Mexico, we worked for three days to protect this delicate art form. But it is much more than an art form. It is a cleansing and healing ceremony. When it is used for the healing of one that is ill, the Hataali, or singer, who conducts the ceremony may direct several others who are his helpers. When it is done as an art form for demonstrations with the public present, these are the steps taken in the process: First, the ground is brushed clean and flattened if necessary. Then the layer of sand that is used for the base or foundation is spread. Finely ground charcoal, corn meal, pollen, mudstone, gypsum, and turquoise run like small streams through the artist's fingers to form the spirits of animals, plants, sunbeams, and rainbows. Working from the center out in circles in the ways of Creation, he creates the intricate painting, leaving the east side open for the spirit people to enter. The painting will not be correct in form and style as a healing painting would be in order not to offend the spirits. If he did a healing painting for demonstration purposes, he would lose the ability to do the real thing when it was needed. But only the medicine people notice what is missing and what may have been added. With the commercialization of sand paintings, the art is no longer confined to the singer; anyone can do the art.

Even before sand paintings were being done for commercial purposes, there were about 1,200 designs used in a wide range of ceremonies that varied with the illness being treated.

With the Dene, illness in a person's body means that there is disharmony in the universe and the cleansing and healing ceremony of the sand painting to call the spirits to heal the patient is putting things back in an orderly way.

The sand painting may be as small as a foot in diameter or as large as 12 feet in diameter but most are about 6 by 6 feet, approximately the floor area of the average hogan (house). Often the painting will take hours to complete even with several helpers. When the painting is finished, the ill person sits on it and the singer transforms the orderly, clean, goodness of the painting into the patient and puts the illness from the patient into the painting. The sand painting is discarded afterward.

The whole ceremony can last from three to nine days, depending on the illness, accident, or catastrophe being treated. The

Ralph Gray and family, Navajo, September 1935
Courtesy Museum of New Mexico, Neg. No. 42219

name of one of the more common ceremonies is the Wind Way, which is sung over several days to treat several diseases, including those related to the eyes. The Mountain Way, another long ceremony, is performed to treat problems with the stomach.

Both commercial and sacred sand paintings use natural pigments on a tan sand base, resulting in pictures largely composed of earth tones, with some black, white, red, and yellow for strength. Both feature angular figures, made of straight lines and zigzags. Both are traditionally bordered on at least three sides, either with a straight or circular design. Subject matter, in addition to the Navajo spirits and scenery, are animals, the sun, the sky, and rainbows.

The most popular design includes sticklike figures (the spirits) adorned with belts, jewelry, skirts, and carrying bows and arrows. Sacred spirit animals like bears, coyotes, deer, and eagles frequently are drawn, as are plants such as corn, beans, squash, and tobacco. Although snakes are sacred, they are usually not found in Dene artwork because they represent danger. All the figures are geometric in design.

Today men and women both make sand paintings for sale, but the sacred ones used in healing are done by men only. Prices can range from about $3.00 to several thousand dollars and in size from about 6 by 6 inches to several feet square.

The first ones released in the 1960s are becoming collector's items because they were permanently mounted on particle board and they contain echoes from the ceremonies in color and design. In the 1970s, other figures began showing up in the paintings, and now in the 1980s, they are becoming more colorful and diverse than ever.

Some of the dances conducted in Navajo land are the Yei-Bei-Chei dances. These are for healing and are prescribed by a medicine man; therefore, they are sporadic in nature and there will only be about two weeks notice. These dances most often occur in fall and continue through the spring and winter months. They are rarely performed in summer. The patient is placed within the ceremonial hogan with the singer and his helpers chanting prayers, while dancers, usually 15 or 16 teams of eleven members each, dance throughout the night. The dancing is done in everyday clothes until the final two nights, when full outfits with special headgear and rattles are used to represent various spirits.

The Fire Dance Ceremony, like the Yei-Bei-Chei, is also a nine-day healing ceremony and also largely restricted to tribal members. This dance is rarely performed. It is important to note that the sponsoring family must give permission to attend the dances described here. If you happen to be on the site, you could be asked to leave.

Some good fictional accounts of the Navajo can be found in books by Tony Hillerman.

Pascua Yaqui Tribal Council
7474 S. Camino de Oeste
Tucson, AZ 85746
(602) 883-2838

Yaqui

Location: The Yaqui were originally Mexican Indians, but many have resettled in Arizona and are recognized by the U.S. government. Most live in or near Tucson or Phoenix. The reservation address is listed above.

Public Ceremony or Powwow Dates: During Holy Week, the Yaqui perform a selection of dances. Some are influenced by the Spanish, but the Deer Dance that they do is very Indian and the deer impersonators dance with gourd hand rattles and Mexican Indian leg rattles.

Art Forms: The Yaqui produce Deer Dance statues and paintings of their culture.

Visitor Information: The tribe operates a landscape nursery, charcoal packing business, and a bingo enterprise on their reservation.

The Lenten Ceremonies at the Pascua-Yaqui Reservation are a hybrid of Christian and Yaqui beliefs. Accepting the crucifixion and resurrection of Jesus while rejecting the dogma of the evangelizing Jesuits, the Yaqui tribe has fashioned an annual Passion Play that expresses their faith.

Every Friday, beginning after Ash Wednesday and continuing to Holy Week, the community makes the Stations of the Cross in 14 venues outside the church and with people playing the parts in each complex tableau under the leadership of an Indian priest, called the maestro. This continues until the Saturday night before

Palm Sunday when groups of Indian societies, numbering 300 or 400, converge and dance until dawn, whereupon palms are distributed to the participants. This intertribal ceremony begins a Holy Week whose key events are again reenacted, with effigies of the Roman soldiers and Judas being burned in bonfires that light up the countryside on Holy Saturday and burn until Easter Sunday dawns over the rocky landscape.

Ceremonies are open to visitors in Guadalupe Village, near Phoenix, and at Old Pasqua Village, Barrio Libre, and the Pasqua-Yaqui Reservation, all in or around Tucson.

Quechan Tribal Council
P.O. Box 1352
Yuma, AZ 85364
(619) 572-0213

Quechan

Location: The Quechan Indian Reservation is actually located in California. To get there from Yuma, take the old bridge across the river. Obtain a map from the Chamber of Commerce at 377 Main, Yuma, AZ 85364, telephone (602) 782-2567.

Art Forms: In the museum there are displays of Quechan clay dolls, pottery, bows, arrowheads, cradleboards, and other arts and crafts.

Visitor Information: Fishing permits are available from the tribal office, and there is a bingo enterprise for those who like to gamble.

The Quechan or Yuma (they prefer Euqchan) people have been in control of the river crossing here for centuries, and this relationship with both the Spanish and United States military is explained in the museum.

Salt River Pima-Maricopa Indian Community
Route 1, Box 216
Scottsdale, AZ 85256
(602) 941-7277

Pima ("no," in the Nevome dialect, a word incorrectly applied through misunderstanding by the early missionaries)
Maricopa (they call themselves Pipatsji, "people," Maricopa being their Pima name)

The Pima are a division of the Piman family living in the valleys of the Gila and Salt in southern Arizona. The Pima call themselves A-a tam, "the people." According to tradition, the Pima tribe had its genesis in the Salt River Valley, later extending its settlements into the valley of the Gila; but a deluge came, leaving a single survivor, a specially favored chief named Ciho, or Soho, the progenitor of the present tribe. One of his descendants, Sivano, who had 20 wives, erected as his own residence the now ruined adobe structure called Casa Grande (called Sivanoki, "house of Sivano") and built other massive pueblo groups in the valleys of the Gila and Salt.

The Maricopa, an important Yuman tribe, have lived with and below the Pima since the early nineteenth century. They joined the Pima for mutual protection against the Yuma, and the two have lived together in peace.

San Carlos Tribal Council
P.O. Box 0
San Carlos, AZ 85550
(602) 475-2361

Apache (probably from apachu, "enemy," the Zuni name for the Navajo, who were designated "Apaches de Nabaju" by the early Spaniards in New Mexico)

Location: The reservation is located at San Carlos, Arizona.

Public Ceremony or Powwow Dates: The girls' rites and mountain spirit dances are held throughout the summer. Call the tribal office for those that are open to the public. The tribal fair is held over Veterans Day weekend and this will also include traditional dancing.

The tribe numbered 1,172 in 1909. The name Apache has little ethnic significance, having been applied officially to those Apache living on the Gila River in Arizona and sometimes referred to also as Gilenos, or Gila Apache.

Na-tu-ende, Apache
Photo by Ben Wittick; Courtesy Museum of New Mexico, Neg. No. 15910

Tohono O'Odham Council
P.O. Box 837
Sells, AZ 85634
(603) 383-2221

Papago (from papah, "beans," ootam, "people": "beansmen," "bean-people"; hence, Spanish Frijoleros)

Location: The tribal office is in Sells, Arizona.

Public Ceremony or Powwow Dates: The Papago dance at the O'Odham Tash Indian Celebration at Casa Grande, Arizona, in February. Memorial Day weekend will find them dancing at the Morongo Indian Reservation in California. Easter provides the opportunity for them to dance at Mission San Xavier del Bac on the Friday following Easter Sunday.

Art Forms: Arts and crafts are sold during the O'Odham Tash at Casa Grande.

Visitor Information: There is also a rodeo, contemporary Indian bands, parade, barbecue, and dancing at the O'Odham Tash. To find Mission San Xavier del Bac, drive 10 miles south of Tucson on San Xavier Road, just off Highway I-19. The mission telephone number is (602) 294-2624; they can give you more information.

The Papago are a Piman tribe, closely allied to the Pima, whose original home was the territory south and southeast of the Gila River, especially south of Tucson, in the main and tributary valleys of the Rio Santa Cruz and extending west and southwest across the desert known as the Papagueria, into Sonora, Mexico. Because of the harshness of their land, they were not inclined to village life. The Papago subsisted by agriculture, and maize, beans, and cotton were their chief crops, which they cultivated using irrigation. Many desert plants also contributed to their food supply, especially mesquite, the beans of which were eaten, and the saguaro, pitahaya, or giant cactus (Cereus giganteus), from whose fruit they made preserves and a syrup. The tribe once traded extensively in salt, taken from the great inland lagoons. Their principal crops were wheat and barley, and they also raised stock. Later, many earned a livelihood by working as laborers, especially on railroads and irrigation ditches.

The Papago are tall and dark complexioned. Their dialect is close to the Pima, and their habits and customs are generally similar except that the men wear their hair only to the shoulders. Like the Pima, the Papago women are expert basketmakers, and the designs and patterns of the pottery and the basketry are the same as those of the Pima. One of their favorite games, played with four sticks, was that known as kings (Spanish, quince, "fifteen"), which they called ghin-skoot (probably derived from the same word).

Traditionally, their typical dwelling was dome shaped, consisting of a framework of saplings, thatched with grass or leafy shrubs, with an adjacent shelter or ramada. These lodges were from 12 to 20 feet in diameter, and sometimes the roof is flattened and covered with earth.

In 1906, the Papago in the United States numbered 4,981. In addition, 859 Papago were officially reported in Sonora, Mexico, in 1900, but this was probably a low estimate.

Tonto Apache Tribal Council
Tonto Reservation #30
Payson, AZ 85541
(602) 474-5000

Public Ceremony or Powwow Dates: The people of this tribe have joined together and are presenting public dances during the Fourth of July at the Flagstaff, Arizona, Coconino Center for the Arts. The Camp Verde Apache, (602) 567-5276, are also participating in these presentations. They are from Camp Verde, Arizona.

White Mountain Apache Tribal Council
P.O. Box 700
Whiteriver, AZ 85941
(602) 338-4346

Apache (probably from apachu, "enemy," the Zuni name for the Navajo, who were designated "Apaches de Nabaju" by the early Spaniards in New Mexico)

Location: The reservation is south of Show Low.

Public Ceremony or Powwow Dates: The Apache Tribal Fair is usually held over Labor Day weekend and features mountain spirit dances. Other dances and girls' puberty rites are held most weekends during July and August. Call the tribal office for celebrations that are open to the public.

Art Forms: Traditional arts and crafts can be found by phoning the tribal office.

Visitor Information: The reservation is in the most scenic part of southeast Arizona. It is great for skiers, hunters, fishermen, and campers. The tribe operates the Sunrise Ski Resort, which is open year-round. This resort is three miles south of McNary, telephone (602) 334-2144. Less expensive accommodations can be found at the White Mountain Apache Motel and Restaurant at Whiteriver, telephone (602) 338-4927. Be sure to contact the tribal office for hunting and fishing permits. Other attractions include the ancient Kinishba Ruins, Geromimo's Cave, and the fish hatchery.

This is a tribe of the Athapascan family. The name has been applied also to some unrelated Yuman tribes, as the Apache Mohave (Yavapai) and Apache Yuma. The Apache call themselves N'de, Dine, Tinde, or Inde, "people." their numbers have increased since the beginning of the seventeenth century, apparently because they took captives from other tribes, particularly, the Pueblos, Pima, and Papago. They were first mentioned as Apache in 1598, although Coronado, in 1541, met the Querechos (the Vaqueros of Benavides, and probably the Jicarillas and Mescaleros of modern times) on the plains of eastern New Mexico and western Texas. Apparently, the Apache did not reach Arizona until after the middle of the sixteenth century. From the time of the Spanish colonization of New Mexico until the late 1800s, they were noted for their warlike disposition, raiding white and Indian settlements alike and extending their territory as far southward as Jalisco, Mexico. Although most of the Apache have been hostile since they have been known to history, the most serious outbreaks in modern times have been attributed to mismanagement on the part of civil authorities. The most important hostilities in the 1800s were those of the Chiricahua under Cochise, and later Victorio, who, together with 500 Mimbrenos, Mogollones, and Mescaleros, were assigned, about 1870, to the Ojo Caliente reserve in western New Mexico. Cochise, who had repeatedly refused to be confined within reservation limits, fled with his band but returned in 1871, at which time 1,200 to 1,900 Apache were on the reservation.

Complaints from neighboring settlers resulted in their removal

Nalte, Coyotero Apache, on left; Gudi-ze-eh, San Carlos Apache, on right; ca. 1883
Photo by Ben Wittick; Courtesy Museum of New Mexico, Neg. No. 15900

to Tularosa, 60 miles to the northwest, but 1,000 fled to the Mescalero reserve on Pecos River, while Cochise went out on another raid. In accordance with the wishes of the Indians, they were returned to Ojo Caliente in 1874. Cochise died soon afterward. In the following year, the Chiricahua reservation in Arizona was abolished. Three hundred twenty-five Indians were removed to the San Carlos Agency; others went to Ojo Caliente; and some either remained on the mountains of their old reservation or fled across the Mexican border. This removal of Indians from their ancestral homes was a matter of government policy. In April 1877, Geronimo and other chiefs, with the remnant of the band left on the old reservation, and evidently the Mexican refugees, began raiding in southern Arizona and northern Chihuahua, but in May, 433 were captured and returned to San Carlos.

At the same time, the policy of removal was applied to the Ojo Caliente Apache of New Mexico. But when the plan was put in action, only 450 of 2,000 Indians were found, the remainder having formed bands under Victorio. After considerable conflict, in February 1878, Victorio surrendered in the hope that he and his people might remain on their former reservation, but another attempt was made to force the Indians to go to San Carlos, with the same result. Just when arrangements were finally made for them to settle there, the local authorities indicted Victorio and others for murder and robbery. With his few immediate followers and some Mescaleros, Victorio fled from the reservation and resumed marauding. There were numerous skirmishes, and even when he was outnumbered, Victorio held his own. Victorio eluded capture and fled across the border, where he continued his victorious campaign. Pressed on both sides of the international boundary, and at times harassed by U.S. and Mexican troops combined, Victorio finally suffered severe losses and his band became divided. In October 1880, Mexican troops encountered Victorio's party, comprising 100 warriors, with 400 women and children, at Tres Castillos; the Indians were surrounded and attacked in the evening, and the fight continued throughout the night. In the morning, the Indians' ammunition was exhausted. Although rapidly losing strength, the remnant refused to surrender until Victorio, who had been wounded several times, finally fell dead.

Victorio was succeeded by Nana, who collected the divided force, received reinforcements from the Mescaleros and the San Carlos Chiricahua, and continued the Indian campaigns against

Cha-si-to (son of Bonito) with mescal fiddle, Warm Springs Apache, ca. 1883
Photo by Ben Wittick; Courtesy Museum of New Mexico, Neg. No. 15899

the whites. Geronimo participated in these hostilities until he and his band finally surrendered September 4, 1886, and with numerous friendly Apache, were sent to Florida as prisoners. They were later taken to Mt. Vernon, Alabama, and then to Ft. Sill, Oklahoma. Apache hostility in Arizona and New Mexico had ceased by 1902.

A nomadic people, the Apache practiced agriculture only to a limited extent before their permanent establishment on reservations. They subsisted chiefly by hunting and on roots (especially that of the maguey) and berries. Although fish and bear were found in abundance in their country, eating them was taboo. Their dwellings were shelters of brush, which were easily erected by the women and were well adapted to their arid environment and constant shifting.

Yavapai-Apache Community Council
P.O. Box 1188
Camp Verde, AZ 86322
(602) 567-3649

Yavapai

Location: The Yavapai-Apache Visitor Center is in central Arizona on Interstate 17. Take the middle Verde exit, then go one quarter mile east.

Public Ceremony or Powwow Dates: The Camp Verde Apaches began dancing for the public recently and they sometimes perform the Mountain Spirit Dance. Call the tribal office for more details.

Visitor Information: The exhibits in the visitor center offer traditional and modern styles of life of the people of this tribe. A film offers interesting examples of their past and present life. Call the Yavapai Community College at Prescott for more details.

Yavapai-Prescott Community Council
P.O. Box 348
Prescott, AZ 86301
(602) 445-8790

Yavapai (said to be from enyaeva, "sun," pai, "people": "people of the sun")

Location: The reservation is on the edge of Prescott.

The Yavapai are a Yuman tribe, popularly known as Apache Mojave and Mojave Apache, that is, "hostile or warlike Mojave." Before its removal to the Rio Verde Agency in May 1873, the tribe claimed as its territory the valley of the Rio Verde and the Black Mesa from the Salt River as far as Bill Williams Mountain in western Arizona. They then numbered about 1,000. Earlier, they ranged much farther west, appearing to have had rancherias on the Rio Colorado. In spring 1875, they were placed under San Carlos Apache Agency. In 1890, most of the tribe drifted from the San Carlos Reservation and settled in part of their old home on the Rio Verde, including the abandoned Camp McDowell military reservation. By 1903, there were said to be between 500 and 600 (but probably including Yuma and Apache), scattered in small bands from Camp McDowell to the head of the Rio Verde. By Executive Order of September 15, 1903, the old reservation was set aside for their use, the claims of the white settlers being purchased under the act of April 21, 1904. In 1905, tuberculosis was responsible for considerable mortality. In 1910, there were about 550 Mojave Apache and Yavapai.

NEW MEXICO INDIAN EVENTS

Event	Pueblo
January		
1	Turtle, Corn and various other dances	(Most pueblos) or Taos, Santo Domingo, San Felipe, Cochiti, Santa Ana, Picuris
6	King's Day and installation of new Governors and officials. Deer, Buffalo, Eagle, Elk Dance	Most northern and southern pueblos
23	Annual feast day in honor of San Ildefonso, Comanche, Buffalo and Deer Dance	San Ildefonso
25	Various Dances	Picuris
27	Basket Dance	San Juan
February		
1st week	Governor's Feast, various dances	Acoma
2	Candelaria Day Celebration. Buffalo and various dances	San Felipe and other pueblos
4–5	Los Comanches Dance	Taos
Date set each year	Deer Dance	San Juan
Date set each year	Deer and Buffalo Dance	Santa Clara
Date set each year	Evergreen Dance	Isleta

March

19	St. Joseph's Feast. Harvest and Social Dance	Old Laguna Village
Easter	Various Dances	Most pueblos

April

19–20	Eight Northern Indian Pueblos Spring Arts and Crafts Show	De Vargas Mall, Santa Fe

May

1	Annual Feast Day in honor of St. Phillip. Green Corn Dance	San Felipe
3	Santa Cruz Day (Coming of the Rivermen). Green Corn Dance and traditional foot races	Cochiti, Taos
Date set each year	Blessing of the fields. Corn or Flag Dance	Tesuque
13	Annual feast day of St. Anthony. Corn Dance Grab Day Celebration of St. Anthony's Day Corn, Comanche or various other dances	Sandia Cochiti San Ildefonso, San Juan, Santa Clara, Taos Picuris
23–24	Annual Feast for St. John the Baptist. Buffalo Dance on evening of the 23rd, War Dances and foot races	San Juan
24	St. John the Baptist Feast Day	Taos

	Corn Dance St. John the Baptist Feast Day, Grab Day	Cochiti
29	San Pedro's Day, Rooster Pulls	Acoma, San Felipe
	San Pedro's Day, Corn Dance	Santa Ana, Santo Domingo

July

1–4	Mescalero Apache Gahan Ceremonial	Mescalero
4	Nambe Falls Ceremonial	Nambe
14	Annual Feast Day of St. Bonaventure Corn Dance	Cochiti
18–20	Annual Eight Northern Pueblos Arts and Crafts Show	San Juan
20	Annual Pope foot race	San Juan
25	Santiago's Day. Various dances	San Ildefonso, Taos
	Celebration of St. James. Grab Day	Acoma, Cochiti, San Felipe, Laguna, Santo Domingo
26	Annual Feast Day in honor of St. Anne. Corn Dance.	Santa Ana
Last weekend	Puye Cliff Ceremonial. Various dances	Santa Clara

August

| 2 | Old Pecos Bull and
Corn Dances | Jemez |

4	Annual Feast Day in honor of St. Dominic. Corn Dance	Jemez Santo Domingo
5–10	Symbolic Relay Run	All Pueblos
9–10	Annual Feast Day in honor of St. Lawrence. Sunset Dance on 9th. Dances and foot races on 10th.	Picuris
10	St. Lawrence Day. Corn Dance. St. Lawrence Day. Grab Day.	Acomita Village, Acoma Laguna, Cochiti
12	Annual Feast Day in honor of Sta. Clara. Corn, Harvest, Comanche or Buffalo Dances.	Santa Clara
Mid-August	Intertribal Indian Ceremonial	Gallup
15	Annual Feast Day in honor of Our Lady of Assumption. Corn Dance Feast of St. Anthony. Harvest and Social Dances	Zia Mesita Village, Laguna
28	Spanish and Indian Fiestas	Isleta

September

2	Annual Feast Day in honor of St. Stephan. Harvest Dance.	Acoma
4	Annual Feast Day in honor of St. Augustine. Harvest Dance.	Isleta

8	Honoring the nativity of the Blessed Virgin Mary. Harvest and Social Dances, Corn Dance	Encinal Village, Laguna
14–15	Jicarilla Apache Fair, Rodeos, Powwows, Foot Races, Dances	San Ildefonso Stone Lake, Dulce
Date set each year	Window Rock Navajo Fair	Window Rock, AZ
19	Annual Feast Day in honor of St. Joseph. Harvest Dance	Old Laguna
25	Annual Feast Day in honor of St. Elizabeth. Harvest and social dances.	Paguate Village, Laguna
29–30	Annual Feast Day in honor of St. Jerome. Sundown Dance on evening of 29th. War and various dances, trade fair, races and pole climbing on 30th	Taos
Last week	Harvest Dance	San Juan

October

1st week	Annual Navajo Fair	Shiprock
4	Annual Feast Day in honor of San Francisco de Assisi. Elk and various dances	Nambe
17	Celebrations of St. Margaret Mary's Day. Harvest and social dances.	Paraje Village, Laguna

November

12	Annual Feast Day in honor of San Diego. Corn Dance	Jemez
	Annual Feast Day in honor of San Diego. Flag, Buffalo, Deer or Comanche Dance	Tesuque

December

Date set each year	Shalako Ceremonial. Blessing of new homes	Zuni
Date set each year	Navajo Nightway and Mountain Topway Ceremonies	Navajo (Window Rock)
12	Celebration in honor of Our Lady of Guadalupe. Matachina Dance.	Jemez
	Annual Feast Day in honor of Our Lady of Guadalupe. Comanche or Buffalo and Bow and Arrow Dances	Pojoaque
24–25	Matachina Dance, Religious Procession	San Juan
	Sundown Torchlight Procession of the Virgin after vespers on 24th. Deer or Matachina Dance on 25th	Taos
	Matachina Dances	Picuris
25	Matachina Dances	San Ildefonso, Santa Clara

	Matachina or Deer Dance	Tesuque
	Buffalo, Deer, Harvest, Basket, Rainbow, Matachina and various other dances	Jemez, Santa Ana, San Felipe, Santo Domingo, Cochiti
26	Turtle Dance	San Juan
28	Holy Innocence Day, various children's dances	Santa Clara

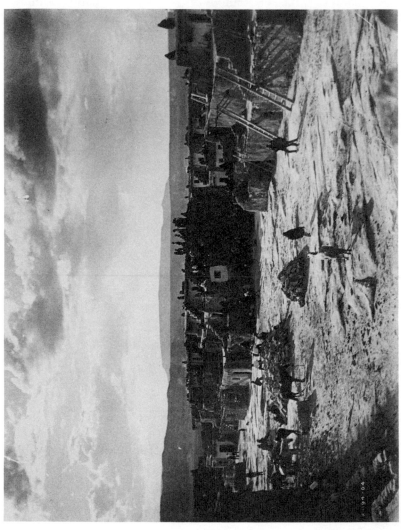

Ácoma Pueblo, 1904
Photo by Edward S. Curtis; Courtesy Museum of New Mexico, Neg. No. 144511

NEW MEXICO

The New Mexico Pueblos

The term "Pueblo" applies to all people living in compact villages in south Colorado, central Utah, and New Mexico. The Pueblo people of the historical period lived in an area extending from northeast Arizona to the Rio Pecos in New Mexico and from Taos on the Rio Grande, New Mexico, in the north, to a few miles below El Paso, Texas, in the south.

The ancient domain of Pueblo peoples, however, covered a much greater territory, extending approximately from west Arizona to the Pecos and into the Texas panhandle, and from central Utah and south Colorado southward into Mexico, where the remains of their habitations have not yet been clearly distinguished from those of the northern Aztec.

Of the Pueblo tribes, the first to become known to white people were the Zuni. After reports of their wealth in 1539, an expedition into their territory was led by Coronado. Exploring parties were sent in various directions—to the Hopi villages of Tusayan, the Grand Canyon of the Colorado, the Rio Grande Valley, and the buffalo plains, nowhere finding the expected wealth but always encouraged by news of what lay beyond. Many Indians were killed in conflicts with the Spanish. In spring 1542, Coronado's force started on their return to Mexico. Two missionaries were left behind, Fray Juan de Padilla, who went to Quivira, and Fray Luis, a lay brother, who remained at Pecos. Both were killed by the native people whom they expected to convert. In Coronado's time, the Pueblos were said to occupy 71 towns, and there may have been others.

The Pueblos were visited successively by several other Spanish explorers. Francisco Sanchez Chamuscado, in 1581, escorted three Franciscan missionaries to the Tigua country of the Rio Grande, but they were killed soon after. Antonio de Espejo, late in 1582, started with a small force from San Bartolome in Chihuahua for the purpose of determining the fate of the missionaries. He traversed the Pueblo country from the Hopi villages of northeast Arizona to Pecos in New Mexico and returned to San Bartolome by way of the Pecos River. Espejo's estimates of the population are greatly exaggerated. One of the most important of all the expeditions was that of Juan de Onate, the colonizer of New Mexico in

1598 and founder of Santa Fe seven years later. This is when the Pueblo tribes were first definitely influenced by "civilization."

Active missionary work among the Pueblos was begun early in the seventeenth century. Toward the middle of the century, difficulties arose between Spanish civil officials and Spanish missionaries, in which the Indians became involved. Many of the Pueblo people abandoned their settlements and took refuge in new ones on less pregnable sites, leaving the former villages to crumble. For twelve years, the Pueblos remained independent of the Spaniards but not free from dissension among themselves or from attacks by their old enemies, the Navajo and the Apache. In 1692, Diego de Vargas reconquered the province after severely chastising many of the natives and destroying some of their towns. Of all the Pueblos of New Mexico at the beginning of the revolt (at which time there were 33 active missions, while others were mere visitas), only Acoma and possibly Isleta continued to occupy their former sites after the conquest. In 1696, some of the Pueblos once more rebelled, killing several missionaries, but they surrendered after again being severely punished by de Vargas.

Acoma Pueblo
P.O. Box 309
Acomita, NM 87034
(505) 552-6604

Acoma

Location: Acoma, the "Sky City," is located west of Albuquerque and south of Interstate 40 on Highway 23.

Public Ceremony or Powwow Dates: Please see the calendar at the beginning of the New Mexico section.

Art Forms: Arts and crafts are sold at the visitors center at the base of the mesa.

Visitor Information: This is a spectacular, but typical, Pueblo village. Be sure to buy permits before photography or sketching is done.

Charles Dixon, Ácoma Pueblo, 1914
Courtesy Museum of New Mexico, Neg. No. 41662

Cochiti Pueblo
P.O. Box 70
Cochiti, NM 87041
(505) 465-2244

Cochiti

Location: This reservation is located south of Santa Fe just off Interstate 25.

Public Ceremony or Powwow Dates: Please see the calendar at the beginning of the New Mexico section.

Art Forms: Cochiti artisans produce the best in drums, pottery, and jewelry. Watch for their storyteller figures in stores and at Indian markets.

Visitor Information: No photographs are allowed, but please consider yourself welcome to Cochiti.

Isleta Pueblo
P.O. Box 317
Isleta, NM 87022
(505) 869-3111

Isleta

Location: This reservation is located 16 miles south of Albuquerque just off Interstate 25.

Public Ceremony or Powwow Dates: Please see the calendar at the beginning of the New Mexico section.

Art Forms: Jewelry and pottery and other arts and crafts can be found here.

Visitor Information: About 3,000 tribal members live in Isleta, and many of the people work in or around Albuquerque. If you are visiting the Pueblo, go to the governor's office to pay for a recreation fee for camping, picnicking, fishing, and photography.

Cooka boy, Cochiti Pueblo, ca. 1935
Photo by T. Harmon Parkhurst; Courtesy Museum of New Mexico, Neg. No. 3516

Augustine, Head Chief, Jicarilla Apache, ca. 1886
Courtesy Museum of New Mexico, Neg. No. 56149

Domingo, Mescalero Apache, standing left; Nallt' Zilli, Mescalero Apache Chief, seated; ca. 1886
Photo by J. R. Riddle; Courtesy Museum of New Mexico, Neg. No. 2131

Jemez Pueblo
P.O. Box 78
Jemez Pueblo, NM 87024
(505) 834-7359

Jemez

Location: Take Interstate 25 north from Albuquerque to Bernalillo; go northwest on Highway 44; turn north on Highway 4 to Jemez Pueblo.

Public Ceremony or Powwow Dates: Please see the calendar at the beginning of the New Mexico section.

Art Forms: Many Jemez artisans produce pottery and other arts and crafts.

Visitor Information: This village is located at the place where the Jemez Mountains slope down to meet the desert. It is worth the drive to go on up to the village of Jemez to see the old mission there which has many items from centuries past. Originally on Indian land, the mission now sits on land owned by the state.

Jicarilla Apache Tribal Council
P.O. Box 147
Dulce, NM 87528
(505) 759-3242

Jicarilla

Location: Take Highway 64 from Taos or Highway 84 from Española and go north past Chama where the two highways split. Turn left, staying on Highway 64, at the Broken Butt Saloon.

Public Ceremony or Powwow Dates: The Little Beaver Rodeo and Powwow is usually held in late July. The tribe celebrates a holiday around September 14–15 each year. Girls' rites, bear dances, and other ceremonials are held regularly. Call the tribe for exact dates and times for all events.

Art Forms: The Jicarilla Apache are encouraging a return to traditional arts and crafts, including basketry, buckskin tanning, leather work, beadwork, and feather work. The Jicarilla museum has arts and crafts on display. The gift shop there has local artisans' work for sale.

Visitor Information: This is a very beautiful and scenic area. The gravel road north out of Dulce to Ignacio, Colorado, is wonderful for unspoiled scenery, but be sure the roads are dry before attempting the drive.

I have danced and competed personally at the Little Beaver Powwow and always had a great time. They provided elk steaks the last year I was there. I'll never forget setting the tipi up in the rain while everyone looked on (from inside their pickup trucks). They probably thought we were Witko!

Laguna Pueblo
P.O. Box 194
Laguna, NM 87026
(505) 552-6654

Laguna

Location: Take Interstate 40 west from Albuquerque, and you will go right through the reservation.

Public Ceremony or Powwow Dates: Please see the calendar at the beginning of the New Mexico section.

Art Forms: Call the tribal office for details on where to purchase arts and crafts.

Visitor Information: You must pay a fee for photography at the tribal office.

When we did motorcycle stunt riding for the movie *Outrageous Fortune,* we had the opportunity to see some of the reservation in the desert. There are very beautiful rock formations and unusual color combinations to be found in this area.

Mescalero Apache Tribal Council
P.O. Box 176
Mescalero, NM 87340
(505) 671-4495

Mescalero

Location: In south central New Mexico on Federal Highway 70; look on your map just northeast of Alamogordo.

Public Ceremony or Powwow Dates: This is the place to go if you are in the area during the Fourth of July. The Apache girls' ceremony is held honoring the young ladies of the tribe who are now of age. There are Mountain Spirit Dancers, rodeo, arts and crafts, and celebrating!

Art Forms: Go to the Inn of the Mountain Gods for Apache arts and crafts.

Visitor Information: The tribe has built a beautiful resort here called the Inn of the Mountain Gods. There is tennis, swimming, a whirlpool, saunas, and boat and bike rentals, and you can ski at the Sierra Blanca Ski Resort. Write Box 269, Ruidoso/Mescalero, NM 88340, or telephone 800-545-9011 or (505) 257-5141.

Be sure to see the Mescalero Apache Cultural Center Museum, also.

Nambe Pueblo
Route 1, Box 117 BB
Santa Fe, NM 87501
(505) 455-7752

Nambe

Location: This reservation is located north of Santa Fe east of Highways 84 and 285. Turn east after crossing the bridge over the river at the Nambe turnoff. Follow the paved road, being careful on the many curves, to Nambe.

Public Ceremony or Powwow Dates: Please see the calendar at the beginning of the New Mexico section.

Art Forms: Call the tribal office for more information on where to purchase local arts and crafts.

Visitor Information: This is enchanted land in the Land of Enchantment. Very scenic land formations are just beyond the last turnoff to the village on the highway to Chimayo.

Picuris Pueblo
P.O. Box 127
Penasco, NM 87553
(505) 587-2519

Picuris

Location: The village is located seven miles northwest of Penasco off of Highway 75.

Public Ceremony or Powwow Dates: Please see the calendar at the beginning of the New Mexico section.

Art Forms: Local artisans produce very nice undecorated pottery and other arts and crafts. Call the tribal office for more details.

Visitor Information: In recent years, the Picuris have revived the pole climbing celebration held in the late fall. Call the tribal office for more information.

Pojoaque Pueblo
Route 11, Box 71
Santa Fe, NM 87501
(505) 455-2278

Pojoaque

Location: The reservation is located 16 miles north of Santa Fe on Highways 285 and 84.

Public Ceremony or Powwow Dates: This tribe is in the process of reviving ceremonials with the help of other tribes in the area. They are now doing the Comanche, Buffalo, and Bow and Arrow dances. Please see the calendar at the beginning of the New Mexico section.

Art Forms: Local artisans produce pottery and other arts and crafts. Ask at the tribal office for more information.

Visitor Information: The tribe has many enterprises in place on their reservation. The tribe owns the Pueblo Grocery and the buildings that house the laundromat, barber shop, beauty shop, and more. They also own the Butterfly Springs Mobile Home Court and the Pojoaque Information Center, which has an RV park behind it. They are in the process of building a cultural center and are paving

An offering at the waterfall, Nambé Pueblo, 1925
Photo by Edward S. Curtis; Courtesy Museum of New Mexico, Neg. No. 132696

Ramita and Juan Jose Martinez, Picurís Pueblo, August 1959
Photo by Flavia Champ; Courtesy Museum of New Mexico, Neg. No. 31053

a new road to that area. Many new homes are also under construction, and they have in operation a new office building in the plaza.

Pueblo of Sandia
Box 6008
Bernalillo, NM 87004
(505) 867-3317

Location: Sandia Pueblo is a small community located 15 miles north of Albuquerque on U.S. Highway 85 and two and a half miles south of the Spanish-American town of Bernalillo. The Pueblo itself occupies approximately 26 acres within a total reservation area of 24,034 acres. The Pueblo is situated near the center of the reservation with a clear view of the mountains.

Public Ceremony or Powwow Dates: The Pueblo of Sandia celebrates its annual feast day to honor their patron saint, Saint Anthony de Padua, on June 13th of every year. This is open to the public. There are Indian Corn Dances all day. The feast begins with mass in the morning. Then St. Anthony is carried down from the church in a procession to an altar erected by tribal members, located in the plaza where the Corn Dances are held. Concession stands are open all day selling different varieties of food.

Other dances held during the year are on January 6th, the day they celebrate King's Day, the installation of their new governor. Dances are also held early Christmas morning.

No cameras, sketching, or recorders of any kind are allowed.

Art Forms: There are various tribal members who still do traditional arts and crafts. There is pottery making, silversmithing, and beautiful beadwork available.

Visitor Information: Albuquerque is located south of Sandia Pueblo, and there are motels, hotels, restaurants, campgrounds, and other facilities available there.

Located right on Sandia Reservation is the Sandia Indian Bingo Parlor, one of the largest in New Mexico with the highest payouts. Sandia Pueblo Agricultural Enterprises is the tribally owned sod farm and nursery.

Located on the southern boundary of the reservation is the Los Amigos Stables, where you can enjoy horseback riding, picnics,

Pueblo Indian girl, Pojoaque Pueblo, ca. 1900
Photo by Kaadt & Whitlock; Courtesy Museum of New Mexico, Neg. No. 46151

Mariano Carpentero, Governor of Sandía Pueblo, 1899
Photo by DeLancey Gill; Courtesy Museum of New Mexico, Neg. No. 87010

hayrides, private parties, and music and dancing. All the food is prepared right there.

Located in the Council Chambers of the governor's office is a display of the history of Sandia Pueblo with photographs. It is still in the development stages as of this writing, but visitors are welcome to come by and browse. There is no charge to visit the display.

San Felipe Pueblo
P.O. Box A
San Felipe Pueblo, NM 87001
(505) 867-3381

San Felipe

Location: This reservation is located on Interstate Highway 25 north of Albuquerque, about halfway to Santa Fe.

Public Ceremony or Powwow Dates: Please see the calendar at the beginning of the New Mexico section.

Art Forms: There is still some jewelry being produced here as well as other arts and crafts. Call the tribal office for more details.

Visitor Information: There are several Kivas in this village, and they have some of the most powerful dances I have ever witnessed. I enjoy the feast days here as well or more than those of any other village.

San Ildefonso Pueblo
Route 5, Box 315 A
Santa Fe, NM 87501
(505) 455-2273

San Ildefonso

Location: To get to the village, take Highways 84 and 285 north from Santa Fe and turn off at Pojoaque on State Highway 4 to Los Alamos; turn off to the right after about eight miles.

Public Ceremony or Powwow Dates: Please see the calendar at the beginning of the New Mexico section.

Art Forms: This is the home of the famous potter, Maria Martinez, who has been gone to the other side for some years now. The black

Unidentified girl, San Felipe Pueblo, ca. 1935
Photo by T. Harmon Parkhurst; Courtesy Museum of New Mexico, Neg. No. 47427

Florentine Martinez, San Ildefonso Pueblo, 1908
Photo by Jesse L. Nusbaum; Courtesy Museum of New Mexico, Neg. No. 61769

pottery here is some of the best you will find. The work can be found in artisans' homes as well as two shops in the plaza.

Visitor Information: Please buy permits for photography and sketching or painting.

San Juan Pueblo
P.O. Box 1099
San Juan Pueblo, NM 87566
(505) 852-4400

San Juan

Location: Drive north of Española on Highway 285 (the Taos Highway), and turn left at the signs to go to the village.

Public Ceremony or Powwow Dates: Please see the calendar at the beginning of the New Mexico section.

Art Forms: To buy traditional arts and crafts from local tribal artisans, go to Oke Oweenge Crafts Cooperative. They sell red pottery, embroidery, beadwork, and other arts.

Visitor Information: To do photography or sketching, go to the tribal office for a permit. To find when the Eight Northern Pueblos Indian Artist and Craftsman Show will be held, check with the Eight Northern Indian Pueblos Council here in San Juan. Don't forget the bingo parlor here, also. They do have high payouts.

Santa Ana Pueblo
P.O. Box 37
Bernalillo, NM 87004
(505) 867-3301

Santa Ana

Location: Drive north of Albuquerque to Bernalillo and take Highway 44 northwest to Santa Ana Pueblo.

Public Ceremony or Powwow Dates: Please see the calendar at the beginning of the New Mexico section.

Art Forms: Call the tribal office for more details.

Eliseo Trujillo, Margurita Trujillo, and baby Pedro, San Juan Pueblo, ca. 1932–34
Photo by T. Harmon Parkhurst; Courtesy Museum of New Mexico, Neg. No. 31856

Three dancers, Santa Ana Pueblo, ca. 1935
Photo by T. Harmon Parkhurst; Courtesy Museum of New Mexico, Neg. No. 4884

Visitor Information: The ceremonies are very much alive at Santa Ana. The landscape is beautiful here where the desert meets the end of the Jemez Mountains.

Santa Clara Pueblo
P.O. Box 580
Española, NM 87532
(505) 753-7326

Santa Clara

Location: The easiest way to find Santa Clara Pueblo is to go to Española and take the Los Alamos Highway to the reservation.

Public Ceremony or Powwow Dates: Please see the calendar at the beginning of the New Mexico section.

Art Forms: There are many potters in the village, and other arts and crafts may be purchased there also. Call the tribal office for more information.

Visitor Information: The people at Santa Clara are friendly, and we have always enjoyed the dancing at feast days in the village. The food is excellent, also, during the feasts. If you like to camp and fish, go to Santa Clara Canyon on the highway past Puye Cliffs. The rangers there will sell you a permit to picnic, camp, or fish. There is no hiking allowed, however, off the floor of the canyon.

Santo Domingo Pueblo
P.O. Box 99
Santo Domingo Pueblo, NM 87052
(505) 465-2214

Santo Domingo

Location: The reservation is on the Albuquerque Highway, Interstate 25, south of Santa Fe.

Public Ceremony or Powwow Dates: Please see the calendar at the beginning of the New Mexico section.

Art Forms: The people here make fine turquoise and silver jewelry. Many of them sell their work on the portal on the plaza in Santa Fe.

Visitor Information: This area is beautiful, with lava formations along the edge of the mountains and above the Rio Grande River.

Florentino, Santa Clara Pueblo, ca. 1920
Photo by T. Harmon Parkhurst; Courtesy Museum of New Mexico, Neg. No. 12444

Francisco Abeita and Victorano Gachupin, Santo Domingo, August 4, 1907
Photo by Milton E. Porter; Courtesy Museum of New Mexico, Neg. No. 7923

Unidentified men on horses, Taos Pueblo, ca. 1915
Courtesy Museum of New Mexico, Neg. No. 21531

Taos Pueblo
P.O. Box 1846
Taos, NM 87571
(505) 758-8626

Taos

Location: The village is located just northeast of the downtown plaza in Taos.

Public Ceremony or Powwow Dates: Please see the calendar at the beginning of the New Mexico section. In recent years, also, there has been a powwow close to the area where the buffalo pasture is located. Call the tribal office for dates and times.

Art Forms: There are several arts and crafts stores on the road into the village and some are located in the village. Stop and see my friend Sonny Spruce in his shop on the right side of the road into the village. He does fine silver and turquoise jewelry. My favorite drums also come from the craftsmen in Taos.

Visitor Information: The village is open to the public, and photography permits must be purchased at the gate directly by the village entrance. San Geronimo Day is a good time to get to know the people at Taos Pueblo.

Tesuque Pueblo
Route 11, Box 1
Santa Fe, NM 87501
(505) 983-2667

Tesuque

Location: Tesuque Pueblo is just north of Santa Fe on Highways 285 and 84. Turn left at the Speedway store.

Public Ceremony or Powwow Dates: Please see the calendar at the beginning of the New Mexico section.

Art Forms: Arts and crafts, including pottery, are all available here. Call the tribal office for more information.

Visitor Information: The Tesuque tribe operates the Camel Rock Campground, with swimming pool and nice RV spaces, on the highway north of the village. They also have horses for rent for

Unidentified man, Zia Pueblo, ca. 1935
Photo by T. Harmon Parkhurst; Courtesy Museum of New Mexico, Neg. No. 3773

riding, hayrides, and cookouts, on the highway on the east side. Don't miss the bingo parlor, if you enjoy gaming. It's all here at Tesuque Pueblo.

Zia Pueblo
General Delivery
San Ysidro, NM 87053
(505) 867-3304

Zia

Location: Drive north from Albuquerque and take Highway 44 at Bernalillo northwest to Zia.

Public Ceremony or Powwow Dates: Please see the calendar at the beginning of the New Mexico section.

Art Forms: The orange on white pottery is distinctive at Zia, and there are other arts and crafts as well.

Visitor Information: It is an inspiring drive up to Zia, which overlooks the Jemez River. This is the land where the desert meets the mountains.

Zuni Pueblo
P.O. Box 339
Zuni, NM 87327
(505) 782-4481

Zuni

Location: Drive south from Grants on Highway 53 or Highway 32 from Gallup and then west on Highway 53.

Public Ceremony or Powwow Dates: Please see the calendar at the beginning of New Mexico.

Art Forms: The Zuni Craftsmen Cooperative Association, Box 426, Zuni, NM 87327, offers silver and turquoise jewelry. They are located on State Highway 53 at the pueblo. The Zuni excel in various kinds of jewelry craftsmanship.

Visitor Information: In November or December, the Zuni hold the spectacular and impressive Shalako dances. The Giant Kachina figures that are over ten feet tall dance and race. There are stores,

Zuni Kachina maker, ca. 1920
Courtesy Museum of New Mexico, Neg. No. 68770

Zuni Pueblo, 1903
Photo by Edward S. Curtis; Courtesy Museum of New Mexico, Neg. No. 143701

restaurants, gas stations, and a tribal campground. If you are in an adventurous mood, take a guided tour from the Zuni Tribal Office and visit Hawikuh ruins, which is twelve miles south of Zuni Pueblo. This was an active pueblo when first visited by the black explorer Esteban and Spanish priest Fray Marcos in 1539. Some sort of conflict took place and Esteban was killed. Fray Marcos returned to Mexico, and the following year Coronado returned with armed men and attacked Hawikuh. The pueblo then lived with Spanish influence for a century. It was then abandoned after the Pueblo Revolt of 1680 when the Pueblo people drove the Spanish out of New Mexico. Also, rock art paintings that were painted earlier in this century can be viewed at the Village of the Great Kivas. And more Zuni art can be viewed in the mission church at the village. Coronado was wrong when he found Zuni and thought it was one of the Seven Cities of Cibola, but mythical gold cities are hard to find.

Ysleta del Sur Pueblo
P.O. Box 17579
El Paso, TX 79907
(915) 859-7913

Ysleta

Location: The Tigua Indian Reservation is south on I-10; twelve miles south to Exit 32 (Avenue of the Americas); then two and a half miles south on Zaragosa Road. Turn on Alameda Road one block east to 122 South Old Pueblo Road, Ysleta. If you get lost, ask directions, like I did.

Public Ceremony or Powwow Dates: Call the tribal office for exact times when dances are held which are open to the public.

Art Forms: There are traditional arts and crafts in the center, and there is a display in the museum.

Visitor Information: Don't miss the tribal restaurant. They generally have dancing in the plaza, also. These people moved here sometime after the Pueblo Revolt of 1680 from the northern areas of the Rio Grande. They were forgotten by the other Pueblo people, but they have now regained recognition.

WEST

Smith River / Soboba / Susanville / Sycuan / Table Bluff / Table Mountain / Torres-Martinez / Trinidad / Tule River / Tuolumne / Twenty nine Palms / Upper Lake / Utu Utu Gwaitu Paiute / Viejas / Yurok / Chemehuevi / Fort Mojave / Woodfords / Agua Caliente / Alturas / Barona / Berry Creek / Big Bend / Big Lagoon / Big Pine / Big Sandy / Big Valley / Bishop / Blue Lake / Bridgeport / Buena Vista / Cabazon / Cahuilla / Campo / Cedarville / Chicken Ranch / Cloverdale / Cold Springs / Colusa / Cortina / Covelo / Coyote / Cuyapaipe / Death Valley / Dry Creek / Elem / Elk Valley / Enterprise / Fort Bidwell / Fort Independence / Greenville / Grindstone / Hoopa / Hopland / Inaja and Cosmit / Jackson / Jamul / Karok / Kashia / La Jolla / La Posta / Laytonville / Lone Pine / Lookout / Los Coyotes / Mancheria - Fort Arena / Manzanite / Mesa Grande / Middletown / Montgomery Creek / Mooretown / Morongo / North Fork / Otter Valley / Pala /

CALIFORNIA

Pauma / Pechanga / Picayune / Pinoleville / Pit River / Quartz Valley / Ramona Band / Redding / Redwood Valley / Resighini / Rincon / Robinson / Rohnerville / Rumsey / San Manuel / San Pasqual / Santa Rosa / Santa Ynez / Santa Ysabel / Sherwood Valley / Shingle Springs

The land slopes down to meet the Great Water, the Pacific, and the land slopes up to meet the Grandfather Mountains, the Sierras. In between, there are deserts and forests and lakes and rivers. It is beautiful land and it is our land.

The people are not known by others. The Spanish missionary influence in the last part of the eighteenth century and the beginning of the nineteenth century and the gold miners in the mid-nineteenth century took over the land, and the people.

The people lived from the land and they lived from respect. With great skill, they made baskets and built their houses. They used tule, grasses, brush, and/or bark, and they covered their houses with earth to protect themselves in winter. In the northwest, they hewed planks to form their houses and canoes were made from the great trees there. Tules were made into rafts and the rivers were their highways. Agriculture and breaking the skin of our Mother Earth was not necessary. Deer and small game and fish and vegetables gave themselves to the people for food. Acorns, seeds, grasses, herbs, roots, and berries were plentiful.

The people practiced their spiritualism within societies and ceremony acted out their heart and mind to a fine degree.

Aho . . .

I have said yes, and thrown away my country.
—Captain Jack (Modoc)

CALIFORNIA

Readers, note: California Indian people are all listed by tribal affiliation, with the reservation address and telephone numbers listed for information only.

Alturas General Council
P.O. Box 1035
Alturas, CA 96101

Lookout Rancheria
P.O. Box 87
Lookout, CA 96054

Montgomery Creek Rancheria
P.O. Box 282
Montgomery Creek, CA 96065

Pit River Tribal Council
P.O. Drawer 1570
Burney, CA 96013
(916) 335-5421

Susanville General Council
Drawer U
Susanville, CA 96130
(916) 257-6264

Achomawi (Pit River), adzuma, achoma, "river"

Visitor Information: The Pit River Home and Agricultural Society is located in Alturas. Their telephone number is (916) 263-2584.

This division of the Shasta family occupied the Pit River country of northeastern California, except Burney, Dixie, and Hat Creek valleys, which were inhabited by the Atsugewi. A principal village was near Fallriver Mills, Shasta County. The languages of the Achomawi and the Atsugewi, while unquestionably related, are strikingly unlike.

Lassen Volcanic National Park
Mineral, CA 96063
(916) 595-4444

Atsugewi

Location: The park is 50 miles east of Redding on Highway 44.

Visitor Information: The park employs local Atsugewi Indian people as cultural historians. Demonstrations include basket weaving and a display of an Atsugewi wickiup.

Medie Webster, 87, is the sole remaining possessor of the Atsugewi language. She is one of only 200 Atsugewi Indians, whose ancestors for centuries hunted and gathered food in what is now Lassen Volcanic National Park 180 miles northeast of San Francisco.

The lakes and mountains in Lassen Park were the spiritual lakes and mountains of the Atsugewi. There were about 2,000 Atsugewis when non-Indian intruders came to this area about one hundred fifty years ago.

Blue Lake Interim Business Committee
P.O. Box 428
Blue Lake, CA 95525
(707) 688-5286

Buena Vista Rancheria
4650 Coalmine Road
Ione, CA 95640

Cabazon General Council
84–145 Indio Springs Drive
Indio, CA 92201
(619) 342-2593

Cabazon (Mission)

Location: The Cabazon Band of Mission Indians live in the lower Coachella Valley in the cities of Indio, Coachella, and Mecca. The reservation is approximately 1,400 acres.

Visitor Information: The Cabazon Band of Mission Indians is a federally recognized reservation. There are 25 enrolled members, and they have been on this reservation since 1876.

The Bingo Palace is open seven days a week and the casino is open twenty-four hours a day.

Laytonville Rancheria
P.O. Box 1239
Laytonville, CA 95454
(707) 984-6197

Cahto

Visitor Information: The Cahto live on their reservation just west of Laytonville.

⟩ This Kuneste tribe or band formerly lived in Cahto and Long valleys, Mendocino County, California. They belong to the Athapascan group and are closely related to the Wailaki, although they resemble the Pomo in culture.

Agua Caliente Tribal Council
960 E. Tahquitz Way #106
Palm Springs, CA 92262
(619) 325-5673

Cahuilla General Council
P.O. Box 860
Anza, CA 92302
(714) 743-5549

Los Coyotes General Council
P.O. Box 86
Warner Springs, CA 92086
(619) 782-3269

Morongo General Council*
11581 Potrero Road
Banning, CA 92220
(714) 849-4697

Ramona Band of Cahuilla Indians
460 West Valley Boulevard
Colton, CA 92314

Santa Rosa General Council
325 N. Western Street
Hemet, CA 92343
(714) 925-7190

Torres-Martinez Business Committee
66–725 Martinez Road
Thermal, CA 92274

Cahuilla

Location: The Morongo Indian Reservation is located at Banning, California. To go to the museum, take Interstate 10 east and take the Fields Road Exit.

Public Ceremony or Powwow Dates: The annual Malki Museum Fiesta is held on Memorial Day weekend. There are Cahuilla bird singers, Papago Chelkona dancers, Apache Mountain Spirit dancers, Luiseno singers, and Aztec dancers.

Art Forms: The arts and crafts sold are likely to include jewelry, beadwork, baskets, cradleboards, gourd rattles, and many more.

Visitor Information: The museum of the Cahuilla and Serrano tribes is named the Malki, and it displays pottery, baskets, and traditional items from the tribes. The gift shop also carries arts and crafts. During the Fiesta there will also be hand games.

The name Kawia is of uncertain origin, but the people are affiliated linguistically with the Aguas Calientes, Juanenos, and Luisenos. They inhabit the north tongue of the Colorado Desert from Banning southeast at least as far as Salton, as also the headwaters of Santa Margarita River, where the Kawia Reservation was situated. They were first visited in 1776 by Fray Francisco Garces. At this time they lived around the north slopes of the San Jacinto Mountains and to the north and roamed east to the Colorado, but their principal seat was near San Gorgonio pass. There were 793 Indians assembled under the name "Coahuila" at all the Mission Reservations in 1885, while the Indians on Cahuilla Reservation under the Mission Tule River Agency in 1894 numbered 151, and in 1902, 159. This reservation consists of 18,240 acres of unpatented land.

Chemehuevi Tribal Council
P.O. Box 1976
Chemehuevi Valley, CA 92363
(619) 858-4531

Chemehuevi

Location: The reservation is located south of Needles and across the river from Lake Havasu City, Arizona.

Visitor Information: The tribe is in the process of developing the recreation potential of their river location. Since they are across the river from an already developing tourist attraction, they will undoubtedly succeed.

Chicken Ranch Rancheria
P.O. Box 85
Jamestown, CA 95327
(209) 984-3057

Santa Ynez General Council
P.O. Box 517
Santa Ynez, CA 93460
(805) 688-7997

Chumash

Location: The members of this tribe reside primarily in Santa Barbara County. The new tribal office building, their bingo enterprise, and many new homes are located on their reservation.

Public Ceremony or Powwow Dates: The Santa Ynez Dolphin dancers are doing traditional Chumash dances and songs. Call the tribal office for dates and times to attend some of their ceremonies.

Woman basket maker with her baskets, Chimehuevis
Courtesy Museum of New Mexico, Neg. No. 82624

Visitor Information: The Chumash are striving to retain their culture and are trying to preserve their sacred Point Conception.

Cloverdale Rancheria
285 Santana Drive
Cloverdale, CA 95425
(707) 894-5773

Coast Miwok

The Miwok of the coast are the people who lived where Marin and Sonoma counties are today. They were taken to Mission San Rafael where the population was reduced by disease. Some of the people survive, and their songs are heard with the Kashaya Pomo.

Death Valley Indian Community
P.O. Box 206
Death Valley, CA 92328
(619) 786-2374

Diegueno

Barona General Business Council
1095 Barona Road
Lakeside, CA 92040
(619) 433-6613

Campo General Council
1779 Campo Truck Trail
Campo, CA 92006
(619) 478-5251

Cuyapaipe General Council
c/o Southern Indian Health, Inc.
P.O. Box 20889
El Cajon, CA 92021
(619) 561-3701

Inja and Cosmit General Council
739 A Street, Apt. 12
Ramona, CA 92065
(619) 765-1993

La Posta Council
1079 Barona Road
Lakeside, CA 92040
(619) 478-5523

Manzanita General Council
P.O. Box 1302
Boulevard, CA 92005
(619) 478-5028

Mesa Grande General Council
P.O. Box 242
Warner Springs, CA 92086

San Pasqual General Council
P.O. Box 365
Valley Center, CA 92082
(619) 749-3200

Santa Ysabel General Council
P.O. Box 126
Santa Ysabel, CA 92070
(619) 765-0845

Syucan Business Committee
P.O. Box 520
Alpine, CA 92001
(619) 445-2613

Viejas Tribal Council
P.O. Box 908
Alpine, CA 92001
(619) 445-3810

Diegueno

Visitor Information: The Tipai and Ipai people live primarily in San Diego County on reservations established by the federal government. Some of these hold annual fiestas that include dancing and food. The other coastal south California tribes include the Luiseno, Cahuilla, Juaneno, Gabrielino, and Cupeno.

Dieguenos is probably a collective name synonymous with Comeya, applied by the Spaniards to Indians of the Yuman group who formerly lived in and around San Diego (and still do). It included representatives of many tribes and has no proper ethnic significance. In 1909, there were about 400 Indian people included under this name as attached to the Mission Agency of California, but they are now officially recognized as a part of the "Mission Indians."

Dry Creek Tribal Council
P.O. Box 224
Geyserville, CA 95441
(707) 443-6137

Pomo
Wappo

Visitor Information: The Wappo Indian people of central California have intermarried with the Pomo. The Warm Springs Dam Visitor Center, 3333 Skaggs Springs Road, Geyserville, CA, (707) 433-9483, shows the work of Laura Fish Somersall, a Wappo speaker and consultant on scholarly studies of the tribe.

Wappo is from Spanish *quapo*, "brave." This small detached portion of the Yukian family of north California, separated from the Huichnom, the nearest Yuki division, by thirty or forty miles of Pomo territory, are the residents of the mountains separating Sonoma from Lake and Napa counties, between Geysers and Calistoga. A portion of them, called Rincons, occupied the Russian River Valley in the vicinity of Healdsburg.

Elk Valley Interim Tribal Council
375 Wyentae Street
Crescent City, CA 95531
(707) 464-4680

Gabrielino

The Gabrielino are a Shoshonean group who formerly occupied all of Los Angeles County south of the San Bernardino Mountains and Santa Catalina Island.

Hupa

Big Bend General Council
P.O. Box 255
Big Bend, CA 96001
(916) 337-6605

Big Lagoon Rancheria
P.O. Drawer F
Trinidad, CA 95570
(707) 677-3115

Hupa Tribal Museum and Historic Villages
Box 1245
Hoopa, CA 95546
(916) 625-4110 or 625-4211

Location: The museum is located inside the shopping center, which is next to the market in the town of Hoopa on Highway 96.

Public Ceremony or Powwow Dates: Call the tribal office for dates and times of public ceremonies.

Visitor Information: The Hupa Tribe has the Six Rivers Bingo Enterprise in the shopping center at Hoopa.

The Hupa are an Athapascan tribe formerly occuping the valley of Trinity River from the South Fork to its junction with the Klamath, including Hupa Valley. In August 1864, a twelve-mile-square reservation was set apart for their use. The population in 1888 was 650; in 1900, 430; and in 1905, 412.

Jamul General Council
P.O. Box 612
Jamul, CA 92035
(619) 697-5041

Karuk Interim Committee
P.O. Box 1098
Happy Camp, CA 96039
(916) 493-5305

Karuk

Location: Some ceremonies are held near Somes Bar.

Public Ceremony or Powwow Dates: Odd-number years have more events than do even-number years as their calendar is on a two-year cycle. There are brush dances, white deerskin dances, jump dances, and more. Call the tribal office for dates and times and etiquette required to attend.

Visitor Information: You will often find Karuk dance groups doing their dances at Indian celebrations and at colleges in northern California.

Luiseno

La Jolla General Council
Star Route, Box 158
Valley Center, CA 92082
(619) 742-3771

Pala General Council
P.O. Box 43
Pala, CA 92059
(619) 742-3784

Pauma General Council
P.O. Box 86
Pauma Valley, CA 92061
(619) 7423-1289

Pechanga Tribal Council
P.O. Box 1477
Temecula, CA 92390
(714) 676-2768

Rincon Business Committee*
P.O. Box 68
Valley Center, CA 92082
(619) 749-1051

Soboda General Council
P.O. Box 562
San Jacinto, CA 92383
(714) 654-2765

Twenty Nine Palms General Council
58 S. El Cielo, Apartment #2
Palm Springs, CA 92262
(619) 332-1914

Visitor Information: The Luiseno office starred above sponsors a fiesta with festivities and peon games (hand games) and other interesting events. Call the tribal office for dates and times.

This is the southernmost Shoshonean division in California which received its name from San Luis Rey, the most important Spanish Mission in the territory of these people.

Maidu

Berry Creek Tribal Council
1779 Mitchell Avenue
Oroville, CA 95966
(916) 534-3859

Covelo Community Council
Round Valley Reservation
P.O. Box 448
Covelo, CA 95428
(707) 983-6126

Enterprise Rancheria
7470 Feather Falls
Star Route
Oroville, CA 95965
(916) 589-0652

Greenville Rancheria
P.O. Box 237
Greenville, CA 95947
(916) 284-6446

Susanville General Council
Drawer U
Susanville, CA 96130
(916) 257-6264

Location: The Maidu do the Bear Dance at Janesville and Greenville.

Public Ceremony or Powwow Dates: The dates and times of the Bear Dance can be determined by calling the Greenville and/or Susanville offices above. Traditional dancing and singing are performed during the Bear Dances.

Art Forms: During the dances, arts and crafts are offered for sale.

Visitor Information: There is a Maidu dance group which performs traditional dancing and singing at Indian Grinding Rock State Park's Chaw-Se Big Time and other events. Call the California State University, Sacramento, for more information.

Maidu ("man," "Indian"). This tribe formerly dwelled in Sacramento Valley and the adjacent Sierra Nevada in California.

Miwok

Jackson Interim Council
16070 Miwuk Drive
Jackson, CA 95642
(209) 223-3931

Shingle Springs Tribal Council
P.O. Box 1340
Shingle Springs, CA 95682
(916) 391-7822

Tuolumne Rancheria
P.O. Box 696
Tuolumne, CA 95379
(209) 928-3475

Location: The California State Indian Museum, which is adjacent to Sutter's Fort, 2618 K Street, in Sacramento, (916) 324-0971, is the location of an annual California Indian Days Celebration. The Kule Loklo Miwok Indian Village is a half-mile northwest of

Olema, and the Miwok dance here during the Kule Loklo Celebration in July or August. Call for dates and times at (415) 663-1092.

Public Ceremony or Powwow Dates: The spring of the year features Pomo and Miwok dancing at the museum in Sacramento. Call for dates and times of the dances.

Art Forms: The arts and crafts of the Miwok are available at the Chaw-Se Big Time Celebration.

Visitor Information: The Mi-Wuk Indian Acorn Festival is also held annually at Tuolumne Indian Rancheria near Tuolumne. September is the time to watch Miwok dancing and eat California Indian foods such as acorn bread and acorn soup.

Miwok ("man"). This is one of the two divisions of the Moquelumnan family in central California, the other being the Olamentke. With a small exception in the west, the Miwok occupied territory bounded on the north by Cosumnes River, on the east by the ridge of the Sierra Nevada, on the south by Fresno Creek, and on the west by the San Joaquin River. The exception on the west is a narrow strip of land on the east bank of the San Joaquin, occupied by Yokuts Indians, beginning at the Tuolumne and extending northward to a point not far from the place where the San Joaquin bends to the west. Their language was so uniform that the Miwok could travel from the Cosumnes to the Fresno and make themselves understood.

Fort Mojave Tribal Council
500 Merriman Avenue
Needles, CA 92363
(619) 326-4591

Mojave

Location: The reservation is located north and northeast of Needles.

Mono (Monache)

Big Sandy Interim Tribal Council
P.O. Box 337
Auberry, CA 93602
(209) 855-4003

Cold Springs Tribal Council
P.O. Box 209
Tollhouse, CA 93667
(209) 855-2326

North Fork Rancheria
3027 Clement Street #2
San Francisco, CA 94121

Sierra Mono Museum
North Fork, CA
(209) 877-2115

Visitor Information: The museum shows the history and culture of the Sierra Mono Indian people.

This tribe forms one of the three great dialect groups in which the Shoshoneans of the great plateau are distinguished. It includes the Mono of southeast California, the Paviotso, or "Paiute," of west Nevada, and the "Snakes" and Saidyuka of east Oregon. Part of the Bannock may be related to them. In 1903, there were about 5,400 people in this division.

Mooretown Rancheria
P.O. Box 1842
1900 Oro Dam Boulevard, Suite 8
Oroville, CA 95965
(916) 533-3625

Visitor Information: This is a recently reorganized tribe just recognized last year. They are in the process of acquiring a land base at the time of this writing. And they are in the process of finalizing their enrollment consisting of both lineal descendants and adoptees.

Ohlone (Costanoan). The original inhabitants of San Francisco Bay south to Monterey Bay. The mission system reduced their culture, but they are recovering.

Otter Valley Rancheria
P.O. Box 94
Potter Valley, CA 95469

Pauite and/or Shoshone

Big Pine General Council
P.O. Box 700
Big Pine, CA 93513
(619) 938-2121

Bishop Tribal Council
P.O. Box 548
Bishop, CA 93514
(619) 873-3584

Bridgeport General Council
P.O. Box 37
Bridgeport, CA 93517
(619) 932-7083

Cedarville Community Council
P.O. Box 142
Cedarville, CA 96104

Fort Bidwell Community Council
P.O. Box 127
Fort Bidwell, CA 96112
(916) 279-6310

Fort Independence General Council
P.O. Box 67
Independence, CA 93526
(619) 878-2126

Lone Pine Tribal Council
Star Route 1
1101 South Main Street
Lone Pine, CA 93545
(619) 876-5414

Utu Utu Gwaitu Paiute Tribal Council
Benton Paiute Reservation
Star Route 4, Box 56A
Benton, CA 935123
(619) 933-2321

Visitor Information: For more information on the Paiute, please see Nevada, the general history of the Paiute. For more information on the Shoshone, please see Wyoming, Shoshone Business Council.

Paiute Shoshone Indian Cultural Museum
2300 West Line Street
Bishop, CA
(619) 873-4478

Visitor Information: This is an Indian owned and operated museum that features interesting Paiute and Shoshone cultural displays. Contact the museum for dates and times of special events that benefit the museum.

Picayune Rancheria
P.O. Box 46
Coarsegold, CA 93614
(209) 683-6633

Pomo

Big Valley Rancheria
P.O. Box 774
Lakeport, CA 95453
(702) 263-7522

Coyote Valley Interim Tribal Council
P.O. Box 39
Redwood Valley, CA 95470-0039
(707) 485-8723

Elem General Council
Sulphur Bank Rancheria
P.O. Box 618
Clearlake Oaks, CA 95423
(707) 998-3315

Hopland Interim Tribal Council
P.O. Box 610
Hopland, CA 95449
(707) 744-1647

Kashia Community Council
Stewarts Point Rancheria
P.O. Box 54
Stewarts Point, CA 95480
(707) 785-2594

Laytonville Rancheria
P.O. Box 1239
Laytonville, CA 95454
(707) 984-6197

Mancheria/Fort Arena Rancheria
P.O. Box 623
Point Arena, CA 95468
(707) 882-2788

Middletown Interim Council
P.O. Box 292
Middletown, CA 95461

Pinolville Rancheria
367 N. State Street, Suite 204
Ukiah, CA 95482

Robinson Citizens Business Council
P.O. Box 1119
Nice, CA 95464
(707) 257-0527

Sherwood Valley General Council
2141 S. State Street
Ukiah, CA 95482
(707) 468-1337

Upper Lake Interim Committee
Upper Lake Rancheria
P.O. Box 20272
Sacramento, CA 95820
(916) 371-5637

Location: The Kashaya Pomo, Elem Pomo, Big Valley Pomo, Coyote Valley Pomo, and Point Arena Pomo listed above have dance groups.

Public Ceremony or Powwow Dates: In August, the City of Cotati, California, sponsors an Indian Day and the Pomo dance here. Telephone the City of Cotati at (707) 795-5478 for dates and times. The Elem Pomo dance, and it is possible to book them for special events. Call (707) 998-1666 for more details. Along the Soda Bay Road between Lakeport and Kelseyville, off of Highway 29, is the Big Valley or Mission Rancheria. The Pomo hold traditional dances here periodically. Pomo dance groups also sometimes hold dances at Ft. Ross on Highway 1, eleven miles north of Jenner, California.

Indian Grinding Rock State Park, off Highway 88 on the Pine Grove-Volcano Road near Pine Grove is the site of the Chaw-Se Big Time Celebration, usually the last weekend in September. Often you will find the Pomo dancing here. No pictures or videotapes are allowed inside the roundhouse. Also, the costumes of the dancers are not to be touched because of spiritual rules against doing so.

There are two Pomo communities near Point Arena, the Point Arena and the Manchester Rancherias. This is the home of the Coastal Pomo Indian Dancers, among the best in the country. You may write Box 423, Point Arena, CA 95468, or call (707) 882-2218 and ask for Jackie Frank, for more details.

There is an annual Kule Loklo Celebration in July or August at Kule Loklo Miwok Indian Village. Call (415) 663-1092 for more information. Often there will be Point Arena Pomo, Kashaya Pomo, and other dance groups performing here. The Strawberry Festival in the spring and the Acorn Harvest Festival also find Pomo dancers at Kule Loklo.

The Jesse Peter Memorial Museum, Santa Rosa Junior College Campus, 1501 Mendocino Avenue, Santa Rosa, California, (707) 527-4479, is the location of the Day Under the Oaks Celebration featuring Coastal Pomo Indian Dancers. Pomo dancing also takes place on occasion at Lake Mendocino Cultural Center at Ukiah, California, (707) 462-7581.

Art Forms: The Elem Pomo have a tribal office decorated with traditional basketry designs. Lakeport Historical Museum, Main and Third streets in Lakeport, has a collection of Pomo baskets, (707) 263-4555. Arts and crafts are sold during the Big Time Celebration. The Kule Loklo Celebration has basket weaving, fire making, crafting of musical instruments, and sales of arts and crafts. The Lake Mendocino Cultural Center displays arts and crafts, and the Mendo-Lake Indian Council operates a gift shop here with Pomo crafts, books, and classes in traditional Pomo arts such as basketry.

Visitor Information: The name of the Indian linguistic group known as Pomo is the Kulanapan, living in parts of Sonoma, Lake, Mendocino, Colusa, and Glenn counties. In the northern Pomo dialect, Pomo means "people" and added to a place-name, forms the name for a group of people. Although Poma is almost as frequently heard as Pomo, the latter has come into general use in both scientific and popular literature.

Quartz Valley Rancheria
P.O. Box 25
Fort Jones, CA 96032
(916) 468-5488

Redwood Valley Rancheria
P.O. Box 499
Redwood Valley, CA 95470
(707) 485-0361

Rohnerville Rancheria
P.O. Box 3443
Eureka, CA 95501
(7097) 442-3931

Salinan

The Salinans are the people of Monterey and San Luis Obispo counties. They were in missions San Antonio and San Miguel. Their descendants are living in central California.

San Manuel General Council
5771 North Victoria Avenue
Highland, CA 92346
(714) 862-2439

Serrano

Serranos (Spanish, "Highlanders," "mountaineers")

Visitor Information: The Serrano Cultural Center is on the beautiful San Manuel Indian Reservation in the tribal hall. Archaeological and ethnological displays are presented.

This is a Shoshonean division with a common dialect, centering in the San Bernardino Mountains in southern California, north of Los Angeles, but extending down the Mohave River at least to Daggett and north across the Mohave desert into the valley of Tejon Creek.

Shasta

Not many of the original people are left here in California and Oregon. In 1967, "termination" policies of the U.S. government took the last of their land. The Siskiyou County Museum in Yreka, California, has some of their history.

Smith River Interim Tribal Council
P.O. Box 307
Smith River, CA 95567
(707) 487-9255

Tache Yokuts

Santa Rosa General Council
16835 Alkali Drive
Lemoore, CA 93245
(209) 924-1278

Table Mountain Interim Tribal Council
P.O. Box 243
Friant, CA 93626
(209) 849-4823

Tule River Tribal Council
P.O. Box 589
Porterville, CA 93257
(209) 781-4271

Location: The Lemoore celebration is held on the reservation, and you must call for dates and times. The Tule River Reservation is east of Porterville. Call (209) 781-4271 for dates and times and etiquette required to attend their celebrations and ceremonies.

Public Ceremony or Powwow Dates: In late August, the Lemoore people sponsor an annual celebration that features traditional Yokuts songs. Also in late August, the Tule River Yokuts hold a spiritual gathering for their community and guests. Call for dates and times and etiquette involved to attend.

The Tachi are one of the larger tribes of the Yokuts family, living on the plains north of Tulare Lake, south central California.

Tolowa

The Tolowa have a cultural program that includes dance in traditional form. The College of the Redwoods sponsors a program at Redwood National Park. For more information, contact Redwood National Park at 1111 Second Street, Crescent City, CA 95531, (707) 464-6101.

Tygh

These Indian people of Tygh Valley hold the Tygh Valley Indian Celebration north of Warm Springs, Oregon, in May. See this section, Warm Springs Tribal Office, for more information. Call the tribal office for dates and times.

Viejas Indian Reservation
P.O. Box 908
Alpine, CA 92001
(714) 445-3810

Kumeyaay Nation

Location: The Viejas Indian Reservation is in south San Diego County, 35 miles east of San Diego adjacent to Interstate 8.

Visitor Information: San Diego, just 35 minutes west of the reservation, has all services and accommodations.

The Viejas Tribe operates the Ma-Tar-Awa Park with a gift shop where you will find beautiful basketry, basketry design in textiles, beadwork, and clothing. There is an RV park with all hookups.

The people of Viejas are progressive and modern Americans who have contributed substantially to fire ecology, irrigation, highway transportation systems, and the building of the San Diego County Mission system established by the Spanish missionaries when they first arrived from Spain.

They are independent people who make significant contributions to our world society.

Wailaki

These Indian people live on the Round Valley Indian Reservation at Covelo, California. They have recently revived their beadwork in a new arts and crafts program. Call (707) 983-06126 for the tribal office and more details.

Wintun (Indian, "people")

Colusa Indian Community Council
P.O. Box 8
Colusa, CA 95932
(916) 458-8231

Cortina General Council
P.O. Box 4113
Sacramento, CA 95814
(916) 725-6104

Grindstone General Council
P.O. Box 63
Elk Creek, CA 95939
(916) 934-3602

Redding Interim Tribal Council
2214 Rancheria Road
Redding, CA 96001
(916) 241-1871

Rumsey Rancheria
P.O. Box 18
Brooks, CA 95606
(916) 924-1278

Visitor Information: The Cach Creek Bingo Enterprise is located at Rumsey Rancheria, telephone (916) 796-3182.

Wintun territory was bounded on the north by Mt. Shasta and on the south by a line running from the east boundary, about 10 miles east of the Sacramento River, due west through Jacinto and the headwaters of Stoney Creek, Colusa County. The east boundary began at the headwaters of Bear Creek, bearing south some miles east of the parallel to McCloud River. From Pit River to the neighborhood of Redding, they occupied a triangular area east of the Sacramento.

Table Bluff Board of Directors
P.O. Box 519
Loleta, CA 95551
(707) 733-5583

Wiyot

Location: The greater part of the people of Wiyot live on the reservation in Humboldt County.

Visitor Information: The culture of these people was almost lost when vigilantes murdered them in the 1860s. The tribe has not fully recovered.

Wiyot is a name given by the Wishosk, a small group on the coast of northern California.

Yahi

This is a branch of the Yana tribe. They are known for their member, Ishi, the last Indian person living in his original state. Ishi died in 1916.

Round Valley Indian Reservation
Covelo, CA

Yuki

Visitor Information: The Yuki were almost exterminated by greedy land grabbers in the area of their reservation near Round Valley, California. There is a book about the story of this disgraceful American episode of manifest destiny: Virginia Miller's, *Ukomno'm: The Yuki Indians.*

The Yuki occupied the Round Valley area as well as an area along the coast and south in the mountains dividing Sonoma from Napa and Lake counties.

Yurok

Big Lagoon Rancheria
P.O. Drawer F
Trinidad, CA 95570
(707) 677-3115

Hoopa Valley Business Council
P.O. Box 1348
Hoopa, CA 95546
(916) 625-4211

Resighini Business Council
P.O. Box 212
Klamath, CA 95548
(707) 484-2431

Trinidad Community Council
P.O. Box 589
Trinidad, CA 95570
(707) 677-0211

Yurok (from Karok Yuruk, "downstream")

The Yurok live on lower Klamath River, California, and the adjacent coast. They have no name for themselves other than Olekwo'l, "persons," sometimes written Alikwa. The territory of the Yurok extended from Bluff Creek, six miles above the mouth of the Trinity, down the Klamath River to its mouth, and on the coast from beyond Wilson Creek, six miles north of the mouth of the Klamath, to probably Mad River.

In 1909, they numbered 500 or 600 along the Klamath River. In 1870, the population was 2,700.

Conclusion

The land is plowed up and fenced and paved over. There are giant buildings reaching up to the sky where there were springs and meadows and trees. Trash dumps and pollution and housing areas cover over the Sacred Land. Indian America is reduced to about one-half of one percent in land area, and the population of the people compared to the non-Indian population is about the same. Native American aboriginal people were the residents and caretakers of this land.

You can still walk the Sacred places. All of Mother Earth is Sacred. But you have to pay or ask permission or trespass on another one's property. How can you own the Earth? The Earth is our Mother.

And when the U.S. government makes another settlement or condemns the Sacred Earth for their ownership, Native American people are paid for that land with the value it was when the treaty was signed. Usually that means 1860s prices. Is this fair? Many people believe that Indian people receive money from the government like a handout. I often hear people say that they wish they were Indian so they could receive money and a free ride. The fact is that Indian people do not have a free ride. What they receive is dividends from their own resources. And medical care and education were guaranteed by the government in the treaties for as long as the water flows and the grass grows. This stipulation was the only benefit Native American tribes received in exchange for their land. Usually the treaties were arranged and signed by Indians who did not have the authority and consent of the people, but they often did have the welfare of the people at heart. What could they do against "civilized" armies and weapons and the hordes of the encroaching intruders? As the administration of the government changes, the benefits that Indian people receive change with it. There are cutbacks in education and medical attention. Cutbacks in the only benefits Indian people traded their Sacred Earth to receive.

What has been lost can never be regained. The population of the Earth will not allow it. The attitude and greed of the people will not allow it. When man had reached the height of his perfect state, that time in his culture just before the Industrial Revolution, it was the center of the world and it was in balance and the tree flowered and filled with singing birds. The air was clean and the sky was always blue and fresh air blew across the land and it was good. It was very, very good. Buffalo herds were wide as day and the earth stayed young. The original people of the land were innocent and without the need of machines. There were reasons to celebrate with ceremony and dance and songs. Man had a love affair with natural things and all living things rejoiced and were in love with mankind. The spirit of the whole of all living things was happy.

Now the people of the Earth who live on Turtle Island still celebrate that time of the past when they were free. Tribes still hold powwows and celebrations and conduct ceremonies that are filled with prayers and hope. It is our responsibility to make sure that their prayers and hope are answered and fulfilled.

Sitting Bull was murdered by members of his own people who had been hired by the government as policemen. A few days before he died he said, "There are no Indians left but me. And soon, too, I will be gone."

Sitting Bull was a medicine man. The culture may be smothered by this society, but Indian people have maintained their society, under the most adverse conditions, better than any other native people on Mother Earth. He must be proud.

Glossary

Absentee: A division of the Shawnee tribe who about 1845 left the rest of the tribe, then in Kansas, and removed to Indian Territory. In 1904, they numbered 459, under the Shawnee School Superintendent in Oklahoma.

Agency: The Bureau of Indian Affairs office established on the reservation is called the "agency."

Algonquian family: The linguistic group that occupied a larger area than any other in North America.

Altar: In Indian ceremonial usage, it is the place of the offerings to the spirit or the place of the cleansing of the particular article placed there.

Athapascan family: The linguistic group that is most widely distributed in North America.

Awl: The sharpened stick, bone, stone, or piece of metal used as a perforator in sewing.

Beadwork: Belts, hair ties, earrings, and other jewelry made by stringing beads is called beadwork. Among the types of beadwork are loomwork, lazy stitch, and peyote stitch.

Casa Grande: The principal structure of an extensive ruined pueblo one-half mile south of the Gila River, Pinal County, Arizona.

Ceremony: The performance in a prescribed order of a series of formal acts constituting a drama that has an ultimate object; usually, the expression of spiritual emotion.

Civilization: The overturning of the aboriginal idea of government, the abolition of many of the aboriginal social beliefs, the readjustment of aboriginal ideas of property and personal rights, and the changing of aboriginal occupation.

Confederation: The political league of two or more tribes.

Coup ("blow"; "stroke"): To touch an enemy was more honorable than to kill him.

Cradleboard: The device made to hold an infant while in the early months of life.

Dance: The prodigal nature of life and energy. It is universal and instinctive. The physical expression of spiritual joy.

Dreams and visions: The revelation of spiritual inspiration from the Creator.

Earth lodge: A dwelling partly underground, circular in form, from 30 to 60 feet in diameter, with walls about 6 feet high, on which rested a dome-shaped roof with an opening in the center to afford light within and to permit the egress of smoke.

Ethics and morals: The rules of the community adapted to its mode of life and surroundings. The primitive aboriginal had more rigorous and demanding moral systems than so-called civilized man.

Family clans: An American Indian clan or gens is an intratribal exogamic group of persons either actually or theoretically consanguine, organized to promote their social and political welfare, the members being usually denoted by a common class name derived generally from some fact relating to the habitat of the group or to its usual tutelary being.

Fasting chants: As with other chanting, this is the expression of prayer verbalized into song. It may or may not be within the language. Often, it is song verbalized with rhythmic sounds from spiritual inspiration.

Featherwork: The art of using feathers in costumes; spiritual objects for prayers, decoration, and rewards.

Five Civilized Tribes: The Cherokee, Chickasaw, Choctaw, Creek, and Seminole tribes in Indian Territory were so-called because of their rapid advancement into "civilization."

Gaming; handgames: Indian games today are games of chance; (1) games in which implements corresponding with dice are thrown at random to determine a number or numbers, the counts being kept by means of sticks, pebbles, etc., or on an abacus or counting board or circuit; (2) games in which one or more of the players guess in which of two or more places an odd or particularly marked counter is concealed, success or failure resulting in the gain or loss of counters. Also games of dexterity: archery, darts, shooting at a moving target, ball games in many forms, and racing games.

Ghost Dance: The ceremonial spiritual dance connected with the messiah Wovoka ("Cutter"). The massacre of so many men, women, and children at Wounded Knee, South Dakota, on December 29, 1890, was undertaken because of the mistaken notion of the U.S. Army that the people were gathering for a violent exchange with them. They were actually gathering for the performance of the Ghost Dance.

Great Spirit: The Creator, God, Jehovah.

Hogan: A Navajo house, constructed of logs with dirt thrown and piled against the sides.

Iroquoian family: A linguistic group of the Northeast United States and Canada.

Kachina: A supernatural being impersonated by men or statuettes.
Keresan family: A linguistic family of Pueblo Indians.
Kiva: Sacred ceremonial and assembly chamber of the Pueblo Indians.

Maize: Corn.
Medicine and Medicine Man: The scope of spiritual agents that are medicinal, magical, prayerful, symbolical, and empirical. The one that interprets and administers and conducts the ceremony surrounding such agents is a Medicine Man.
Metalwork: The art of converting metals into adornments and jewelry.
Metate: The name given to stones for grinding grains, seeds, chile, dried meats, and so forth.
Missions: The southern California and coastal Spanish settlements that employed the use of forced Indian labor to construct, maintain, and operate. Other missions were common across the Americas and were conducted by a variety of groups, usually religious in nature.
Moccasin: The shoe; usually made of deerskin.
Muskhogean family: A linguistic group comprising the Creeks, Choctaw, Chickasaw, Seminole, and other tribes.

Powwow: A social gathering of the tribes with intertribal singing and dancing. Usually there is also competition dancing in many styles.
Pueblo: A town or village built in a permanent manner. In the Southwest, the term has come to signify all Indian villages built from stone or adobe.

Quillwork: The embroidery work that includes the quills of porcupines or bird feathers.

Reservation: A tract of land that is held in trust by an Indian tribe, nation, or community. The U.S. government set aside these areas as a result of treaties that were often signed by people of the tribe who did not have authority to do so. The reservation was a device that allowed the government to bring Indian people under control and to take the greater portion of the land area. Ironically, much of the poor land that was set aside for the reservations also was the land that contained mineral deposits.

Salinan family: A linguistic group of California.
Sand painting: An art existing among Indian people, especially those of the southwestern part of the United States. Some tribes use the painting in a ceremonial and healing way.

Shoshonean family: The linguistic group that occupied most of the Mountain and Plateau all the way to the southwest coast of the United States.

Shrines: The place where sacred offerings are deposited in prayers to the Creator.

Sinew: The tendonous animal fiber used for sewing purposes.

Siouan family: The most populous linguistic family north of Mexico, next to the Algonquian.

Snake Dance: The ceremony of the Hopi people in which live snakes are carried.

Soul: The concept of spiritual life residing in the body.

Sun Dance: The Offerings Lodge, misnamed the Sun Dance by observers who believed the dancers were worshiping the sun. This is the most sacred of ceremonies of the Plains tribes, especially the Arapahoe, Cheyenne, Siksika, Cree of Algonquian stock, the Dakota, Assiniboine, Mandan, Crows, Ponca, Omaha of Siouan stock, Pawnee of Caddoan stock, Kiowa, Shoshone, and the Ute of Shoshonean stock. The ceremony does not involve self-inflicted torture as many writers have postulated in the past. This is the giving and offering of one's self to the Creator with fasting and praying and, in some tribes, piercing of the pectoral muscle.

Sweat lodge: The ceremony of prayer in a sweat lodge built with a willow frame and covered with buffalo robes (blankets, carpet, canvas or combinations of these today). Hot stones are brought into the lodge and water is poured over them to produce steam. It is a rigorously prescribed ceremony in which rules and observances are followed.

Symbols: An object or action that conveys a meaning distinct from the actual concept corresponding to the object or to the action.

Tattooing: The act of affixing a permanent symbol or design on the body. This is very common among many Indian tribes. The act of signing for Arapahoe was a tapping of the upper chest because they usually tattooed one or more dotted circles in that area.

Tewa: A linguistic family of the Pueblo people in the Southwest.

Tipi: From the Siouan root *ti* "to dwell," *pi* "used for." This is the spelling approved by the Sioux Nation. A tipi is the conical skin dwelling of the Plains tribes and by some of the tribes of the Northwest. Constructed with buffalo hides sewn to form a single piece and held in place by lodgepoles, the average tipi was about 16 feet in diameter in the days when people were free to roam the plains.

Tribe: The body of persons who are bound together by ties of consanguinity and affinity and by certain esoteric ideas or concepts derived from their philosophy concerning the genesis and preservation of the environing cosmos and who by means of these kinship ties are thus socially, politically, and spiritually organized through a variety of ritualistic, governmental, and other institutions, and who dwell together occupying a definite territorial area, and who speak a common language or dialect.

Walum Olum: The sacred tribal chronicle of the Lenape or Delaware. The name signifies "painted tally."

Wickiup: The popular name for the brush shelter or mat-covered house of the Paiute, Apache, and other tribes of the Nevada and Arizona regions.

Wigwam: An arborlike or conical structure covered with bark or whatever the local area dictated.

Yuman family: A linguistic group of southern California and southern Arizona.

Bibliography

Brown, Dee. *Bury My Heart at Wounded Knee.* Holt, Rinehart, Winston, New York, 1970.

Brown, Dee. *Wounded Knee.* Holt, Rinehart, Winston, New York, 1970.

Brown, Joseph Epes. *The Sacred Pipe.* University of Oklahoma Press, Norman, Oklahoma, 1953.

Capps, Benjamin. *The Indians.* Time-Life Books, Alexandria, Virginia, 1973.

Eagle/Walking Turtle. *Keepers of the Fire.* Bear and Co., Santa Fe, New Mexico, 1987.

Formen, Werner, and Norman Bancroft-Hunt. *The Indians of the Great Plains.* Orbis Publishing Limited, London, 1981.

Hardt, Athia L. *The Art of Navajo Sand Paintings.* N.Y. Times, October 2, 1988.

Hillinger, Charles. *Tribe's Single Survivor Passes Along Knowledge.* Los Angeles Times, Albuquerque Journal, September 25, 1988.

Hodge, Frederick W. *Handbook of American Indians North of Mexico.* Pageant Books, Inc., New York, 1959.

Jacka, Lois Essary. *On the Mesas of the Hopis.* N.Y. Times, October 2, 1988.

Karr, Jane Alice. *Courtesy Note.* N.Y. Times, October 2, 1988.

Mails, Thomas E. *Dog Soldiers, Bear Men and Buffalo Women.* Prentice-Hall, Inc., Englewood Cliffs, New Jersey, 1973.

Marquis, Arnold. *A Guide to America's Indians.* University of Oklahoma Press, Norman, Oklahoma, 1974.

Neihardt, John G. *When the Tree Flowered.* University of Nebraska Press, Lincoln, 1951.

Pacheco, Patrick. *Rites of Passage.* N.Y. Times, October 2, 1988.

Schmitt and Brown. *Fighting Indians of the West.* Chas. Scribner's Sons, Bonanza Books, New York, 1948.

Shakespeare, Tom. *The Sky People.* Vantage Press, New York, 1971.

Shanks, Ralph. *The North American Indian Travel Guide.* Petaluma, 1986, 1987.

Snyder, Fred. *National Native American Directory.* San Carlos, Arizona, 1982.

Trenholm, Virginia Cole. *The Arapahoes, Our People.* University of Oklahoma Press, Norman, Oklahoma, 1970.

Vanderwerth, W. C. *Indian Oratory.* University of Oklahoma Press, Norman, Oklahoma, 1971.

APPENDIX

Indian Moons

January
Sioux:	Moon of strong cold
Zuni:	Moon when the limbs of trees are broken by snow
Omaha:	Moon when the snow drifts into the tipis

February
Sioux:	Raccoon moon
Omaha:	Moon when the geese come home
Tewa Pueblo:	Moon of the cedar dust wind
Kiowa:	Little bud moon
Winnebago:	Fish-running moon

March
Sioux:	Moon when the buffalo cows drop their calves
Omaha:	Little frog moon
Tewa Pueblo:	Moon when the leaves break forth
Cherokee:	Strawberry moon
Ponca:	Water stands in the ponds moon

April
Sioux:	Moon of greening grass
Cheyenne:	Moon when the geese lay eggs
Winnebago:	Planting corn moon
Kiowa:	Leaf moon
Mandan-Hidatsa:	Moon of the breaking up of the ice

May
Sioux	Moon when the ponies shed
Creek:	Mulberry moon
Osage:	Moon when the little flowers die
Cheyenne:	Moon when the horses get fat
Winnebago:	Hoeing-corn moon

June

Sioux:	Moon of making fat
Omaha:	Moon when the buffalo bulls hunt the cows
Tewa Pueblo:	Moon when the leaves are dark green
Ponca:	Hot weather begins moon

July

Sioux:	Moon when the wild cherries are ripe
Omaha:	Moon when the buffalo bellow
Kiowa:	Moon of deer horns dropping off
Creek:	Little ripening moon
Winnebago:	Corn-popping moon

August

Sioux:	Moon when the geese shed their feathers
Cherokee:	Drying up moon
Ponca:	Corn is in the silk moon
Creek:	Big ripening moon
Osage:	Yellow flower moon

September

Sioux:	Moon of drying grass
Omaha:	Moon when the deer paw the earth
Tewa Pueblo:	Moon when the corn is taken in
Cherokee:	Black butterfly moon
Creek:	Little chestnut moon

October

Sioux:	Moon of falling leaves
Zuni:	Big wind moon
Ponca:	Moon when they store food in caches
Cheyenne:	Moon when the water begins to freeze on the edge of streams
Kiowa:	Ten-colds moon

November

Creek:	Moon when the water is black with leaves
Kiowa:	Geese-going moon
Mandan-Hidatsa:	Moon when the rivers freeze
Tewa Pueblo:	Moon when all is gathered in
Winnebago:	Little bear's moon

December

Sioux:	Moon of popping trees
Cheyenne:	Moon when the wolves run together
Creek:	Big winter moon
Arikara:	Moon of the nose of the great serpent
Winnebago:	Big bear's moon

Powwow Calendar for North America

January
1st weekend

Phoenix Powwow
Central Plains Indian Club
Phoenix, AZ

1st weekend

New Year's Day Veteran's Dinner
White Swan Longhouse
White Swan, WA
(509) 865-2800

New Year's Powwow
Oklahoma City, OK
(405) 232-2512

*Early January
through March*

Alaska Dog Mushers Races
each weekend
Fairbanks, AK

February
Bethel Winter Carnival
Bethel, AK

2nd weekend

Fur Rendezvous
Alaska's largest winter celebration
    with champion Sled Dog Races
Anchorage, AK

3rd weekend

O'Odham-Tash Indian Days
Chamber of Commerce
Casa Grande, AZ
(602) 836-2125

George Washington Birthday
  Celebration
Toppenish Community Center
Toppenish, WA
(509) 865-2800

March
2nd weekend

Speelyi Mi Indian
  Arts & Crafts Fair
Yakima Nation Cultural Center
Highway 97
Toppenish, WA
(509) 253-1594

3rd weekend

Indian Market
Phoenix Fairgrounds
Phoenix, AZ
(602) 253-1594

April
1st weekend

Mul-Chu-Tha
Community Fair
Box 97
Sacaton, AZ
(602) 562-3311 Tribe

3rd weekend

Native American Student
  Association Powwow
Native American Program
Arizona State University
Tempe, AZ
(602) 965-6053

Satus Longhouse Powwow
Satus, WA
(509) 865-2800

Institute of American Indian
  Arts Powwow
Cerrillos Road
Santa Fe, NM 87501
(505) 988-6281

4th weekend

Yavapai Community College
  Powwow
Prescott, AZ
(602) 445-7300

May
2nd weekend

Ty Valley All-Indian Rodeo
Ty Valley, OR

3rd weekend

Stanford University Powwow
Native American Program
Stanford University
Stanford, CA
(415) 497-2300

4th weekend

Weaseltail Mini Powwow
White Swan, WA
(509) 865-2800

World Championship Jeep Rodeo
Yakima Nation
Toppenish, WA
(509) 865-2800

June
1st weekend

Mescalero Apache Fair
Mescalero Tribe
Mescalero, NM
(505) 671-4494

2nd weekend

Delta Park Powwow
Portland Indian Center
Delta Park, OR
(503) 248-4562

Cortez Spiritual Encampment
Spiritual Grounds
Cortez, CO
Allen Neskahi
(303) 565-3205

Tiinowit International Powwow
White Swan Ceremonial Grounds
White Swan, WA
(509) 865-2800

Annual Treaty Day Celebration
 & Rodeo
White Swan, WA
(509) 865-2800

All Indian Nations Art & Craft
 Festival
Fort Mason
San Francisco, CA

4th weekend

Warm Springs Treaty Days
Warm Springs Tribe
Warm Springs, OR
(503) 553-1161

Worley Indian Days
Coeur d'Alene Tribe
Worley, ID
(206) 274-3101

Lummi Indian Days
Lummi Tribe
Bellingham, WA
(206) 734-8180

July
1st weekend

Arlee Powwow
Flathead Tribe
Arlee, MT
(406) 675-2700

Toppenish Powwow
Toppenish, WA
(509) 865-2800

Yakima Indian Encampment
White Swan Grounds
White Swan, WA
(509) 865-2800

Nespelium
Colville Confederated Tribe
Nespelium, WA
(10 days)
(509) 634-4072

2nd weekend

Mission Indian Days
Mission Indian Friendship Center
Mission, British Columbia,
 Canada
(604) 826–12w81

Honor the Earth Traditional
 Powwow
Lac Courte Oreilles Ceremonial
 Ground
Hayward, WI
(715) 634-8934

3rd weekend

Browning Indian Days
Chamber of Commerce
Browning, MT
(406) 338-2230

4th weekend

Fallon Indian Days
Chamber of Commerce
Fallon, NV
(702) 423-2544

World Eskimo Indian Olympics
Fairbanks, AK

Indian-Eskimo-Aleut Olympics
University of Alaska
Fairbanks, AK

August
1st weekend

Stony Spiritual Encampment
Stony Tribe
Stony, Alberta, Canada

Brockett Indian Days
Brockett Powwow Grounds
Brockett, Alberta, Canada

2nd weekend

Fort Hall Indian Days
Fort Hall Tribe
Fort Hall, ID
(208) 238-3800

Ermineskine Band Powwow
Powwow Grounds
Hobbema, Alberta, Canada
(403) 585-3941

Gallup Ceremonial
Red Rock State Park
Gallup, NM
(505) 863-3896

3rd weekend

Crow Fair
Crow Agency, MT
(406) 638-2601

Regina Powwow
Regina, Saskatchewan, Canada

Winterburn Powwow
Winterburn, Alberta, Canada

Onion Lake Indian Days
Onion Lake, Saskatchewan,
  Canada

Kamiaah Indian Days
Nez Perce Tribe
Kamiaah, ID
(208) 843-2253

Omak Stampede
Colville Confederated Tribe
Omak, WA
(509) 634-4072

American Indian Exposition
Anadarko, OK
(405) 247-5661

Makah Indian Days
Makah Tribe
Neah Bay, WA
(206) 645-2201

Santa Fe Indian Market
Chamber of Commerce
Santa Fe, NM
(505) 983-7317

September
1st weekend

Wellpinit Indian Days
Spokane Tribe
Wellpinit, WA
(509) 258-4581

3rd weekend

Pendleton Roundup
Chamber of Commerce
Pendleton, OR

4th weekend

National Indian Days
Colorado River Tribes
Parker, AZ
(602) 669-9211

California Indian Days
Intertribal Council of California
Expo Grounds
Sacramento, CA
(916) 488-8508

National Indian Days
  Celebration Powwow
Yakima Nation
White Swan, WA
(509) 865-2800

October
1st weekend

Shiprock Navajo Fair
Shiprock, NM
(602) 871-4941

2nd weekend

National Congress of American
  Indian
Annual Convention

National Indian Education
  Conference
Annual Convention

Western Navajo Fair
Tuba City, AZ
(602) 871-4941

3rd weekend

Palm Springs Powwow
Agua Caliente Tribe
Palm Springs, CA
(714) 352-5673

American Indian Exposition
Anadarko, OK
1 week duration

Arizona State Fair
Indian Village (Phoenix
  Fairgrounds)
Phoenix, AZ
(602) 252-6771
15-day duration

November
1st weekend

San Carlos Veteran's Day Parade
  Powwow
San Carlos Tribe
Box 0
San Carlos, AZ 85550
(602) 475-2361

Papago All-Indian Rodeo and Fair
Papago Tribe
Sells, AZ
(602) 383-2221

American Indian Film Festival
Palace of Fine Arts
San Francisco, CA

Indian Market Days
Phoenix Indian Center
Phoenix, AZ
(602) 279-4116

Scottsdale Community College
  Powwow
Native American Program
Scottsdale Community College
Scottsdale, AZ
(602) 941-0999

Heard Museum Craft Show
Heard Museum
22 East Monte Vista Road
Phoenix, AZ 85004
(602) 252-8848

Veteran's Day Celebration
Toppenish Community Center
Toppenish, WA
(509) 865-2800

3rd weekend

Indian National Rodeo Finals
Box 1725
Albuquerque, NM 87103

Indian Market
Phoenix Fairgrounds
Phoenix, AZ
(602) 253-1594

Indian Market
San Xavier Plaza
Papago Tribe
Tucson, AZ
(602) 298-3772

Thanksgiving Powwow
Fort Duschesne, UT

Chicago Annual Powwow
Chicago Armory
Chicago, IL
(312) 275-5871

December
1st weekend

Pueblo Grande Museum Art and
  Craft Show
Pueblo Grande Museum
Phoenix, AZ
(602) 275-3452

2nd weekend

Coconino High School Powwow
Flagstaff Indian Center
Flagstaff, AZ
(602) 774-2537

4th weekend

Bay Area Powwow
Mr. Sy Williams
Oakland, CA
(415) 534-8664

Miccosukee Indian Fair
Miccosukee Tribe
Tamiami Trail
Miami, FL
(305) 223-8380

Christmas Celebration
Wapato Longhouse
Wapato, WA
(509) 865-2800

Seminole Tribal Fair
Seminole Tribe
Hollywood, FL
(305) 583-7112

This calendar does not include all powwows. Many come and go each year. The ones listed are at least three years old and will be worth a full day's journey to visit. Call to verify dates.

Check local Indian centers, clubs, and Native American programs at your nearest college or university. Quite often they will sponsor an event in conjunction with Indian awareness week, an anniversary, or sometimes they will have a monthly powwow.

All-Indian Arts and Crafts Shows and Exhibitions

February
3rd weekend

O'Odham-Tash Indian Days
Chamber of Commerce
Casa Grande, AZ
(602) 836-2125

March
2nd weekend

Mi Indian Art & Craft Fair
Yakima Cultural Center
Highway 97, Box 151
Toppenish, WA 98948
(509) 697-5126

3rd weekend

Indian Market
P.O. Box 504
Phoenix, AZ 85001
(602) 253-1594

April
3rd weekend

Eight Northern Pueblo Indian
Arts and Crafts
Santa Fe, NM 87501
(505) 852-4265

August
2nd weekend

Gallup Ceremonial
Red Rock State Park
Gallup, NM
(505) 863-3896

4th weekend

Santa Fe Indian Market
Chamber of Commerce
Santa Fe, NM
(505) 983-7317

September
4th weekend

California Indian Days
Intertribal Council of California
Expo Grounds
Sacramento, CA
(916) 488-8508

November
2nd weekend

Heard Museum Craft Show
Heard Museum
22 E. Monte Vista Road
Phoenix, AZ 85004
(602) 252-8848

American Indian Film Festival
225 Valencia Street
San Francisco, CA 94103
(415) 552-1070 Michael Smith
held at: Palace of Fine Arts

December
1st weekend

Pueblo Grande Museum Art &
Craft Show
Pueblo Grande Museum
48th and Washington Sts.
Phoenix, AZ
(602) 275-3452

4th weekend

Miccosukee Indian Fair
Tamiami Trail
Miami, FL
(305) 223-8380

June-August

Flagstaff Festival of Native
American Arts
Coconino Center for the
Arts—County Courthouse
Flagstaff, AZ
(602) 779-5944

1st weekend of December
through January 31st

Institute of American Indian Art
Annual Student Sales Show
I.A.I.A. Museum
1369 Cerrillos Road
Santa Fe, NM 87501
(505) 988-6281

1st Sunday of February
through May 1st

Institute of American Indian Art
Annual High School Art
Competition
1369 Cerrillos Road
Santa Fe, NM 87501
(505) 988-6281

1st Sunday of May
through June 1st
Institute of American Indian Art
Annual Graduation Class Exhibit
1369 Cerrillos Road
Santa Fe, NM 87501
(505) 988-6281

One-man exhibits are available to any Native American artist in any media. Contact: C. Dailey, I. A. I. A. Museum, 1369 Cerrillos Road, Santa Fe, NM 87501, (505) 988-6281.

Navajo Rug Auctions

Crownpoint Rug Weavers Association
P.O. Box 1630
Crownpoint, NM 87313
(505) 786-5302

The Crownpoint Rug Weavers Association sponsors auctions that are held at the Crownpoint Elementary School, usually starting at 7:00 p.m. Rugs are usually on display from about 2:00 p.m. on the date of the auction at the school. Rugs from all areas of the reservation are available. Generally, there is a minimum bid on each rug which is set by the association and the weaver. A fine selection with reasonable prices can be acquired at these auctions.

These auctions are held approximately every six to seven weeks. Call to verify dates.

Indian Museums with Major Collections on American Indians

Anchorage Historical and
Fine Arts Museum
121 W. 7th Ave.
Anchorage, AK 99501

Museum of North Arizona
Ft. Valley Road, Box 1389
Flagstaff, AZ 86001

Heard Museum of
Anthropology and
Primitive Art
22 E. Monte Vista Road
Phoenix, AZ 85004

University of Arizona
Arizona State Museum
Tucson, AZ 85721

University of California
Robert H. Lowie Museum of
Anthropology
103 Kroeber Hall
Berkeley, CA 94720

Southwest Museum
Box 128, Highland Park Station
Los Angeles, CA 90042

Denver Art Museum
100 W. 14th Avenue Parkway
Denver, CO 80204

Museum of Science
3280 S. Miami Avenue
Miami, FL 33129

Red Rock Museum
Box 328
Church Rock, NM 87311
(505) 722-6196

Field Museum of Natural
History
Roosevelt Road at Lake Shore
Drive
Chicago, IL 60605

Pipestone National
Monument
Box 727
Pipestone, MN 56164

Brooklyn Museum
188 Eastern Parkway
Brooklyn, NY 11238

Museum of Primitive Art
15 W. 54th Street
New York, NY 10019

American Museum of Natural
History
79th Street & Central Park West
New York, NY 10024

Museum of the American
Indian
Heye Foundation
155th Street & Broadway
New York, NY 10032

Smithsonian Institution
1000 Jefferson Drive S.W.
Washington, D.C. 20560

University of Washington
Thomas Burke Memorial
Washington State Museum
Seattle, WA 98195

Museum of Native American Cultures
P.O. Box 2044
Spokane, WA 99220

Indian-Owned/Operated Museums and Cultural Centers

National Association:
North American Indian Museums
  Association
c/o Richard Hill
466 Third Street
Niagara Falls, NY 14301
(716) 284-2427

Acoma Museum
P.O. Box 309
Pueblo of Acoma, NM 87032

Akwesasne Museum
Route 37—St. Regis Mohawk
  Reservation
Hogansburg, NY 13655
(518) 358-2240
Admission: Free
Hours: Mon.-Fri. 8:00 a.m.-
  4:00 p.m.
Parking: Ample
Accommodations: Yes
Museum Shop: Yes

Alaska Native Village
Alaskaland Park
Fairbanks, AK 99701

Arts and Crafts Cultural Center
P.O. Box 529
Bayfield, WI 54814
(715) 779-5609

Bacone College Museum
(Ataloa Art Lodge)
East Shawnee
Muskogee, OK 74402
(918) 683-4581, Ext. 212 or 229
Admission: Free
Hours: Mon.-Fri. 8:00 a.m.-
  12:00 noon, 1:00-4:00 p.m.
Parking and Dining: Yes
Museum Shop: Yes
Accommodations: Yes

Chaw-se Indian Grinding Rocks State Park
c/o Margaret Dalton
Star Route 1
Jackson, CA 95642

Cherokee National Museum, Tsa-La-Gi
P.O. Box 515
Tahlequah, OK 74464
(918) 456-6007
Admission: Adults: $1.00,
   Children under 16: $.50
Hours:
   Winter: Tues.-Sat. 10:00 a.m.-
      5:00 p.m.
   Sun. 1:00 p.m.-
      5:00 p.m.
   Summer: Mon.-Sat. 10:00 a.m.-
      8:00 p.m.
   Sun. 1:00 p.m.-
      6:00 p.m.
Parking: Yes
Accommodations: Yes
Book Shop: Yes

Colville Confederated Tribes
Star Route
Coulee Dam, WA 99116

Colorado River Indian Tribes Museum
Route 1, P.O. Box 23B
Parker, AZ 85344
(602) 669-9211
Admission: Free
Parking: Ample
Accommodations: Yes

Comanche Cultural Center
P.O. Box 382
Walters, OK 73572
(405) 429-8199
Admission: Free
Hours: Mon.-Fri. 8:00 a.m.-
   5:00 p.m.
Parking: Ample
Lunch Facilities: Snack Bar
Accommodations: Yes

Crow Tribe Historical and Cultural Commission
P.O. Box 173
Crow Agency, MT 59022
(406) 638-2328

Daybreak Star Arts Center
P.O. Box 99523
Seattle, WA 98199
(206) 285-4425
Admission: Free
Parking: Ample
Accommodations: Yes

Dinjii Zhuu Museum
P.O. Box 42
Fort Yukon, AK 99740
(907) 622-2345
Admission: Contribution of one
   dollar
Hours: May-October, 1:00 p.m.-
   3:00 p.m.
Parking: Ample
Accommodations: Yes—summer
Museum Shop: Yes

Duncan Cottage Museum
P.O. Box 282
Annette Island Reserve
Metlakatla, AK 99926
Admission: Free
Hours: Mon.-Fri. 9:00 a.m.-
   5:00 p.m.
Parking: Yes
Lunch Facilities: Yes
Accommodations: Yes
Museum Shop: Yes

Fort Sill Apache Museum
115 NE First St.
Anadarko, OK 73005

Gila River Arts and Crafts Museum

P.O. Box 457
Sacaton, AZ 85247
(602) 963-3981
Admission: Free
Hours: 10:00 a.m.-5:00 p.m.
    Mon.-Fri.
Parking: Ample
Accommodations: 10 miles into
    Phoenix

Hoonah Cultural Center

P.O. Box 218
Hoonah, AK 99829

Hopi Tribal Museum

P.O. Box 38
Second Mesa, AZ 86035
(602) 734-2411
Parking: Ample
Accommodations: No

Indian Pueblo Cultural Center, Inc.

2401 12th Street, NW
Albuquerque, NM 87102
(505) 843-7270 or 843-7271
Admission: Free
Hours:
    Winter: Mon.-Fri. 9:00 a.m.-
        6:00 p.m.
    Sun. Noon-5:00 p.m.
    Summer: Mon.-Fri. 9:00 a.m.-
        6:00 p.m.
    Sun. 10:00 a.m.-
        6:00 p.m.
Parking: Yes
Lunch Facilities: Yes
Accommodations: Yes
Museum Shop: Yes

Institute of American Indian Arts Museum

1369 Cerrillos Road
Santa Fe, NM 87501
(505) 988-6281
Admission: Free
Hours:
    Winter: Mon.-Fri. 9:00 a.m.-
        5:00 p.m.
    Summer: Every day 9:00 a.m.-
        5:00 p.m.
Parking: Ample
Lunch Facilities: Yes
Accommodations: Yes
Museum Shop: Yes

Inupiat University of the Arctic

P.O. Box 429
Barrow, AK 99723

Kanien 'Kehaka Raotitiohkwa Cultural Center

P.O. Box 750
Kahnawake, Quebec
J0L 1B0 Canada
(514) 638-0880
Admission: Free
Hours:
    Mon.-Thurs. 8:30 a.m.-
        5:30 p.m.
    Fri. 8:30 a.m.-4:00 p.m.
    Sun. 1:30 p.m.-9:00 p.m.
Parking: Yes
Lunch Facilities: Yes
Accommodations: 10 miles into
    Montreal

Makah Cultural Research Center
P.O. Box 95
Neah Bay, WA 98357
(206) 645-2711
Admission: Adults—$2.00; senior citizens and 16 and under—$1.00; infants—free
Hours:
Winter: Wed.-Sun. 10:00 a.m.-5:00 p.m.
Summer: Every day 10:00 a.m.-5:00 p.m.
Accommodations: Write to: Neah Bay Chamber of Commerce, P.O. Box 448 Neah Bay, WA 98357
Craft Shop: Yes

Malki Museum Inc.
11–795 Fields Road
Morongo Indian Reservation
Banning, CA 92220
(714) 849-7289

Mescalero Apache Cultural Center
P.O. Box 175
Mescalero, NM 88340
(505) 671-4495
Admission: Free
Hours: Mon.-Fri. 9:00 a.m.-4:30 p.m.
Parking: Yes
Accommodations: No

Miccosukee Cultural Center
P.O. Box 440021, Tamiami Station
Miami, FL 33144
(305) 223-8380

Mic Mac Museum
RR 1
Pictou, Nova Scotia, Canada
(902) 485-4723

Museés Des Ab'Nakes D'Odanak
Odanack, Quebec, Canada
(902) 568-2600

Museum of the Arctic
P.O. Box 49
Kotzebue, AK 99752
(907) 442-3301

Museum of the Cherokee Indian
U.S. Highway 441 North, P.O. Box 770-A
Cherokee, NC 28719
(704) 497-3481
Admission: Adults $2.50, Children (6-13 yrs.) $1.25, under 6 yrs. free
Hours:
Winter: Mon.-Fri. 9:00 a.m.-5:30 p.m.
Summer: Mon.-Fri. 9:00 a.m.-8:00 p.m.
Parking: Ample
Lunch Facilities: Snack Bar
Accommodations: Yes
Gift Shop: Yes

Museum of the Plains Indian and Craft Center
P.O. Box 400
Browning, MT 59417

Museum of the Woodland Indian
184 Mohawk Street
Brantford, Ontario
Canada N3T 5V6
(519) 759-2650
Admission: 13 years and over
$.75, 12 years and under $.50
Hours: Mon.-Fri. 8:30 a.m.-
    4:00 p.m., weekends
    and holidays
    10:00 a.m.-5:00 p.m.
Parking: Yes
Accommodations: Yes
Lunch Facilities: Cafeteria for bag
  lunches only
Craft Shop: Yes

Muskogee Creek National Museum
P.O. Box 1114
Okmulgee, OK 74447
(918) 756-8700

Navajo Tribal Museum
P.O. Box 308
Window Rock, AZ 86515
(602) 871-4941, Ext. 1457 or 1459
Admission: Free
Hours:
  Winter: Mon.-Fri. 9:00 a.m.-
    5:00 p.m.
  Summer: Sun. 1:00 p.m.-
    5:00 p.m.,
    Mon.-Sat. 9:00 a.m.-
    5:00 p.m.

Native American Centre for the Living Arts, Inc.
25 Rainbow Mall
Niagara Falls, NY 14801
(716) 284-2427
Lunch Facilities: Yes
Craft Shop: Yes

Native American Cultural Heritage Center
Dallas Independent School
  District
Dallas, TX 75204

North American Indian Traveling College
RR 3
Cornwell Island, Ontario
Canada K6H 5R7
(613) 932-9452

Oneida Nation Museum
886 Double E Road
DePere, WI 54115
(414) 869-2768
Admission: Free
Hours: Tues.-Sat. 10:00 a.m.-
    6:00 p.m.
    Sun. Noon-6:00 p.m.
Parking: Yes
Lunch Facilities: Picnic area
Museum Shop: Yes

Osage Tribal Museum
P.O. Box 178
Pawhuska, OK 74056

Pamunkey Indian Village
c/o Pamunkey Research Center
Route. 1, P.O. Box 217-AA
King William, VA 23806
(804) 843-3648

Puyallup Tribe
2215 East 22nd Street
Tacoma, WA 98404
(206) 597-6479

Sac and Fox Tribal RV Park and Museum/Cultural Center
Route 2, P.O. Box 246
Stroud, OK 74079
(918) 968-3526 or (405) 275-4270

San Ildefonso Pueblo Museum
Route 5, Box 315-A
Santa Fe, NM 87501
(505) 455-2424
Admission: Free
Hours:
Winter: Mon.-Fri. 8:00 a.m.-
4:30 p.m.
Summer: Mon.-Fri. 8:00 a.m.-
6:00 p.m.
Parking: Yes
Lunch Facilities: No
Accommodations: No
Craft Shops: Yes

Seminole Tribal Museum
6073 Stirling Road
Hollywood, FL 33024
(305) 587-4500 or 583-7111

Seneca Iroquois National Museum
P.O. Box 442
Broad Street Exit
Salamanca, NY 14779
(716) 945-1790
Admission: No, donations
accepted
Hours: Mon.-Sat. 10:00 a.m.-
5:00 p.m.
Sun. 12:00 p.m.-
5:00 p.m.
Closed January
Parking: Ample
Accommodations: Nearby hotels
Craft Shop: Yes

Sioux Indian Museum & Craft Center
P.O. Box 1504
Rapid City, SD 57709

Southeast Alaska Indian Cultural Center
P.O. Box 944
Sitka, AK 99835
(907) 747-8061

Southern Plains Indian Museum
P.O. Box 749
Anadarko, OK 73005
(405) 247-6211

Stockbridge Munsee Historical Library and Museum
Route 1, Box 300
Bowler, WI 54416
(715) 793-4270
Admission: Free
Hours: Mon.-Fri. 8:00 a.m.-
4:30 p.m. or by appointment
Parking: Limited
Craft Shop: Yes

Tantaquidgeon Indian Museum
Route 32 Norwich-New London
Road
Uncasville, CT 06382
(203) 858-9145

Tigua Pueblo Museum
Texas Indian Reservation
El Paso, TX 79917
(915) 859-7913

Tomaquag Indian Memorial Museum
Summit Road
Exeter, RI 02822
(401) 539-7795

Totem Heritage Center
629 Dock St.
Ketchikan, AK 99901

Ute Mountain Tribal Park
General Delivery
Towaoc, CO 81334
(303) 565-3751
Admission: Tours by donation
Hours: Mon.-Fri. 8:00 a.m.-
   4:30 p.m. or by appointment
Lunch Facilities: Bag lunches only
Craft Shop: Yes

Ute Tribal Museum
Ute Tribe, P.O. Box 190
Ft. Duchesne, UT 84026
(801) 722-4992
Admission: Free
Hours: Mon.-Fri. 9:00 a.m.-
   5:00 p.m.
Parking: Yes
Lunch Facilities: Yes
Accommodations: Yes

Wampanoag Indian Program of Plymouth Plantation
P.O. Box 1620
Plymouth, MA 02360
(617) 746-1622
Admission: Adults $4.00; children
   $2.00
Hours: Mon.-Fri. 9:00 a.m.-
   5:00 p.m.
Parking: Yes
Lunch Facilities: Yes
Museum Shop: Yes

Wichita Tribal Cultural Center
P.O. Box 927
Anadarko, OK 73005

Winona Club Sioux Cultural Center
Box 775
Rapid City, SD 57701

Yakima Nation Cultural Center Museum
P.O. Box 151
Toppenish, WA 98948
(509) 865-2800

Yankton Sioux Museum
Box 244
Marty, SD 57301

Yugtarvik Regional Museum
Box 388
Bethel, AK 99559
(907) 543-2098
Admission: Free
Hours: Tues.-Sat. 10:00 a.m.-
   6:00 p.m.
Parking: Yes
Accommodations: Yes
Museum Shop: Yes

Indian-Owned Stores

ARIZONA

George J. Stevens
P.O. Box 57
San Carlos, AZ 85550
(602) 475-2235
Store: In home
Specialty: Apache, Navajo, Zuni, and Hopi crafts

Hopi Arts & Crafts
Von and Elaine Monongya
P.O. Box 82
Oraibi, AZ 86039
(602) 734-6605
Store: In home
Specialty: Hopi arts and crafts, kachina doll carver

Arizona Indian Market Associates
Jane and John Popovich
P.O. Box 504
Phoenix, AZ 85001-0504
(602) 253-1594
Store: In home
Specialty: Navajo silverwork

Gila River Arts & Crafts
John A. Long
P.O. Box 457
Sacaton, AZ 85247
(602) 963-3981 or 562-3411
Store: 20 miles south of Phoenix
Specialty: Southwestern traditional arts and crafts

Taz Studio
Clifford Beck
P.O. Box 8216
Scottsdale, AZ 85252
Store: In home
Specialty: Publisher of fine art prints and posters

Earl and Shirly Chico
1000 Parkside Dr.
Tempe, AZ 85281
(602) 968-1568
Store: In home
Specialty: Jewelry, custom silversmithing

Hopi Arts and Crafts
Beverly Sekaquaptewa
2771 W. Nebraska St.
Tucson, AZ 85706
Store: San Xavier Mission, Tucson
Specialty: Hopi silverwork and arts and crafts

Nav-Hopi Crafts
Mr. and Mrs. Mark Taho
P.O. Box 131
Tuba City, AZ 86045
(602) 283-5864
Store: In home
Specialty: Navajo and Hopi crafts

Hopi Arts & Crafts-Silvercraft
Mark Lomayestewa
P.O. Box 37
Second Mesa, AZ 86043
(602) 734-2463
Store: In Hopi Cultural Center
Specialty: Hopi silverwork

Richard and Rita Begay
5250 N. Hwy 89 50
Flagstaff, AZ 86001
(602) 526-6461
Store: In home
Specialty: Custom silversmithing

**Navajo Arts and Crafts
Enterprise**
P.O. Drawer A
Window Rock, AZ 86515
(602) 871-4095
Store: Hwy. 264, Window Rock
Specialty: Navajo arts and crafts

George O. Bennett
5517 E. Waverly
Tucson, AZ 85712
(602) 298-3772
Store: In home
Specialty: Custom jewelry made to
order

Sandra and Ralph Davis
1005 West 12th St.
Tempe, AZ 86515
(602) 298-3772
Store: In home
Specialty: Hopi kachina wall
hangings

American Indian Arts
Raymond J. Judge
P.O. Box 2792
Flagstaff, AZ 86003
Store: In home
Specialty: Pen and ink watercolor
tempera fine art

CALIFORNIA

Apache Canyon
Joe and Homer Hi Joe
132 E. Main St.
Barstow, CA
(714) 256-0108
Store: 132 E. Main
Specialty: Custom silver and tur-
quoise jewelry

FLORIDA

**Osceola's Indian Gift Shop
and Village**
Bill Osceola and William
On U.S. 41, 1/2 mile west of
Jetport
S.R. 23B
Ochopee, FL 33943
(813) 695-4857
Specialty: Seminole arts and crafts

Osceola Sales Co.
6571 Sheridan St.
Hollywood, FL 33024
(305) 962-8303
Specialty: Seminole Indian clothing collection and accessories

IDAHO

Fort Hall Trading Post
Stephanie Daugomah
Clothes Horse
P.O. Box 368
Fort Hall, ID 83203
(208) 237-8433
Store: In Fort Hall Shopping
Center
Specialty: Beaded items

Marsh's Trading Post
Lorna and Doug Marsh
P.O. Box 547
Kamiah, ID 83526
(208) 935-2601
Store: One-half mile west of
  Kamiah
Specialty: Traditional arts and
  crafts

**Shoshone and Bannock
Indian Beadwork**
Yvonne S. Capps
P.O. Box 399
Fort Hall, ID 83203
Store: In home
Specialty: Beadwork

KANSAS

Edmonds Indian Jewelry
Randlett and Geneva Edmonds
1309 Fair Lane
Lawrence, KS 66044
(913) 842-1567
Store: In home
Specialty: Indian jewelry

MICHIGAN

Indian Hills Trading Co.
Victor S. Kishigo
P.O. Box 546
Petoskety, MI 49770
(616) 347-3789
Store: On Indian Hills
  Reservation
Specialty: Authentic arts and
  crafts

MONTANA

Chippewa-Cree Crafts Coop
Rocky Boy Route
Box Elder, MT 59521
Store: In tribal building at Rocky
  Boy's Reservation
Specialty: Beadwork and buckskin

Indian Arts and Crafts
Dorothy M. Brown and Associates
Star Route, Box 1B
Ronan, MT 59864
(406) 676-5020
Store: In home
Specialty: Traditional arts and
  crafts

NEW MEXICO

Yellowhorse Trading Co.
Artie Yellowhorse
P.O. Box 1205
Corrales, NM 87048
(505) 898-6184
Store: In home
Specialty: Navajo-style concho
  belts

Waquie's Arts and Crafts
Pat and Marie
P.O. Box 64
Jemez Pueblo, NM 87024
Store: In home
Specialty: Pottery

Yabeny's Rodeo and Jewelry
P.O. Box 938
Shiprock, NM 87420
Store: At powwows all the time
Specialty: Turquoise and silver
  jewelry and animal stock
  contractor

Hoswood Brown

P.O. Box 246
Shiprock, NM 87420
(505) 368-4626
and
715 N. 51st Place
Phoenix, AZ
(602) 267-8431
Store: In home
Specialty: Turquoise and silver
jewelry, sand paintings and rugs

Zuni Craftsmen Cooperative Association

Zuni Pueblo
P.O. Box 425
Zuni, NM 87327
(505) 782-4425
Store: Hwy. 53, Zuni Pueblo
Specialty: Silver and turquoise
jewelry—Zuni style

Ivan T. Paquin

P.O. Box 145
Gamerco, NM 87317
(505) 722-5549
Store: In home
Specialty: Handmade Zuni jewelry

Hubert Ben, Sr.

Box 1967
Shiprock, NM 87420
(505) 368-4185
Store: In home
Specialty: Navajo sand painter

NEVADA

Ms. Squaw Indian Handcrafts Trading Post

Delaine Spillsbury
Old Nevada, NV 89004
(702) 642-6674
Store: In home
Specialty: Intertribal traditional
arts and crafts

NEW YORK

American Indian Community House, Inc., Gallery

Lloyd E. Oxendine
404 Lafayette St.
New York, NY 10003
(212) 598-0100
Store: 404 Lafayette St.
Specialty: Painting, sculpture,
weavings, and traditional arts
and crafts

Museum of the American Indian

Lee Callander
Broadway & 155th St.
New York, NY 10032
(212) 283-2420

Native American Center

Duffy Wilson
Rainbow Mall
Niagara Falls, NY 14304
(716) 284-2427
Store: In museum
Specialty: Eastern Indian tradi-
tional arts and crafts

Shenandoah Trading Post

Rt. 46
Oneida, NY 13424
(315) 363-1315
Store: On reservation at Oneida
Specialty: Authentic Indian crafts

Sweetgrass Gift Shop

Akwesasne Museum and Cultural
Center, Inc.
Hogansburg, NY 13655
(518) 358-2240
Store: In museum
Specialty: Mohawk basketry and
artforms

OKLAHOMA

Oklahoma Indian Arts and Crafts Cooperative
P.O. Box 966
Anadarko, OK 73005
(405) 247-3486
Store: In museum at Anadarko
Specialty: Southern Plains
  beadwork

Whitehair Trading Post
Andrew and Margret Gray
107 East Sixth
Pawhuska, OK 74056
(918) 287-3320
Store: 107 E. 6th
Specialty: Traditional beadwork
  and buckskin items

Alco Printing
Al Doonkeen
1612 NW 4th
Oklahoma City, OK
(405) 235-9991
Store: 1612 NW 4th
Specialty: Complete printing service, business forms through
  bumper stickers

UTAH

Taylors Indian Crafts
68 South Main
Brigham City, UT 84302
Store: 68 S. Main
Specialty: Beadwork and
  featherwork

WASHINGTON

Heritage Inn
Yakima Nation Culture Center
P.O. Box 151
U.S. Hwy. 97
Toppenish, WA 98948
(509) 865-2800
Store: Gift shop in museum
Specialty: Beadwork and buckskin
  items

Kewa Publishing Co.
Glenn Raymond
N. 2927 Standard
Spokane, WA 99004
Store:
Specialty: Television and record
  producers

Seattle Indian Arts and Crafts Shop
Letoy Eike
617 Second Avenue
Seattle, WA 98104
(206) 623-2252
Store: 617 Second Ave.
Specialty: Northwest coast tradi-
  tional arts and crafts

Mt. Adams Art Gallery
Bob Maldonado
4 Washington Ave.
Toppenish, WA 98948
(509) 865-5020
Store: 4 Washington Ave.
Specialty: Contemporary jewelry

Check Indian-owned and operated museums and cultural centers for additional listings. (See: gift shops)

Indian Rodeos

National Organization
Indian National Final Rodeo Commission
P.O. Box 1725
Albuquerque, NM 87103

INFRC recognizes regions as follows:

Region I
Indian Rodeo Cowboy Association (IRCA) Canada
Box 36
Standoff, Alberta, Canada T0L 1Y0

Region II
Western States Indian Rodeo Association (WSIRA)
Route 4, Box 4244
Wapato, WA 98951

Region III
United Indian Rodeo Association (UIRA)
Browning, MT 59417
(406) 336-3393

Region IV
Rocky Mountain Indian Rodeo Association (RMIRA)
P.O. Box 141
Ft. Washakie, WY 82514
(307) 322-3726

Region V
All Indian Rodeo Cowboys Association (AIRCA)
P.O. Box 155
Tsaile, AZ 86556
(602) 724-3235

Region VI
Navajo Nation Rodeo Cowboys Association (NNRCA)
P.O. Box 27
Crownpoint, NM 87313

Region VII
Great Plains Indian Rodeo Association (GPIRA)
P.O. Box 418
Newtown, ND 58763
(701) 627-3466

Region VIII
  All Indian Rodeo Association of Oklahoma (AIRAO)
  P.O. Box 471
  Coweta, OK 74429
  (918) 486-2832

SANCTIONED RODEO SCHEDULE

Region I (IRCA)
Standoff, Alberta, Canada

1st weekend	June	Eden Valley, Alberta
2nd weekend	June	Sarcee, Alberta
3rd weekend	June	Brockett, Alberta
1st weekend	July	Morley, Alberta
2nd weekend	July	High River, Alberta
3rd weekend	July	Hobbema, Alberta
4th weekend	July	Standoff, Alberta
5th weekend	July	Glecian, Alberta
1st weekend	August	Erminskin, Alberta

Region II (WSIRA)
Wapato, WA

2nd weekend	May	Tygh Valley, Oregon
3rd weekend	May	Klamath Falls, Oregon
1st weekend	June	White Swan, Washington
2nd weekend	June	Las Vegas, Nevada
3rd weekend	June	Yerington, Nevada
1st weekend	July	Hoopa, California
1st weekend	September	Wellpinit, Washington
3rd weekend	September	Schurz, Nevada
4th weekend	September	Sacramento, California

Region III (UIRA)
Browning, MT

1st weekend	June	D-D—Harlem, Montana
1st weekend	July	Babb, Montana
2nd weekend	July	Browning, Montana
3rd weekend	July	Cut Bank, Montana
1st weekend	August	Rocky Boys, Montana

Region IV (RMIRA)
Ft. Washakie, WY

4th weekend	June	Fort Washakie, Wyoming
1st weekend	July	Fort Duchesne, Utah
3rd weekend	July	Ethete, Wyoming
1st weekend	August	Thermopolis, Wyoming
2nd weekend	August	Fort Hall, Idaho
1st weekend	September	Fort Washakie, Wyoming
2nd weekend	September	Fort Duchesne, Utah

Region V (AIRCA)
Tsaile, AZ

3rd weekend	February	Casa Grande, Arizona
1st weekend	April	Sacaton, Arizona
2nd weekend	April	Tsaile, Arizona
3rd weekend	April	Tuba City, Arizona
1st weekend	May	Ganado, Arizona
1st weekend	May	Kayenta, Arizona
2nd weekend	May	Ft. Defiance, Arizona
3rd weekend	May	Ganado, Arizona
4th weekend	May	Tuba City, Arizona
5th weekend	May	Pinon, Arizona
1st weekend	June	Oraibi, Arizona
2nd weekend	June	Seba Dalkai, Arizona
3rd weekend	June	Houck, Arizona
4th weekend	June	Tsaile, Arizona
1st weekend	July	Whiteriver, Arizona
1st weekend	July	Window Rock, Arizona
3rd weekend	July	Lukachukai, Arizona
4th weekend	July	Whiteriver, Arizona
2nd weekend	August	Gallup, New Mexico
3rd weekend	August	Sawmill, Arizona
1st weekend	September	Whiteriver, Arizona
2nd weekend	September	Window Rock, Arizona
3rd weekend	September	Ft. Defiance, Arizona
2nd weekend	October	Tuba City, Arizona
3rd weekend	October	Phoenix, Arizona
4th weekend	October	San Carlos, Arizona
2nd weekend	November	Sells, Arizona
3rd weekend	November	Albuquerque, New Mexico
1st weekend	December	Parker, Arizona
2nd weekend	December	Chinle, Arizona

Region VI (NNRCA)
Crownpoint, NM

1st weekend	May	Ganado, Arizona
2nd weekend	May	Kayenta, Arizona

3rd weekend	May	San Fidel, New Mexico
1st weekend	June	Tsa-Ya-Toh, New Mexico
3rd weekend	June	Dulce, New Mexico
2nd weekend	July	Thoreau, New Mexico
3rd weekend	July	Crownpoint, New Mexico
4th weekend	July	Rock Springs, New Mexico
1st weekend	August	Crownpoint, New Mexico
2nd weekend	August	Gallup, New Mexico
3rd weekend	August	Nageezi, New Mexico
4th weekend	August	San Fidel, New Mexico
5th weekend	August	Little Water, New Mexico
2nd weekend	September	Window Rock, Arizona
3rd weekend	September	Ignacio, Colorado
2nd weekend	October	Finals (Site Pending)

Region VII (GPIRA)
New Town, ND

1st weekend	June	Pierre, South Dakota
4th weekend	June	New Town, South Dakota
4th weekend	June	Poplar, Montana
3rd weekend	July	Belcourt, North Dakota
1st weekend	August	Lower Brule, South Dakota
2nd weekend	August	Yorkton, Saskatchewan
1st weekend	September	Wolf Point, Montana
2nd weekend	September	Finals (Site Pending)

Region VIII (AIRAO)
Coweta, OK

4th weekend	May	Claremore, Oklahoma
2nd weekend	June	Muskogee, Oklahoma
3rd weekend	June	Henryetta, Oklahoma
4th weekend	June	Tahlequah, Oklahoma
1st weekend	September	Tahlequah, Oklahoma
2nd weekend	September	Fort Worth, Texas
1st weekend	October	Finals (Site Pending)

Rodeos are sometimes rescheduled but usually follow in sequence year after year. Call the respective Region Rodeo Association.

Indian Tribes Operating Indian Community Colleges

Blackfeet Tribe
Browning, MT 59417
(406) 338-5411

Flathead Tribe
Pablo, MT 59821
(406) 745-4297

Northern Cheyenne Tribe
Lame Deer, MT 59043
(406) 477-6219

Crow Tribe
Crow Agency, MT 59022
(406) 638-2238

Winnebago Tribe
Winnebago, NE 68071
(402) 878-2414

Turtle Mountain Tribe
Belcourt, ND 58316
(701) 477-5605

Fort Berthold Tribe
P.O. Box 220
New Town, ND 58763
(701) 627-4738

Devils Lake Tribe
Sioux Community Center
Ft. Totten, ND 58335
(701) 662-8683

Standing Rock Tribe
Ft. Yates, ND 58538
(701) 854-3861

Cheyenne River Tribe
P.O. Box 590
Eagle Butte, SD 57625
(605) 964-3632

Oglala Sioux Tribe
Pine Ridge, SD 57770
(605) 867-5893

Rosebud Sioux Tribe
Rosebud, SD 57570
(605) 747-2381

Sisseton-Wahpeton Sioux Tribe
Rt. 2, P.O. Box 144
Sisseton, SD 57262
(605) 698-3966

Navajo Tribe
P.O. Box 302
Fredonia, AZ 86022
(602) 724-3311

Lummi Tribe
2616 Kwina Rd.
Bellingham, WA 98225
(206) 758-2368

Population Totals for American Indians, Eskimos, and Aleuts by State April 1980

Rank	State	Population
1	California	201,311
2	Oklahoma	169,464
3	Arizona	152,857
4	New Mexico	104,777
5	North Carolina	64,635
6	Alaska	64,047
7	Washington	60,771
8	South Dakota	45,101
9	Texas	40,074
10	Michigan	40,038
11	New York	38,732
12	Montana	37,270
13	Minnesota	35,026
14	Wisconsin	29,497
15	Oregon	27,309
16	North Dakota	20,157
17	Florida	19,316
18	Utah	19,256
19	Colorado	18,059
20	Illinois	16,271
21	Kansas	15,371
22	Nevada	13,304
23	Missouri	12,319
24	Ohio	12,240
25	Louisiana	12,064
26	Idaho	10,521
27	Pennsylvania	9,459
28	Arkansas	9,411
29	Virginia	9,336
30	Nebraska	9,197
31	New Jersey	8,394
32	Maryland	8,021
33	Indiana	7,835
34	Massachusetts	7,743

35	Georgia	7,619
36	Alabama	7,561
37	Wyoming	7,125
38	Mississippi	6,180
39	South Carolina	5,758
40	Iowa	5,453
41	Tennessee	5,103
42	Connecticut	4,533
43	Maine	4,087
44	Kentucky	3,610
45	Rhode Island	2,898
46	Hawaii	2,778
47	West Virginia	1,610
48	New Hampshire	1,352
49	Delaware	1,330
50	District of Columbia	1,031
51	Vermont	984

For the first time since the Bureau began collecting data on American Indians, the American Indian population exceeded the 1 million mark on April 1, 1980. The 1980 proportion of American Indians residing in the:

West	49%
South	27%
North Central	18%
Northeast	6%

One-half of the American Indian population resided in five states:

California	201,311
Oklahoma	169,464
Arizona	152,857
New Mexico	104,777
North Carolina	64,635

The 1980 census was the first in which data were collected separately for Eskimos and Aleuts in all states:

| Eskimos | 42,149 |
| Aleuts | 14,177 |

About 81 percent of the Eskimo population and 57 percent of the Aleut population lived in Alaska.

**American Indian Population
of the United States: 1900 to 1970**

Census Year	Population	Change from Preceding Year	
1900	237,196		
1910	276,927	+39,731	16.6%
1920	244,437	−32,490	−11.7%
1930	343,352	+98,915	40.5%
1940	345,252	+1,900	0.6%
1950	357,499	+12,247	3.5%
1960	523,591	+166,092	46.5%
1970	792,730	+269,139	51.4%

Reservations, Rancherias, Pueblos

Indian Service Population	(1981)
Absentee-Shawnee Tribe	1,365
Acoma Pueblo	2,940
Agua Caliente Tribe	190
Ak-Chin Tribe	433
Alabama-Quassarte Creek Tribe	—
Alturas Tribe	10
Apache Tribe	517
Arapahoe Tribe	—
Augustine Tribe (Band of Mission)	—
Bad River Tribe	1,316
Barona Tribe	301
Bay Mills Tribe	466
Benton (see Utu Utu Gwaitu-Paiute)	—
Berry Creek Rancheria	154
Big Bend Rancheria	106
Big Lagoon Rancheria	7
Big Pine	419
Bishop Tribe	1,006
Blackfeet Tribe	6,632
Bois Forte Tribe (Nett Lake)	940
Bridgeport Tribe	81

Burns-Paiute Tribe	194
Cabazon Tribe	22
Caddo Tribe	1,215
Cahuilla Tribe	148
Campo Tribe	205
Capitan Grande Tribe	—
Cayuga Tribe	89
Cedarville Rancheria	16
Chehalis Tribe	721
Chemehuevi Tribe	124
Cherokee-Delaware Tribe	—
Cherokee Tribe (Oklahoma)	42,992
Cherokee (Eastern Band)	5,664
Cheyenne Arapaho Tribe	—
Cheyenne River Sioux Tribe	4,449
Chickasaw Tribe	8,507
Chippewa Cree Tribe (Rocky Boy's)	1,897
Chitimacha Tribe	278
Choctaw Tribe (Oklahoma)	19,660
Choctaw Tribe (Mississippi)	4,914
Citizen Potawatomi Tribe	6,354
Cochiti Pueblo	910
Cocopah Tribe	835
Coeur d'Alene Tribe	822
Cold Springs Rancheria	209
Colorado River Tribe	2,084
Colusa Tribe	44
Colville Tribe	6,090
Comanche Tribe	3,597
Cortina Tribe	81
Coushatta Tribe	272
Covelo Tribe	709
Creek Tribe (Oklahoma)	37,679
Crow Creek Sioux Tribe	2,091
Crow Tribe	4,969
Cuyapaipe Tribe	24
Delaware Tribe	522
Devils Lake Sioux Tribe	2,916
Dry Creek Tribe	126
Duckwater Shoshone Tribe	139
Eastern Band of Cherokee (see Cherokee)	—
Eastern Shawnee Tribe	335
Elem Tribe (Sulphur Rancheria)	157
Ely	234
Enterprise Rancheria	18
Fallon Paiute Shoshone Tribe	677
Flandreau Santee-Sioux Tribe	413

Flathead Tribe	3,300
Fond du Lac Tribe	1,431
Forest County Potawatomi Tribe	390
Fort Apache (see White Mountain Apache)	—
Fort Belknap Tribe	2,097
Fort Berthold Tribe	3,194
Fort Bidwell Tribe	162
Fort Hall Tribe	3,820
Fort Independence Tribe	93
Fort McDermitt Shoshone-Paiute Tribe	653
Fort McDowell Mohave-Apache Tribe	383
Fort Mohave Tribe	537
Fort Peck Tribe	5,095
Fort Sill Apache Tribe	70
Fort Yuma Tribe (see Quechan)	—
Gila River Tribe	9,592
Goshute Tribe	211
Grand Portage Tribe	310
Grindstone Tribe	173
Hannahville Tribe	344
Havasupai Tribe	475
Hoh Tribe	61
Hoopa Valley Tribe	1,816
Hoopa Extension Tribe	1,850
Hopi Tribe	8,439
Houlton Band of Maliseet Indians (ME)	239
Hualapai Tribe	1,017
Inaja-Cosmit Tribe	10
Indian Township Passamaquoddy Tribe	367
Iowa Tribe (Iowa of Kansas and Nebraska)	280
Iowa Tribe (Oklahoma)	203
Isleta Pueblo	3,110
Jackson Rancheria	19
Jemez Pueblo	1,889
Jicarilla Apache Tribe	2,269
Kaibab-Paiute Tribe	229
Kalispel Tribe	205
Kashia Tribe	204
Kaw Tribe	617
Keweenaw Bay Tribe (L'Anse)	893
Kickapoo Tribe	598
Kiowa Tribe	4,005
Kootenai Tribe	115
La Jolla Tribe	221
La Posta Tribe	14
Lac Courte Oreilles Tribe	1,811
Lac de Flambeau Tribe	1,485

Laguna Tribe	6,406
L'Anse (see Keweenaw Bay)	—
Las Vegas Tribe	123
Laytonville Tribe	177
Leech Lake Tribe	4,034
Lone Pine Tribe	204
Lookout Rancheria	11
Los Coyotes Tribe	161
Lovelock Tribe	163
Lower Brule Sioux Tribe	988
Lower Elwha Tribe	1,191
Lower Sioux Tribe	209
Lummi Tribe	2,290
Makah Tribe	927
Manchester Tribe	88
Manzanita Tribe	40
Menominee Tribe	3,384
Mesa Grande Tribe	28
Mescalero Apache Tribe	2,415
Miami Tribe	350
Miccosukee Tribe	457
Middletown Tribe	62
Mille Lacs Tribe	897
Minnesota Chippewa Tribe	—
Mississippi Choctaw (see Choctaw)	
Moapa Tribe	216
Montgomery Creek Rancheria	19
Morongo Tribe	743
Muckleshoot Tribe	2,227
Nambe Pueblo	370
Navajo Tribe	160,722
Nett Lake (see Bois Forte)	—
Nez Perce Tribe	2,020
Nisqually Tribe	1,257
Nooksack Tribe	694
Northern Cheyenne Tribe	3,110
Oglala Sioux Tribe	13,417
Omaha Tribe	1,469
Oneida Tribe (Wisconsin)	3,384
Oneida Tribe (New York)	145
Onondaga Tribe	850
Osage Tribe	5,612
Ote-Missouri Tribe	1,165
Paiute Indian Tribe (Utah)	312
Pala Tribe	455
Palm Springs (see Agua Caliente)	—
Papago Tribe	17,651

Pascua Yaqui (see Yaqui)	—
Pauma Tribe	93
Pawnee Tribe	2,066
Payson (see Yavapai Tonto Apache)	—
Pechanga Tribe	428
Penobscot Tribe	1,029
Picuris Pueblo	177
Pine Ridge (see Oglala Sioux)	—
Pit River Tribe	1,192
Pleasant Point Passamaquoddy Tribe	691
Pojoaque Pueblo	78
Ponca Tribe	2,065
Port Gamble Tribe	446
Prairie Island Tribe	118
Prairie Potawatomi Tribe	1,302
Prescott (see Yavapai)	—
Pueblos (see Individual Listings)	—
Puyallup Tribe	5,660
Pyramid Lake Paiute Tribe	776
Quapaw Tribe	1,193
Quechan Tribe	1,500
Quileute Tribe	327
Quinault Tribe	2,013
Red Cliff Tribe	1,349
Red Lake Tribe	4,399
Reno-Sparks Tribe	603
Resighini Tribe	104
Rincon Tribe	261
Roaring Creek Rancheria	36
Rocky Boy's (see Chippewa Cree)	—
Rosebud Sioux Tribe	9,484
Round Valley (see Covelo)	—
Rumsey Tribe	47
Sac & Fox Tribe (Oklahoma)	1,352
Sac & Fox Tribe (Iowa)	695
Sac & Fox Tribe (Kansas and Nebraska)	36
Saginaw Chippewa Tribe	—
Salt River Pima-Maricopa Tribe	3,364
San Carlos Tribe	5,967
San Felipe Pueblo	2,072
San Ildefonso Pueblo	430
San Juan Pueblo	1,842
San Manuel Tribe	88
San Pasqual Tribe	347
Sandia Pueblo	295
Santa Ana Pueblo	501
Santa Clara Pueblo	2,327
Santa Rosa Tribe	271

Santa Rosa Tribe	100
Santa Inez Tribe	200
Santa Ysabel Tribe	889
Santee Sioux Tribe	434
Santo Domingo Pueblo	3,332
Sauk-Suiattle Tribe	255
Sault Ste. Marie Tribe	2,246
Seminole Tribe (Oklahoma)	3,719
Seminole Tribe (Florida)	1,424
Seneca-Cayuga Tribe	670
Seneca Tribe	5,418
Shakopee Tribe	98
Sheep Ranch Rancheria	—
Sherwood Valley Tribe	173
Shingle Springs Rancheria	—
Shoalwater Tribe	62
Shoshone-Bannock (see Fort Hall)	—
Shoshone Tribe (Wind River)	5,705
Shoshone Paiute Tribe (Duck Valley)	—
Siletz Tribe	671
Sisseton-Wahpeton Sioux Tribe	3,730
Skokomish Tribe	1,008
Skull Valley Tribe	72
Soboba Tribe	457
Sokaogon Chippewa Tribe	—
Southern Ute Tribe	1,096
Spokane Tribe	1,921
Squaxin Island Tribe	926
St. Croix Tribe	1,041
St. Regis Mohawk Tribe	2,799
Standing Rock Tribe	7,958
Stewart's Point Rancheria (see Kashia)	—
Stockbridge-Munsee Tribe	948
Sulphur Bank (see Elem)	—
Summit Lake Paiute Tribe	—
Susanville Tribe	350
Suquamish Tribe	1,784
Swinomish Tribe	648
Sycamore Valley Tribe (see Cold Springs)	—
Sycuan Tribe	70
Taos Pueblo	1,860
Te-Moak Tribe	—
Tesuque Pueblo	299
Thlophlcco Tribe	—
Tonawanda Tribe	600
Tonkawa Tribe	1,265
Tonto Apache (see Yavapai-Tonto Apache)	—
Torrez-Martinez Tribe	81

Trinidad Tribe	67
Tulalip Tribe	855
Tule River Tribe	549
Tuolumne Tribe	276
Turtle Mountain Tribe	8,656
Tuscarora Tribe	725
Twenty-Nine Palms Tribe	18
Unitah and Ouray Tribe	1,890
Umatilla Tribe	1,500
United Keetoowah Cherokee Tribe	—
Upper Sioux Tribe (Granite Falls)	127
Upper Skagit Tribe	376
Ute Mountain Tribe	1,528
Utu Utu Gwaitu Paiute Tribe	25
Viejas Tribe	183
Walker River Paiute Tribe	980
Warm Springs Tribe	2,412
Washoe Tribe	544
White Earth Tribe	3,948
White Mountain Apache Tribe	8,010
Wichita Tribe	610
Wind River (see Arapahoe and Shoshone)	—
Winnebago Tribe	1,143
Winnemucca Tribe	81
Wisconsin Winnebago Tribe	1,718
Wyandotte Tribe	440
Yakima Tribe	8,502
Yankton Sioux Tribe	2,531
Yaqui Tribe	616
Yavapai Apache Tribe	516
Yavapai-Prescott Tribe	75
Yavapai Tonto Apache Tribe	66
Yerington Tribe	342
Yomba Tribe	114
Zia Pueblo	584
Zuni Tribe	6,999

Urban Indian Centers in Major Metropolitan Areas

ALASKA

Tlingit & Haida Central Council
1 Sealaska Plaza 200
Juneau, AK 99801
(907) 586-1432

ARIZONA

American Indian Association of Tucson, Inc.
92 W. Simpson
Tucson, AZ 85701
(602) 884-7131

Phoenix Indian Center
3202 N. 7th St.
Phoenix, AZ 85012
(602) 279-4116

Native Americans for Community Action, Inc.
15 North San Francisco
P.O. Box 572
Flagstaff, AZ 86001
(602) 774-6613

ARKANSAS

American Indian Center of Arkansas, Inc.
4318 West Markham
Little Rock, AK 72202
(501) 666-0181

CALIFORNIA

Inter-Tribal Friendship House
523 E. 14th St.
Oakland, CA 94606
(415) 452-1235

Fresno American Indian Council
N. 5150 6th Ave.
Fresno, CA 93721
(209) 222-7741

Santa Rosa Indian Center
1305 Cleveland Avenue
Santa Rosa, CA 95406
(707) 527-8711

Indian Action Council of Northwestern California
P.O. Box 3180
219 5th St.
Eureka, CA 95501
(707) 443-8401

Indian Center of San Jose, Inc.
3485 East Hills Drive
San Jose, CA 95127
(408) 259-9722

Los Angeles Indian Center, Inc.
1111 W. Washington Blvd.
Los Angeles, CA 90015
(213) 747-9521

South Bay Indian Services
3520 Long Beach Blvd.
Long Beach, CA 90807
(213) 424-0941

San Bernardino Indian Center, Inc.
441 W. 8th St.
San Bernardino, CA 92401
(714) 889-8516

Sacramento Indian Center
P.O. Box 16094
1402 32nd
Sacramento, CA 95816
(916) 452-3988

Community Action for the Urbanized American Indian
225 Valencia Street
San Francisco, CA 94103
(415) 552-1070

COLORADO

Denver Native Americans United, Inc.
4407 N. Morrison Rd.
Denver, CO 80206
(303) 934-5793

ILLINOIS

Native American Committee
4546 N. Hermitage
Chicago, IL 60640
(312) 728-1477

American Indian Center
1630 W. Wilson Ave.
Chicago, IL 60640
(312) 275-5871

IOWA

Sioux City American Indian Center
304 Pearl St.
Sioux City, IA 51101
(712) 255-8957

HAWAII

Hawaii Council of American Indian Nations
3260 Yalena St.
P.O. Box 17627
Honolulu, HI 96817
(808) 833-4581

KANSAS

Indian Center of Topeka, Inc.
915 N. Western
Topeka, KS 66608
(913) 233-5531

The Indian Center of Lawrence
2326 Louisiana St.
Lawrence, KS 66044
(913) 841-7202

Mid-American All Indian Center
650 N. Seneca
Wichita, KS 67203
(316) 262-5221

MARYLAND

American Indian Center, Inc.
211 S. Broadway
Baltimore, MD 21231
(301) 563-4600

MASSACHUSETTS

Boston Indian Council
105 S. Huntington Ave., Jamaica
Plains
Boston, MA 02130
(617) 232-0343

MICHIGAN

Grand Rapids Inter-Tribal Council
756 Bridge, NW
Grand Rapids, MI 49508
(616) 774-8331

North American Indian Association of Detroit
360 John R. Street
Detroit, MI 48226
(313) 963-1710

Lansing North American Indian Center
820 W. Saginaw
Lansing, MI 48912
(517) 487-5409

South Eastern Michigan Indians
8830 Ten Mile Road
Centerline, MI
(313) 756-1350

MINNESOTA

Minneapolis Regional N.A. Center
1530 E. Franklin
Minneapolis, MN 55404
(612) 871-4555

St. Paul American Indian Center
1001 Payne Ave.
St. Paul, MN 55101
(612) 776-8592

American Indian Fellowship Association
8 East Second St.
Duluth, MN 55802
(218) 722-9776

MISSOURI

American Indian Cultural Center of Mid-America
4648 Gravois St.
St. Louis, MO 63110
(314) 353-4517

Heart of America Indian Center
1340 E. Admiral Blvd.
Kansas City, MO 64124
(816) 421-7608

MONTANA

Montana United Indian Association
P.O. Box 786
Helena, MT 59601
(406) 443-5350

NEBRASKA

Lincoln Indian Center
10th & Military Rd.
Lincoln, NE 68508
(402) 474-5231

Omaha American Indian Center
613 S. 16th St.
Omaha, NE 68102

NEVADA

National Indian Center
418 Hoover Ave., Suite One
Las Vegas, NV 89101
(702) 385-0211

Inter-Tribal Council of Nevada
650 S. Rock Blvd.
Reno, NV 89502
(702) 786-3128

NEW MEXICO

Albuquerque Indian Center
1114 7th St., NW
Albuquerque, NM 87102
(505) 243-2253

Gallup Indian Community Center
200 W. Maxwell Ave.
Gallup, NM 87301
(505) 722-4388

Farmington Intertribal Indian Organization
100 W. Elm
Farmington, NM 87401
(505) 327-6296

NEW YORK

Indian Culture Center, Inc.
P.O. Box 37, Market Station
Buffalo, NY 14203
(716) 877-6321

North American Indian Club, Syracuse
P.O. Box 851
Syracuse, NY 13201
(315) 476-7425

American Indian Community House
842 Broadway, 8th Floor
New York, NY 10003
(212) 598-0100/0181

American Indian Club of Rochester, Inc.
P.O. Box 272
Rochester, NY 14601
(716) 244-7353

NORTH DAKOTA

Dakota Association of Native Americans, Inc.
201 E. Front Ave.
P.O. Box 696
Bismarck, ND 58501
(701) 258-0040

Fargo-Moorhead Indian Center
1444 N. 4th Ave.
P.O. Box 42
Fargo, ND 58107
(701) 293-6863

NORTH CAROLINA

Cumberland County Association for Indian People
P.O. Box 6–4243
Fayetteville, NC 28306
(919) 483-8442

Metrolina Native American Association
Charlotte Merchandise Mart
Charlotte, NC 28202
(704) 333-0135

Guilford Native American Association
P.O. Box 6782
Greensboro, NC 27405
(919) 273-8686

OHIO

Cleveland American Indian Center
5500–02 Lorain Ave.
Cleveland, OH 44102
(216) 961-3490

OKLAHOMA

Native American Coalition
P.O. Box 2646
Tulsa, OK 74102
(918) 8458

Native American Center
2830 S. Robinson
Oklahoma City, OK 73103
(405) 232-2512

Southern Plains Inter-Tribal Center
120 Northeast Rogers Lane
Lawton, OK 73501
(405) 353-4604

Tri-City Indian Development Corporation
109 N. Broadway
Holdenville, OK 74848
(405) 379-6256

McCurtain County Indian Development Corporation
P.O. Box 432
Wright City, OK 74766
(405) 981-2882

OREGON

Organization of the Forgotten American
3949 S. 6th Street
Suite 205
Klamath Falls, OR 97601
(503) 882-4442/4441

Urban Indian Program
1634 SW Alder
Portland, OR 97210
(503) 248-4562

PENNSYLVANIA

Council of Three Rivers
200 Charles
Pittsburgh, PA 15208
(412) 782-4457

United American Indians of Delaware Valley
225 Chestnut St.
Philadelphia, PA 19106
(215) 574-9020

SOUTH DAKOTA

Mother Butler Indian Center
P.O. Box 7038
Rapid City, SD 57701
(605) 342-4772

TEXAS

American Indian Center of Dallas
1314 Munger Blvd.
P.O. Box 22334
Dallas, TX 75222
(214) 826-8856

UTAH

Utah Native American Consortium, Inc.
120 W. 1300 South
Salt Lake City, UT 84115
(801) 486-4877

WASHINGTON

Seattle Indian Center
121 Stewart St.
Seattle, WA 98104
(206) 624-8700

American Indian Community Center
1007 N. Columbus
Spokane, WA 99202
(509) 489-2370

Tacoma Indian Center
3602 McKinley
Tacoma, WA 98421
(206) 474-0793

United Indian Association of Central Washington
106 S. 4th St.
Yakima, WA 98093
(509) 575-0835

Kitsap County Indian Center
212 Burwell
Bremerton, WA 98310
(206) 377-8521

WISCONSIN

Milwaukee Indian Urban Affairs Council
1410 N. 27th St.
Milwaukee, WI 53208
(414) 342-4171

Index

Other Books from John Muir Publications

Asia Through the Back Door, 3rd ed., Rick Steves and John Gottberg (65-48-3) 336 pp. $15.95

Being a Father: Family, Work, and Self, Mothering Magazine (65-69-6) 176 pp. $12.95

Buddhist America: Centers, Retreats, Practices, Don Morreale (28-94-X) 400 pp. $12.95

Bus Touring: Charter Vacations, U.S.A., Stuart Warren with Douglas Bloch (28-95-8) 168 pp. $9.95

Catholic America: Self-Renewal Centers and Retreats, Patricia Christian-Meyer (65-20-3) 325 pp. $13.95

Complete Guide to Bed & Breakfasts, Inns & Guesthouses, 1990-91 ed., Pamela Lanier (65-43-2) 504 pp. $15.95

Costa Rica: A Natural Destination, Ree Strange Sheck (65-51-3) 280 pp. $15.95

Elderhostels: The Students' Choice, Mildred Hyman (65-28-9) 224 pp. $12.95

Europe 101: History & Art for the Traveler, Rick Steves and Gene Openshaw (28-78-8) 372 pp. $12.95

Europe Through the Back Door, 9th ed., Rick Steves (65-42-4) 432 pp. $16.95

Floating Vacations: River, Lake, and Ocean Adventures, Michael White (65-32-7) 256 pp. $17.95

Gypsying After 40: A Guide to Adventure and Self-Discovery, Bob Harris (28-71-0) 264 pp. $12.95

The Heart of Jerusalem, Arlynn Nellhaus (28-79-6) 312 pp. $12.95

Indian America: A Traveler's Companion, Eagle/Walking Turtle (65-29-7) 424 pp. $16.95

Mona Winks: Self-Guided Tours of Europe's Top Museums, Rick Steves and Gene Openshaw (28-85-0) 450 pp. $14.95

The On and Off the Road Cookbook, Carl Franz (28-27-3) 272 pp. $8.50

The People's Guide to Mexico, Carl Franz (28-99-0) 608 pp. $15.95

The People's Guide to RV Camping in Mexico, Carl Franz with Steve Rogers (28-91-5) 256 pp. $13.95

Preconception: A Woman's Guide to Preparing for Pregnancy and Parenthood, Brenda Aikey-Keller (65-44-0) 236 pp. $14.95

Ranch Vacations: The Complete Guide to Guest and Resort, Fly-Fishing, and Cross-Country Skiing Ranches, Eugene Kilgore (65-30-0) 392 pp. $18.95

Schooling at Home: Parents, Kids, and Learning, Mothering Magazine (65-52-1) $14.95

The Shopper's Guide to Mexico, Steve Rogers and Tina Rosa (28-90-7) 224 pp. $9.95

Ski Tech's Guide to Equipment, Skiwear, and Accessories, edited by Bill Tanler (65-45-9) 144 pp. $11.95

Ski Tech's Guide to Maintenance and Repair, edited by Bill Tanler (65-46-7) 144 pp. $11.95

A Traveler's Guide to Asian Culture, Kevin Chambers (65-14-9) 224 pp. $13.95

Traveler's Guide to Healing Centers and Retreats in North America, Martine Rudee and Jonathan Blease (65-15-7) 240 pp. $11.95

Undiscovered Islands of the Caribbean, Burl Willes (28-80-X) 216 pp. $12.95

Undiscovered Islands of the Mediterranean, Linda Lancione Moyer and Burl Willes (65-53-X) 184 pp. $13.95

22 Days Series
These pocket-size itineraries are a refreshing departure from ordinary guidebooks. Each author has an in-depth knowledge of the region covered and offers 22 tested daily itineraries through their favorite destinations. Included are not only "must see" attractions but also little-known villages and hidden "jewels" as well as valuable general information.

22 Days Around the World by R. Rapoport and B. Willes (65-31-9)
22 Days in Alaska by Pamela Lanier (28-68-0)
22 Days in the American Southwest by R. Harris (28-88-5)
22 Days in Asia by R. Rapoport and B. Willes (65-17-3)
22 Days in Australia, 3rd ed., by John Gottberg (65-40-8)
22 Days in California by Roger Rapoport (28-93-1)
22 Days in China by Gaylon Duke and Zenia Victor (28-72-9)

22 Days in Europe, 5th ed., by Rick Steves (65-63-7)
22 Days in Florida by Richard Harris (65-27-0)
22 Days in France by Rick Steves (65-07-6)
22 Days in Germany, Austria & Switzerland, 3rd ed., by Rick Steves (65-39-4)
22 Days in Great Britain, 3rd ed., by Rick Steves (65-38-6)
22 Days in Hawaii, 2nd ed., by Arnold Schuchter (65-50-5)
22 Days in India by Anurag Mathur (28-87-7)
22 Days in Japan by David Old (28-73-7)
22 Days in Mexico, 2nd ed., by S. Rogers and T. Rosa (65-41-6)
22 Days in New England by Anne Wright (28-96-6)
22 Days in New Zealand by Arnold Schuchter (28-86-9)
22 Days in Norway, Denmark & Sweden by R. Steves (28-83-4)
22 Days in the Pacific Northwest by R. Harris (28-97-4)
22 Days in Spain & Portugal, 3rd ed., by Rick Steves (65-06-8)
22 Days in the West Indies by C. & S. Morreale (28-74-5)

All 22 Days titles are 128 to 152 pages and $7.95 each, except *22 Days Around the World* and *22 Days in Europe*, which are 192 pages and $9.95.

**"Kidding Around"
Travel Guides for Children**
Written for kids eight years of age and older. Generously illustrated in two colors with imaginative

characters and images. An adventure to read and a treasure to keep.

Kidding Around Atlanta, Anne Pedersen (65-35-1) 64 pp. $9.95
Kidding Around Boston, Helen Byers (65-36-X) 64 pp. $9.95
Kidding Around the Hawaiian Islands, Sarah Lovett (65-37-8) 64 pp. $9.95
Kidding Around London, Sarah Lovett (65-24-6) 64 pp. $9.95
Kidding Around Los Angeles, Judy Cash (65-34-3) 64 pp. $9.95
Kidding Around New York City, Sarah Lovett (65-33-5) 64 pp. $9.95
Kidding Around San Francisco, Rosemary Zibart (65-23-8) 64 pp. $9.95
Kidding Around Washington, D.C., Anne Pedersen (65-25-4) 64 pp. $9.95

Automotive Books

The Greaseless Guide to Car Care Confidence: Take the Terror Out of Talking to Your Mechanic, Mary Jackson (65-19-X) 224 pp. $14.95
How to Keep Your VW Alive (65-12-2) 424 pp. $19.95
How to Keep Your Subaru Alive (65-11-4) 480 pp. $19.95
How to Keep Your Toyota Pickup Alive (28-89-3) 392 pp. $19.95
How to Keep Your Datsun/ Nissan Alive (28-65-6) 544 pp. $19.95
Off-Road Emergency Repair & Survival, James Ristow (65-26-2) 160 pp. $9.95
Road & Track's Used Car Classics, edited by Peter Bohr (28-69-9) 272 pp. $12.95

Ordering Information

If you cannot find our books in your local bookstore, you can order directly from us. Your books will be sent to you via UPS (for U.S. destinations), and you will receive them approximately 10 days from the time that we receive your order. Include $2.75 for the first item ordered and $.50 for each additional item to cover shipping and handling costs. UPS will not deliver to a P.O. Box; please give us a street address. For airmail within the U.S., enclose $4.00 per book for shipping and handling. All foreign orders will be shipped surface rate; please enclose $3.00 for the first item and $1.00 for each additional item. Please inquire about foreign airmail rates.

Method of Payment

Your order may be paid by check, money order, or credit card. We cannot be responsible for cash sent through the mail. All payments must be made in U.S. dollars drawn on a U.S. bank. Canadian postal money orders in U.S. dollars are also acceptable. For VISA, MasterCard, or American Express orders, include your card number, expiration date, and your signature, or call (800)888-7504. Books ordered on American Express cards can be shipped only to the billing address of the cardholder. Sorry, no C.O.D.'s. Residents of sunny New Mexico, add 5.625% tax to the total.

Address all orders and inquiries to:
John Muir Publications
P.O. Box 613
Santa Fe, NM 87504
(800) 888-7504
(505) 988-1680 FAX